People of the Eye

Dedication

To Deaf people in New Zealand: this book is for you. I hope it brings pleasure, pride and strength.

This book is also for the families and educators of Deaf children in acknowledgment of your role in future Deaf lives.

Stories from the Deaf World

People OF THE Eye

Rachel Locker McKee

with photographs by Bruce Connew

 BRIDGET WILLIAMS BOOKS

First published in New Zealand in 2001 by Bridget Williams Books
PO Box 12 474, Wellington, New Zealand

Reprinted 2011

ISBN 978-1-877242-08-3

Acknowledgements
The publishers and the author warmly thank the following organisations for financial support making this publication possible: Bridget Williams Books Publishing Trust, Creative New Zealand, the Deaf Decade Trust (of Sir Roy Mackenzie), Deaf Development Fund and Victoria University of Wellington.

Historical photographs: Reproduced with the permission of Kelston Deaf Education Centre (KDEC) and van Asch Deaf Education Centre (VADEC).

Photographs in preliminary pages:
p. 1 Revellers after the traditional fancy dress Christmas party at Titirangi school, 1952, KDEC
p. 2 At the National Deaf Cricket Tournament, Bruce Connew
p. 8 With the Buzzard family, Bruce Connew; Children at Sumner, 1954, VADEC
p. 9 Friday night at the Auckland Deaf Club, Bruce Connew

Cover photographs: Bruce Connew

National Library of New Zealand Cataloguing-in-Publication Data
McKee, Rachel, 1963-
People of the eye : stories from the deaf world / author, Rachel McKee ;
photographer, Bruce Connew.
Includes bibliographical references.
ISBN 978-1-877242-08-3
1. Deaf–New Zealand. 2. Deafness–Social aspects. I. Connew, Bruce. II. Title.
305.908162–dc 21

Cover design by Mission Hall DGL, Wellington
Internal design by Afineline, Wellington
Typesetting by Archetype, Wellington
Printed by Printlink, Wellington

Contents

List of Illustrations

Photographs by Bruce Connew
Five sections following pp. 44, 106, 146, 200, and 243 include photographs taken by Bruce Connew at Kelston Deaf Education Centre, with the Buzzard family in Christchurch, at the National Deaf Cricket Tournament, and on a Friday night at the Auckland Deaf Club.

Acknowledgments

My admiration and thanks go to each of the Deaf people included in this book. They have not only shared their personal experiences with me as researcher and you as reader, but they have also trusted their stories to the process of translation from sign language to English print. I deeply appreciate the risk they have taken.

Many other Deaf people allowed me to record their stories, which could not be included in this book because it would have been too long. I am grateful for their willingness to participate.

Wenda Walton did a fine job as my assistant by translating first drafts of many stories: I am grateful for her contribution to this project. A grant from the Faculty of Humanities and Social Sciences at Victoria University of Wellington made this possible.

Comments from colleagues and friends on drafts of the book have helped to make it accessible to as many readers as possible. Thanks to my husband, David McKee, for his practical support and encouragement in bringing this project to fruition. I also thank Dan Levitt for guiding my first steps in the Deaf world, back in 1985. Thanks to my mother who makes my work possible by minding the children and doing a million other behind-the-scenes things.

Historical photographs relating to Deaf school life were generously made available by Kelston Deaf Education Centre (KDEC) and van Asch Deaf Education Centre (VADEC), who also gave permission for current students and teachers to be photographed for this book.

I wish to acknowledge my intellectual debt to the many scholars elsewhere, and in New Zealand, who have written about the language, culture, and community of Deaf people. *People of the Eye* does not aim to be a scholarly text, but rather to open some windows onto the Deaf world. I hope it will portray Deaf New Zealanders authentically.

Bruce Connew's photographic essay was commissioned for this book. I would like to acknowledge his great skill in capturing the essential 'visualness' of this world.

Finally, I thank Bridget Williams, the publisher, for her affirmation of the Deaf community by undertaking to publish this book.

Rachel McKee
Wellington, 2001

With the Buzzard family

Children at Sumner, 1954

Preface – A Moment in the Deaf World

My 'bring-a-plate' in hand, I walk from the street at the unglamorous end of town into a room harsh with fluorescent light. Moving hands and mobile faces animate it with a sense of warmth and life. This is Friday night at the Deaf Club.

Cups of tea and small plates of food are precariously juggled in one hand so that the other is kept free for talking; food and drink are deposited on any nearby surface when conversation demands two hands. There is little noise – but plenty of lively communication. Personal news, gossip and plans are exchanged. People greet each other with smiles and hugs, wave to friends across the room, or avoid eye contact with certain others. Many have known each other since school or pre-school days; with others they've played sports, served on committees, and shared problems and milestones; they have met again and again at gatherings like this. The crowd includes all kinds and all ages: Pakeha, Maori, unemployed, blue-collar workers and a handful of white-collar workers, students, senior citizens, the articulate, the eccentric, the trendy, the down-at-heel. All are an expected and accepted part of the scene here. These are Deaf people at home in the company of other Deaf.

The walls of this clubroom are unadorned, except for a bulletin board, and a glass case displaying club sports trophies and pictures of club members at past events. One corner has a large TV screen, and stored nearby are toys for small children. Coloured streamers on the ceiling are left over from last weekend's anniversary function. Next to a lectern, from which announcements are made, sits a red light. As the supper plates empty, and socialising warms up, the red light flashes insistently, stopping hands in mid-air, calling eyes away from conversations and towards the party host who stands unselfconsciously on a chair by the lectern, waiting patiently for the gaze of many eyes to meet hers. After several calls of the light, she invites people to sit on chairs arranged in horseshoe rows. The ritual part of the event begins.

This is a farewell for an overseas Deaf person, who is leaving after two years living and working in the community. Stories are called for. Departures demand tales of arrival and belonging, and amusing moments shared. Tonight's stories tell how the visitor first seemed so foreign, with her different sign language, but gradually gaining acceptance as she learned New Zealand Sign Language. The stories are told frankly, and often with unflattering humour. People move spontaneously to the front, climb onto a chair or up the steps to the lectern so that they can be seen above the sea of heads, and sign stories of first encounters and memorable moments, rounded off with expressions of regret at the visitor's departure and anticipated pride in her future achievements that will reflect on all Deaf people. Promises are made to meet again in the worldwide network of Deaf travellers. Hugs and souvenirs are given, and a home-made cake decorated for the visitor is presented and admired. All this is recorded on video by a friend, as part of the going-away gift – signed memories captured. Another round of stories trickles out, but gradually the formalities fade out and eyes are diverted back to conversations. The forest of hands begins to move again as everyone returns to talk for the rest of the evening. Eventually the lights are flicked on and off to signal that this Deaf haven must lose its inhabitants – until the next club night.

Friday night at the Auckland Deaf Club

Introduction

Being Deaf for life is an experience most people have no reason to imagine and little opportunity to observe. Deafness as a physical condition is invisible and is often misinterpreted as unsociability or a puzzling difference. Even less obvious than lack of hearing, but more intriguing, is the life of Deaf people as a community bonded by shared experience and language. Because they don't experience the world through sound in the usual ways, Deaf people are some-what like foreigners in their own country: their access to the surrounding language and culture is never quite complete, and so their outlook and their connection to society is, in many ways, unlike that of hearing people. It is rare for people with hearing to communicate deeply enough with Deaf people to know them well, and so society superimposes its own impressions of deafness. Popular images of life-long deafness highlight silence, muteness, tragic isola-tion, educational problems, and miracle medical cures. But these concerns are far removed from Deaf people's own interpretations of their lives.

This book is not about hearing loss, except as a point of origin for the personal journeys that result from being Deaf. Its purpose is to provide a window on the experiences of New Zealanders who describe themselves as Deaf. This group in any population is small: an estimated one per 1,000 people are born or become profoundly Deaf in early infancy or childhood and thus do not have early access to spoken language. The Deaf community in New Zealand is conservatively estimated at around 4,320, but since some people with lesser degrees of hearing loss and some who lose hearing at later ages may also identify with the Deaf community, it is probably larger than this.[1]

Inside the Deaf world, calling oneself Deaf is not a description of disability. It contrasts with words such as 'hearing impaired' and 'deaf mute', and with the way the adjective 'deaf' is ordinarily used to describe someone who can't hear well. For the people in this book, the term 'Deaf' is a label of cultural iden-tity, a way of being and communicating shared by people who feel most akin to other Deaf, regardless of gender, ethnicity, age, education, or nationality. The written use of capitalised Deaf has been adopted by Deaf New Zealanders over the last decade to express an emerging cultural consciousness.[2] This spelling is used throughout the book as a translation of Deaf people's sign, although not every mention of deafness in the stories implies cultural identity. For example, when a narrator tells of his parents discovering that he was deaf as an infant, the word is probably used more in its audiological sense; for some narrators, personal identity as Deaf was discovered in early adulthood rather than childhood. This variation in meaning of the sign makes it difficult for a translator to determine when the sense of 'deaf' evolves to 'Deaf' in each case. I have chosen to use 'Deaf' throughout – although for the same reasons other writers may prefer the more neutral 'deaf'.

Another word used here in an unfamiliar way is 'hearing', which is how Deaf people describe those who are not Deaf. 'Hearing' people contrast with Deaf in terms of language, life experience, attitudes, behaviour, and power status; in essence, 'hearing' is the category of 'others', or the dominant majority group. One narrator emphasises the most basic distinction – communication – in her definition: 'From the time I was very young I knew instinctively that some people were Deaf like us and others were different. Hearing to us meant people who couldn't really sign, and Deaf meant the people you could sign fluently with.'[3] In the narratives, Deaf and hearing are portrayed as clearly distinct groups – much in the way that the world is divided into male/female, Maori/Pakeha, gay/straight or child/adult, depending on one's primary identity.

Observations about people's 'ways' are often ascribed by Deaf people to a Deaf/hearing cultural distinction, although the behaviour described may have little to do with being able to hear or not. For example, a Deaf friend (from a Deaf family) at a barbecue recently commented to me that 'Deaf cooks always make sure the meat is well charred – we like it that way – but hearing people cook it more lightly.' Deaf people often remark that at Deaf parties, people congregate in the kitchen to talk, whereas at hearing parties the guests supposedly stay in the formal living areas. Whether or not such generalisations are true, they do illustrate an instinctive demarcation that Deaf people perceive between themselves and people unlike themselves, i.e., the hearing. Identifying as members of a minority group means that issues of 'insider' and 'outsider' status in the worlds of hearing and Deaf recur through the stories. Many express a feeling of being an insider in the Deaf world and an outsider in the hearing world, while some describe moving between both worlds.[4]

As the hearing outsider who collected and interpreted the material in this book, I should explain my connection with Deaf people. I first met the Deaf community as a novice sign language interpreter in 1985, after happening upon a small newspaper advertisement for New Zealand's first training course for sign language interpreters. I had no relevant experience for this vocation other than some aptitude for languages – and certainly no notion of the world I was about to enter. Not having grown up with Deaf parents or siblings, I learned the language and culture by late immersion – observing, asking questions, and making mistakes on patient Deaf people. I was fascinated by this community who apparently had an oppressive educational history, but a highly organised social world and a sense of identity that was expressed in stories, through Deaf humour, and in their close bonds with each other.

When I took up my newly created position as an interpreter in Wellington, my presence in the community was an enigma to local Deaf people who, at that time, had rarely encountered hearing strangers in their own territory, such as the Deaf Club. They were puzzled by my keen interest in their sign language, as signing had been a clandestine behaviour at school and around hearing people in general. I was regularly asked why I was there and how I knew sign language – the first suggestion usually being, 'Are your mother and father Deaf?' Or, when this didn't fit, 'Do you love Deaf people?' It was awkward to find a satisfactory answer, because I had neither a natural social connection nor a missionary motive, and 'interpreter' wasn't a recognised category then.

Becoming an interpreter in the Deaf community prompted me to study applied linguistics, and inevitably led me into a network of professional and personal relationships with Deaf people, including (much later) marriage to a Deaf American. Working as an interpreter in New Zealand and in America has allowed me to closely observe the interface between Deaf and hearing people. Some of the misunderstandings I have witnessed occur because most hearing people only glimpse a fragment of a Deaf person's life in a situation where it intersects briefly with their own – perhaps in a doctor's office, in the courtroom, at work, or in a classroom. Deaf people are usually seen 'through a keyhole' – in isolation – without reference to the wider backdrop of their community. Interpreting across this gap has motivated me to present this collection of Deaf people's own stories to give a fuller picture of their lives.

I now work as a lecturer and researcher in Deaf Studies, and sometimes as an interpreter. Deaf people still often categorise me as an interpreter, because this label most easily defines my bilingual, outsider/insider status in the community. Interpreting is how I came to be in their community in the first place, and no matter what else I may be in relation to Deaf people, I have the useful potential to communicate between them and hearing people. Making this book is an extension of that role.

Medically oriented descriptions of deafness as an audiological impairment (or in terms of other 'deficits') have not contributed to an understanding of Deaf people as a social group. Deaf people's own accounts of their lives have barely been documented in New Zealand, because many of them express themselves better in the face-to-face medium of New Zealand Sign Language (NZSL) than in written or spoken English. And, because of the perception of

Deaf people as 'unfortunates', their own perspective has not often been sought as a relevant contribution to the body of expert knowledge on deafness.[5] My own understanding of the New Zealand Deaf community and their experience in society has been deepened by numerous analyses of Deaf culture, history and language published by both Deaf and hearing writers elsewhere.[6] There is a great deal in their accounts that sheds light on the local situation, but it remains important to describe what it means specifically to be Deaf in New Zealand.

The raw material for this book is selected from approximately 40 interviews recorded in NZSL on videotape, between 1993 and 1999. Sixteen of these were chosen to represent a cross-section of age, educational background, gender and family ethnicity. Each one has been translated into English and edited into a narrative, and for the most part left in a chronological sequence to retain the natural progression of each life story. In some cases, storytellers chose to edit out critical comments about their experiences with educational institutions, while others have omitted details about family relationships that may have been hurtful to others. Material that has been excluded for fear of offence indicates some deeply felt injustices and clashes of perspective with non-Deaf people in the storytellers' lives.

Capturing, in one-dimensional print, the emotional tone of each narrator as it was expressed in sign language was an elusive task for a translator. Qualities of hand and body movement and facial expression of a signer are visual charact-eristics equivalent to 'voice' that don't transfer easily into writing. As NZSL and English are separate languages with the capacity to express concepts in differ-ent ways, the translation ranges from literal to free, as required by the sense and structure of each signer's expression. Although every effort has been made to preserve the intent and style of the storytellers, the original voices lose some character in print. Video frames of most of the signers in action provide a glimpse of their natural mode of expression. Bruce Connew's photographic essay brings the reader a visual encounter with scenes captured from the Deaf world.

Some of the narratives simply chronicle life as it happened; others reflect more explicitly on the development of a personal Deaf consciousness. The stories overwhelmingly reveal the challenges that Deaf people face in growing up and navigating both Deaf and hearing environments at home, school and work. They show what Deaf people can do and aspire to do, which is often in contrast to the opportunities they have been offered.

The extent to which Deaf New Zealanders' lives have been constrained by our society's treatment of deafness was brought home to me when I had the opportunity to study and work in the United States from 1987. My limited notions of 'the Deaf community' were turned upside down when I arrived at a class at California State University, Northridge, and met my Deaf lecturer, and later other Deaf academics, all highly educated and articulate in American Sign Language and written English. At this university, interpreters were provided for hearing students in Deaf lecturers' classes, to interpret from sign language into English. This sophisticated reversal, and the apparent normality of it, was a thrilling shock. In America I met Deaf teachers, lawyers, scientists, post-graduate students, administrators, film directors, travel agents, actors, psychologists, and so on. No one seemed to have given them the message that these were not possible vocations for Deaf people unless they could speak well and pass as hearing people. In New Zealand at that time, the highest occupations in the signing Deaf community were skilled tradesmen (many without qualifications because of a literacy barrier) and a small handful of white-collar workers. Very few could have hoped to become as educated as or more educated than their own school teachers.

Returning from four years in America, my perspective had changed. My glimpse of a different reality told me that if New Zealand Deaf had been products of a different educational history, some of them would by now be self-confident professionals, academics, artists, and so on. The people I knew in New Zealand were no different in their intelligence or potential from the Americans – only in the opportunities and possibilities that had been imagined for them. This epiphany confirmed my professional goal to change expectations in some small way.[7]

The honest and consistent perspectives of Deaf people recorded in this book may challenge existing stereotypes and perhaps raise some uncomfortable truths. Acknowledging their experiences in printed literature is a necessary step in the New Zealand Deaf community's journey of empowerment through reflection, self-knowledge, and action for change. As Lloyd Geering remarks: 'The human existence of each one of us unfolds as a story, and it is only as we attempt to tell that story that we come to understand more clearly who we are, where we have come from, and where we are going.'[8]

The next chapter previews some themes that recur throughout the stories, and briefly provides some historical context. A list explaining terms and concepts from the Deaf world that are mentioned in the stories is included at the end of the book for the reader's information.

Notes and References

1 P. Dugdale, 'Being Deaf in New Zealand: A Case Study of the Wellington Deaf Community', PhD thesis, Victoria University of Wellington, 2000.

2 This usage was defined and made popular by American sociolinguist James Woodward in 1972 as a way of capturing the cultural meaning of the sign in print, in his article 'Implications for Sociolinguistic Research Among the Deaf', *Sign Language Studies*, 1, pp. 1–7.

3 Sara Pivac's story, p. 227.

4 For discussion of insider/outsider identity in the Deaf world, see Chapter 3 in Paul C. Higgins, *Outsiders in a Hearing World: A Sociology of Deafness*, Sage Publications, Beverly Hills, 1980.

5 P. Penman, 'Deaf Way, Deaf View: A Study of Deaf Culture from a Deaf Perspective' (Masters thesis, Victoria University of Wellington, 1999) documents the perceptions of New Zealand Deaf about characteristic experiences and 'ways'.

6 For example: C. Baker and R. Battison (eds), *Sign Language and the Deaf Community: Essays in Honor of William C. Stokoe*, National Association of the Deaf, USA, 1980; J. Gannon, *Deaf Heritage: A Narrative History of Deaf America*, National Association of the Deaf, Silver Spring, 1981; S. Gregory and G. M. Hartley (eds), *Constructing Deafness*, Pinter, London, 1991; Leo Jacobs, *A Deaf Adult Speaks Out*, Gallaudet College Press, Washington DC, 1974; H. Lane, *When the Mind Hears: A History of the Deaf*, Random House, New York, 1984; H. Lane, R. Hoffmeister and B. Bahan, *A Journey into the Deaf World*, Dawn Sign Press, San Diego, 1996; C. Padden and T. Humphries, *Deaf in America: Voices from a Culture*, Harvard University Press, Cambridge, Mass., 1988; G. Taylor and J. Bishop (eds), *Being Deaf: The Experience of Deafness*, Pinter, London, 1991; Oliver Sacks, *Seeing Voices: A Journey into the World of the Deaf*, University of California Press, 1995.

7 Possibly my most useful contribution in this regard was marrying that first Deaf professor I met (David McKee), and importing him to New Zealand. His presence and work as a teacher has had more impact on the Deaf community and their ideas of what is possible than anything I will ever contribute.

8 Lloyd Geering, in N. Glasgow (ed.), *Directions: New Zealanders Explore the Meaning of Life*, Shoal Bay Press, Christchurch, 1995 (Foreword, p. 10).

Themes in Deaf Experience

'People of the eye'

The absence of sound preoccupies people who hear as the most problematic aspect of deafness, and is generally how they understand the meaning of 'deaf'. This is not a major theme for the Deaf people in this book, even though the physical fact of deafness powerfully shapes the ways in which they interact with the world. Some of the storytellers do mention experiences with sound, usually pointing to differences between Deaf and hearing ways. They do not dwell on a lack of sound, because in fact most Deaf people do hear certain sounds to some degree in some situations, and most make certain sounds purposefully for various everyday reasons (for example, knocking on a hearing person's door, using their voice to call hearing children). However, most of the sounds hearing people take for granted are not a useful source of information for Deaf people; so how, then, do they orient themselves to the environment by relying not on sound but on sight?

In 1910, George Veditz, an American Deaf leader, eloquently described the Deaf as 'first, last, and for all time, the people of the eye'.[1] A Deaf person in this book expresses the same thought: 'Deaf people see – things are visual for us. That's how we access everything.'[2] Deaf communities throughout history have created visual languages to communicate, as Veditz noted. But he could not have imagined how later generations of Deaf people would use technology to make their environment visually accessible. Today, for example, flashing lights signal doorbells, alarm clocks, smoke alarms and baby-cry monitors; text telephones (TTYs), fax machines, pagers and e-mail are used for everyday communication; television has subtitles, and videos capture sign language. In Deaf homes, dividing walls between living areas (kitchen/dining/living room) tend to be removed immediately in any renovation, since open sight lines are a priority for communication. These are everyday examples of how Deaf people adapt their physical environment for seeing rather than hearing.

KDEC

All eyes turn to the boy leading grace (far right) in the dining hall of Kelston School for Deaf Children (1966). The number of boarders at Deaf schools in the 1960s increased because of a rubella epidemic.

Deaf patterns of interaction are also shaped by the need to receive information through the eyes. Each act of live communication has to be intentional, mutual and face-to-face. There is no talking while someone's back is turned or their eyes otherwise occupied, nor chatting casually over washing the dishes, calling from one room to another, talking in bed after lights out, or phoning the neighbour to send the children home for dinner. The Deaf have other solutions. Instead of saying a name to get someone's attention, a Deaf person will move into another's line of vision, gently tap a shoulder, or flutter a hand at eye level. They may bang on the floor or table to send vibrations, flick the lights, or signal to a bystander to get the attention of someone too far away to reach. For all ordinary acts of communication, mutual eye contact must be gained and managed, often at the same time as competing actions such as eating, driving or nursing a baby. Activity and talk are alternated in different rhythms, stopping and starting as eyes and hands allow. Knowing when and where to look and when to expect someone else to look are essential skills in the Deaf world.

Even with the advent of text-based phone and e-mail communications, Deaf people often travel inconvenient distances to hold a conversation face to face, rather than trust the vagaries of disembodied writing. This preference is not unique to Deaf culture, of course, but before TTY and fax became available in New Zealand in the 1980s, it was a necessity. Signed conversations, however, can be

VADEC VADEC

conducted through windows, between cars in traffic, across a street or a crowded room, at much greater distances than soundwaves would allow a polite spoken conversation. These technological and behavioural adaptations for using the eyes instead of the ears are understood as norms in the Deaf community, and are often referred to as examples of Deaf culture or 'the Deaf way'.[3]

Frustrations expressed in the stories recorded here tend to focus not on the deprivation of sound but on problematic interactions with hearing people resulting from differences in language, behaviour and outlook. Deaf people experience and value sound differently from the way most hearing people would assume. Many make functional use of whatever they can hear (awareness of vehicle noises, for example, or sound effects at movies, music at high volume, a dog barking), while for others the main relevance of sound is learning and observing 'hearing' rules about producing acceptable and unacceptable sounds. The fact that lack of sound does not dominate Deaf people's perception of themselves underlies the intuitive misgivings many Deaf express about the current enthusiasm for normalising young Deaf children through cochlear implant surgery, as advocated by medical experts. The medical profession is apt to perceive deafness in ways that bear no relation to the beliefs, values and experiences of Deaf people.[4]

LEFT: *Delwyn Williams (now Buzzard) at Sumner School, 1968. (See Della's story, p. 162.)*

RIGHT: *Helen Keller with teenager Patty Tremaine (now Still) during her visit to Sumner school in 1948. (See Patty's story, p. 68.)*

Speech training, late 1940s. The child is encouraged to watch his mouth and feel his breath on his hand. Deaf people commonly recall many hours of their childhood spent like this.

Language history

Language and communication issues tend to dominate the stories of Deaf people and their families, because it is their lack of access to spoken language on the one hand and their gravitation towards sign language as a visual alternative on the other that differentiate Deaf people from hearing people. The universal problem faced by Deaf children in hearing families is that the incidental, everyday talk they don't hear is the gateway to learning and to the culture of the family and society. Sharing a language with others also enables self-knowledge and identity. Unless a complete language and natural communication is accessible to deaf children in everyday situations, this process is delayed and complicated. Upon expert advice, generations of Deaf children in New Zealand laboured for years at school and home to learn to articulate and lipread spoken language, mostly with limited success, and at the expense of a proper education and natural relationships with parents.

The discovery of other Deaf people and sign language, and the sense of identity and freedom of communication that ensues, is a recurring theme in the narratives. The extent to which the storytellers comment on language and communication suggests how dominant these are in shaping their self-perception and their social landscape. Signing is the visible badge of being Deaf and in many societies it has been stigmatised. The oldest generation of today's Deaf in New Zealand were so strictly prohibited from signing at school that they express ambivalence about signing and nearly always accompany signs with speech. However, attitudes about signing in New Zealand have been positively re-valued within the span of these people's lives. Their personal histories are thus closely tied to the collective history of language use in the New Zealand and international Deaf community.

Although philosophers and educationalists through the ages have observed that Deaf people communicate spontaneously with each other in gestures or signs, the use of signing (like many minority languages) has had a chequered history in education. In 1880 the International Congress on Education of the Deaf in Milan passed a resolution to eliminate the use of signing as a teaching method (and thereby the employment of Deaf teachers) in the majority of Deaf schools worldwide. This infamous resolution, which coincided with the opening of Sumner School for the Deaf in Christchurch also in 1880, arbitrarily claimed 'the incontestable superiority of speech over signs' and elevated the importance of speech to both the means and the end in the education of the Deaf. It was a decision that would have worldwide consequences for Deaf people, made by a group of hearing teachers.

For the following century in New Zealand, signing was regarded as a threat to the acquisition of speech and written language, and a hindrance to the integration of Deaf people into society. Signing was officially banned in schools until 1979, when a system of manually coded English (referred to in New Zealand variously as Australasian Signed English, Total Communication, or TC) was adopted.[5] The addition of manual communication to Deaf education in New Zealand (and its resumption in countries with an earlier history of signed instruction) came about when it was apparent that a century of oralism had not produced the desired results for the majority of Deaf students, in terms of academic achievement, social assimilation, or even the accomplishment of speech itself. Natural articulation and fluency in English language is notoriously difficult and laborious for the born Deaf or early deafened to master, simply because they cannot hear what they are supposed to be imitating and producing – either in others' speech or in their own voice.

Many Deaf people at first welcomed the use of Australasian Signed English in education because it was more visual than lipreading alone, and provided some legitimisation of signing, although there was ambivalence about the 'new'

Marching team at Sumner School for the Deaf, 1957.

signing. Signed English allows a hearing person to speak their first language, English, at the same time as making signs on their hands that correspond to each word. However, this is not how Deaf people naturally use sign language – something that was difficult for the community to articulate convincingly at the time because there was no linguistic description of their own sign language available.

New Zealand Sign Language (NZSL), which uses space and movement to encode meaning visually, differs from English in its grammar and vocabulary, and does not generally match with spoken English. In the past this led to the misconception that it must be an inferior form of communication, lacking the structure of English. As an example of how the grammar differs, NZSL constructs a question by using certain facial expressions rather than a different word order, and a signer can indicate the subject and object of a verb by altering the direction of a verb's movement. Signed English lacks the grammatical structures that exist in naturally developed sign languages, which take advantage of space and movement for visual efficiency. In its pure form, Signed English is generally seen by Deaf people as alien (being initiated by hearing people and based on a lexicon of signs adopted from Australia or invented by hearing people), cumbersome to use (being based on English grammar, which doesn't fit a visual modality), and frequently incomprehensible. Not surprisingly, Signed English has not survived in adult community usage, but its use in Deaf education for over 10 years has resulted in differences in

the vocabulary and signing styles of older and younger generations of Deaf people. Views about Signed English as opposed to NZSL are expressed by narrators of different generations in the stories.

Boarders at Titirangi, 1958. Experiences and friendship shared at Deaf schools led to a group identity and bonds that underpin the 'extended family' feeling of the Deaf community. (Susan Hamilton is seated fourth from right; see her story, p. 87.)

NZSL officially found a place in the education system in 1993, when the first bilingual (NZSL and English) class was opened at Kelston Deaf Education Centre in Auckland. Van Asch Deaf Education Centre in Christchurch (formerly Sumner School for the Deaf) soon followed suit. With increased recognition that many Deaf people identify culturally with a Deaf community, and typically use both NZSL and English in their adult lives, the concept of bilingualism for Deaf children is gaining wider acceptance in New Zealand among teachers and parents of Deaf children – although it is still seen only as one option. Oralism continues to be chosen as a path by a significant number of parents. To date, the implementation of bilingual and bicultural Deaf education remains a challenge, with only a tiny handful of Deaf people trained as teachers and the majority of non-Deaf people in the field still working to develop fluency in NZSL. The first signing Deaf person qualified as a teacher of the Deaf in 1992[7] (see Cheryl Anton's story, p. 97).

Before the 1880 Milan congress resolution banning sign language, numerous schools for the Deaf in countries such as America, Australia, France, Ireland, Scotland and other European countries had been founded by, or employed, Deaf teachers who used signing as the medium of instruction (as did many hearing teachers), with impressive educational results. By the early twentieth century, the effects of Milan as well as changes in the scientific, religious and political thinking of the era contributed to a rapid decline in the use of sign language in Deaf education. Assimilation to hearing/speaking norms became the main goal, leading to the near-total exclusion of Deaf teachers from Deaf education worldwide (with the notable exception of the USA, where Deaf teachers did decline drastically in number but continued to have a role within Deaf education throughout the twentieth century).[8] In New Zealand, there was no history of Deaf education let alone Deaf teachers prior to 1880, and thus oral teaching solely by hearing teachers became uncontested policy from the outset. Gerrit van Asch, as founding director of the Sumner school, prohibited any use of signs to the extent that children with a prior knowledge of signs or fingerspelling were declined enrolment during the earliest decades of the school.[9] In 1898 van Asch wrote in a report: 'Let it be distinctly understood that the clearly spoken word was and is our only means of communication and that finger signs have no place and no meaning amongst us.'[10]

Modern NZSL is closely related to British and Australian Sign Languages,[11] and has presumably evolved from approximately 1880 when Deaf children first came together at the residential Sumner school and started to communicate with each other. NZSL was developed and passed on for a century as the playground and dormitory language of successive generations of children at Deaf schools, and naturally became the language of the adult community.

It is likely that some Deaf school children from the earliest times had exposure to adults using sign language, which fertilised the development of NZSL as a close relative of British and Australian Sign Languages. In the late nineteenth and early twentieth century, a significant number of Deaf children were sent to Australian Deaf schools for part or all of their education, returning to New Zealand with a knowledge of sign language (British and Irish) used in those institutions. It is also possible that there were Deaf immigrants from the UK with Deaf children who may have transmitted their parents' home sign language to peers in the community. Ex-pupils of the Deaf schools were sometimes employed as domestic help in the early days, and may also have been a source of adult signing.[12] The system of signs that children used at school was enriched further as Deaf adults maintained social networks after leaving school and established formal organisations in which signing was an important means of communication, even though these signs were not viewed as a 'language' by the older generations who describe themselves as 'oral' in accordance with the school policy of their time.[13]

As some of the stories in this book attest, the constraints of the oral teaching

KDEC

method, along with a pathological perception of Deaf people, by and large failed to deliver an adequate education to previous generations of Deaf in New Zealand. This fact is not only claimed by Deaf people themselves but also acknowledged by many teachers who struggled within an unworkable system. As one former teacher of the Deaf from the 1950s to the 1960s recalls: 'We were bound by the chains of oralism ... those "in the know" became obsessed with it. Where it should have been part of a total package it was a "coat of iron". In reality we succeeded in the classroom by using sign language done in an atmosphere of secret!'[14] Oralism also spectacularly failed in its aim to prevent the natural formation of a signing Deaf community – in New Zealand and everywhere else it has been tried.

NZSL was systematically analysed and named as a language by American linguist Marianne Collins-Ahlgren in the late 1980s.[15] Previously, it had been generally regarded as a collection of rudimentary gestures, somewhere between mime and broken English. Around the same time as Collins-Ahlgren's work, the re-definition of signing as a real language was given momentum in the grassroots Deaf community after the first group of eight sign language interpreters was trained in a course initiated by the New Zealand Association of the Deaf in 1985. The course activities involved Deaf people as language models for the students, prompting some in the Deaf community to perceive their use of signing in a more positive light, and actually

Using a group microphone for speech and listening practice, 1952. Curriculum subject matter at the Deaf schools was often subordinated to activities aimed at learning to speak.

VADEC

Pupils in the early days at the Sumner school undertook farm work on the property, both to sustain the residents of the school and to learn work skills. This photograph was taken in 1912.

begin to refer to it as 'NZSL'. Three of the course graduates were employed full-time to provide interpreting services to Deaf communities in Auckland, Wellington and Christchurch. This quickly brought signing into the public domain, as interpreters enabled Deaf people to participate and have a voice in all kinds of activities and events from which they had previously been excluded. A permanent two-year training course was established in 1992, at the Auckland Institute of Technology (now the Auckland University of Technology) with the first eight interpreters graduating in 1994.

Today, sign language interpreters are available to provide communication access by interpreting between spoken English and sign language, and vice versa, at appointments and meetings where Deaf and hearing people need to communicate. Their role is contained to interpreting the communication from one language to another (as opposed to acting as an advocate or spokesperson) in order to enable Deaf people to interact more independently with hearing people than was possible in the past. Interpreters remain a scarce commodity in New Zealand, with approximately 40 qualified interpreters serving the whole country at this time. The training of interpreters has not yet caught up with the backlog of demand for their service which has developed rapidly since 1985. Once the potential of interpreters to provide access to a wide range of situations was realised, Deaf New Zealanders became less reticent about using sign language, and began to assert their right to access public life and higher education via interpreters as a channel of communication. The opportunity to communicate in many new contexts through interpreters, including tertiary education and political advocacy, for example, has accelerated the rate of natural growth and change in NZSL during the last decade.

Increased international contact with signing and politically empowered Deaf people, particularly through Deaf sports, from the 1980s also enhanced Deaf New Zealanders' perception of sign language and its importance as an emblem of 'Deaf pride'. The publication of *A Dictionary of New Zealand Sign Language* in 1997 was a milestone in public recognition of the language and its richness.[16] New information and perspectives on signing communities are still transforming the way Deaf people in New Zealand feel about their language and their status as Deaf.

As with the re-introduction of Maori language into education, the inclusion of NZSL in Deaf education was not motivated primarily by innovation within the establishment. The education system has rather shifted its orientation to acknowledge the rapidly changing consciousness and demands of the Deaf community, who have drawn strength from parallel movements overseas and from new perspectives arising from local and international research. For the first time in a century, the 1990s saw the beginning of dialogue between educators of Deaf children and Deaf people themselves – a process made possible through the use of interpreters to bridge the language and communication gap. It is perhaps telling that interpreters are still regularly needed to facilitate this dialogue within Deaf education; there are still many issues to be resolved in the shifting of power in this complex relationship. As one administrator in Deaf education recently remarked to me, 'Most professionals in Deaf education still see Deaf adults as the "clip-on" to Deaf education: they are driving the car and the Deaf people are in the trailer.'[17]

Deaf school, hearing school: finding the Deaf world

Several stories in the book bring to light the role of older Deaf children and Deaf adults in passing on sign language, life experience and a sense of identity to younger ones. Since most are not born to Deaf parents, this connection traditionally happened at school with Deaf peers. Deaf schools are often seen by past pupils as being a second home, an important place of origin, since many boarded and grew up there, developing lifelong bonds with a community of peers.[18] This is why Deaf people typically ask 'where did you go to school?' when introducing themselves. It places community members within a social

Gerrit van Asch (founding director of Sumner School for the Deaf, 1880-1906) teaching speech articulation. The boot, boat and bread were presumably used as props for demonstrating different vowel sounds.

network, just as the question 'no hea koe?' in the Maori world does not simply mean 'where are you from?' but also 'which people are you connected to?'

The two remaining residential Deaf schools in New Zealand are van Asch Deaf Education Centre at Sumner, Christchurch (formerly Sumner School for Deaf Children) and Kelston Deaf Education Centre in Auckland (formerly Kelston School for Deaf Children, and originally located at Titirangi). The third, which closed in 1989, was the Catholic (and smaller) St Dominic's School for the Deaf, originally opened in Wellington but located in Feilding for most of its life. These institutions are significant cultural and emotional landmarks in the Deaf community, and figure prominently in many stories of growing up.

From 1880 until the 1960s, nearly all children with a significant hearing loss attended one of the Deaf schools as boarders or day pupils. But in the early 1960s a maternal rubella epidemic swelled the numbers of Deaf children entering school, and residential education was recognised as a costly option for the state. Hearing aid technology also began to improve, meaning that partially deaf children were expected to make more use of residual hearing than in the past. Educational philosophies of this period also favoured the concept of integration generally. All these factors led to the placement of more Deaf children into regular schools rather than the traditional residential schools. Deaf units were established in many

KDEC

KDEC

ABOVE: *Sumner School for the Deaf. These original buildings, comprising boys and girls dormitories and classrooms, were demolished (for safety reasons) just before the school centenary in 1980, to the regret of many in the Deaf community.*

LEFT: *The Titirangi Hotel was converted to a branch of the Sumner school in 1942 to accommodate North Island children during the war. The rather unsuitable premises at Titirangi finally closed in 1958, when the new school at Kelston opened.*

KDEC

ABOVE: *Older pupils were important mentors for younger children at the residential schools. Outside of class, sign language was an easy means of communication passed on from older to newer pupils.*

RIGHT: *The matron was a central figure in the domestic lives of generations of Deaf children like these young boarders at Sumner, pictured with Miss Leary in 1934.*

VADEC

primary and secondary schools and as time went by, more Deaf children were also mainstreamed into regular classes. The rationale behind this change was that through increased contact with hearing children, Deaf students would become socially integrated into their local community and acquire better speech (in the absence of other Deaf children to sign with). Some students did manage to get a better education than they might have in the Deaf schools, but many others struggled in hearing school environments that did not meet their social or educational needs, as described in some of the stories in this book.

Because signing was not recognised as part of Deaf education until 1979, the mainstreaming of Deaf children officially meant no change in communication mode. But in reality it meant that Deaf children were increasingly cut off from a large community of peers with whom they could communicate freely. From an oralist point of view, this had been seen as one of the main benefits of mainstreaming – being surrounded by hearing children would surely make Deaf children more like hearing children in communication and social behaviour. However, the risk of social isolation and lack of proper access to classroom teaching that Deaf children can face in this situation continues to concern Deaf adults, who advocate the need for easy communication and identity with other Deaf children and role models – as well as the opportunity to fully access education in a comprehensible environment.

Now that approximately 90 per cent of Deaf children are educated in mainstream schools, discovering or consolidating a Deaf identity is often delayed until young adulthood, when contact with Deaf peers and role models is made through Deaf Clubs or sports groups.[19] As there are very few Deaf people spread out over a long country with a small and scattered population, New Zealand Deaf people have always faced a degree of geographic and social isolation from each other. In the past this was offset by the fact that they nearly all came together at residential schools where they established strong Deaf community bonds. Today, Deaf children may have more access to their family (by attending a local school, and by families learning to sign), but they face potential social isolation where they are the only one of a kind at a hearing school. Most now discover a connection to the Deaf community at a later stage of life.

Being Deaf is a collective historical experience beyond simply an individual condition.[20] In other words, Deaf lives have been a continuous thread in the fabric of societies in all eras – one which is invisible to most eyes, but recognised by Deaf people when they come across it. This is why school is such a major topic in the life stories of Deaf people, because connecting with other Deaf children at school opens doors to a Deaf world at an early age, allowing easy communication and social networks. Contact with a critical mass of other Deaf people offers access to a visual language, knowledge of how a wide spectrum of other Deaf people live (past and present), and the self-esteem that comes of feeling normal and competent in a group of peers. The storytellers in this book who lacked contact with the Deaf world while growing up came to this knowledge later, often at an emotional cost.

In this photograph from the 1950s, an advisor on Deaf children demonstrates auditory/oral training exercises for parents to continue at home. Parents were generally advised that their Deaf child's success depended on the effort they put into structured coaching of speech.

Deaf people in hearing families

More than 90 per cent of Deaf people are born to hearing parents, and a small percentage of these may have Deaf siblings. As for children of inter-racial adoption, this 'different-ness' creates a tension between belonging to a family and needing to identify with those who share their biological similarity and the social experiences this brings. Because they communicate, perceive and thus experience the world differently from hearing people, Deaf people tend to spend at least part of their life in another 'culture' that is different from that of their non-Deaf family. So the feeling of being both familiars and strangers within their own family is evident in many Deaf stories. This distinction between the two worlds is more sharply felt and articulated by some than others.

Most of the adults in this book were born into an educational era (pre-1979) when sign language was not presented to parents as an option for communicating even with a profoundly Deaf child. For many, this led to linguistic and emotional disconnection between the Deaf and their hearing families. While some families did succeed in devising their own system of communication, many others could not get beyond superficial communication despite, or probably because of, professional advice that they 'talk, talk, talk' as if the child could hear, and that on no account should they let the child rely on 'the crutch' of gestures. It is understandable that many Deaf people (and undoubtedly the parents, if their stories were told) express anguish or bitterness about their experiences in a hearing family.

These life stories are told retrospectively from the perspective of the Deaf children; it is important also to consider the impact of a Deaf child from the hearing family's point of view. Parents faced the difficult task of raising a child without being able to rely on the instinctive reflexes of verbal communication, often devoting much time to teaching language and other taken-for-granted knowledge to their Deaf child. Hearing siblings of Deaf people often recall feeling sidelined while a disproportionate amount of parents' attention was focused on the needs of the Deaf child in the family. Decisions had to be made about schooling: whether to send a young child far away from home to a residential school or to move a whole family closer to a school for the Deaf, or to place the child in a local school possibly ill-equipped to teach them. Some Deaf people have traumatic memories of a long journey away from home at a tender age to go to a residential school; without the benefit of explanation, this felt like abandonment at an unknown destination. No doubt it was traumatic for their parents too.

However, many of those children quickly developed a sense of kinship with Deaf school friends that contrasted with the way they felt when they returned home in the holidays to a family life that they found hard to be a part of. One Deaf person recalls:

> I hated going home for the holidays: it was so dead for me. It was so different at home - the food was different, the culture was different. Theirs was a hearing world and I was a Deaf person coming into it. I used to wonder if this was actually my real home; it was difficult to fit in and really connect. The communication was stilted. Mum would write messages to me, trying hard: 'Are you okay? Are you happy?' I'd just respond with 'yes' or 'no'. After about a week of trying to communicate it got better and we ended up gesturing, pointing and feeling more relaxed. If Mum mouthed something that I didn't get, she'd remember to gesture what it was and mouth the word at the same time. That was the old fashioned way of communicating! I used to look forward to getting back to school. My mother would cry and worry that I would be upset about leaving, but actually I was happy to be going back.[21]

Of course, there are exceptions to these patterns, and Deaf schools were not always happy havens, but the general picture of feeling isolated at a mainstream school and/or in a hearing family is a consistent theme. These dilemmas of difference have changed only slightly for the current generation of Deaf children and hearing parents, but fortunately, families now have more opportunity to learn sign language as a means of communication, and are more likely to have some access to Deaf adults as mentors for their children and themselves.[22]

Deaf children of Deaf parents

Deaf people born to Deaf parents (fewer than 10 per cent) have quite a different childhood experience from the majority of Deaf people, because their identity and lives are closer to their parents'. Although Deaf parents have a range of reactions to having Deaf offspring, a Deaf child is seen as unexceptional at home, and becomes 'exceptional' only when he enters school and becomes conscious of being Deaf. By contrast, the birth of a Deaf child to hearing parents presents a crisis of difference, so that the Deaf child may begin to feel truly normal only when she encounters other Deaf children like herself at school.

The Deaf offspring of Deaf parents have a pivotal role in passing on sign language, general world knowledge and 'the Deaf way' to Deaf children not born to it. They usually arrive at school with a well-developed first language, a broader base of knowledge, and social skills acquired from interaction at home. These children often become relatively high achievers and social leaders. They also provide an important link to an older generation of role models, as a second-generation Deaf person recalls: 'When my [Deaf] parents came to my school, the other Deaf children were just blown away, because they had never seen a Deaf adult before. Up till then they thought there were only Deaf children in the world. They were amazed to realise that grown-ups could be Deaf ...'[23]

Deaf parents of Deaf children, however, describe the dilemma of whether to send their children to a Deaf school that did not fulfil their own educational potential and may not be fully conversant in their home language, or to place them in a mainstream school that is academically challenging but further removed from the child's cultural background and peer group. While the orientation of Deaf education has changed in the 1990s, there remains an uneasy compromise for parents who want the advantages of both worlds in their Deaf child's education.

VADEC

Habitats for a language and culture

In everyday life the paths of hearing and Deaf individuals cross regularly, but because hearing people generally encounter Deaf people as isolated individuals, the social world that they inhabit as a group is nearly invisible. The concept of 'Deaf territory' has been used to describe the psychological and physical spaces that Deaf people create when they congregate.[24] Such 'territories' provide a context for the links between individual life stories from the Deaf community. Sir Tipene O'Regan once remarked that the survival of Maori language and culture in New Zealand depends on the existence of 'habitats' – physical places that are socially purposeful – in which the language and culture can thrive. Both these analogies of territory and habitat are useful for describing the way Deaf people together create distinctive environments in which Deaf ways flourish – the use of sign language, Deaf communication behaviour and technology, and the sense of ease among Deaf people together. Permanent Deaf territories such as Deaf schools, Deaf Clubs and Deaf homes are more than just gathering places: they sustain a communal history of

Illingworth wedding party, 1920, in front of Sumner school. Hilda (nee Illingworth) and Douglas Ashley (pictured at right holding their son) were Cheryl Anton's Deaf grandparents (see Cheryl's story, p. 97). Hilda was the first child to attend Sumner school as a day pupil, and Douglas studied under Gerrit van Asch. Hilda later returned to the school to work as a housemistress.

links from the past to the present, and ties with Deaf people from other places and countries. Such Deaf spaces seem to provide a sense of 'turangawaewae' (a Maori term meaning 'a place to stand'), where both local and visiting Deaf people can feel at home.[25]

Deaf Clubs are decorated with photographs of past presidents (almost exclusively men), photos of sports teams and other Deaf community groups, and engraved sports trophies that have passed from one generation to the next. There may be a display of pictures and gifts showing links between New Zealand Deaf people and Deaf in other countries, especially through sport. Noticeboards display information about club rules, meetings and upcoming activities. Deaf homes might also feature photos and mementoes that express relationships with Deaf people elsewhere. These things create and re-affirm a community identity and mark the space as a Deaf place.

More temporary Deaf territories include the site of sports tournaments, conferences or a favourite pub where a group of Deaf people meet regularly and the Deaf way prevails for a while. The universal activity is chatting (normally in sign language), even when the official agenda is a sports event or a formal meeting – and this usually goes on long beyond the stated finish time, until the lights are switched off. Sport is a major focus for social activity in the Deaf world from local to international level; many Deaf couples recount meeting each other at sporting events.[26] In these temporary or permanent Deaf habitats, friendships and romances are formed, information, news, ideas, and favours are exchanged, social rituals and traditions are carried on, sign language is used and absorbed by newcomers, loud Deaf voices are used freely, goals and plans of the community are discussed and formulated.

Apart from the language difference, many aspects of these scenes are typical of small communities and clubs of various kinds. The fact that these characteristics have continuously evolved in the New Zealand Deaf community is remarkable, when one considers that only approximately one in 1,000 people are born Deaf or become Deaf in infancy, and most have no connection to the Deaf world through their hearing family. Yet Deaf people find each other and develop enduring bonds, create distinct habitats, establish formal organisations and maintain ways of being, all of which are encompassed in the folk terms 'Deaf world' and 'Deaf way'.[27]

Hearing people attempting to make a connection with the Deaf world (such as parents of a Deaf child) sometimes express the feeling that the Deaf community is a 'closed shop' to which they cannot fully gain admission. What they are probably sensing is that when Deaf people meet to socialise or do business, they already share a web of group history and a sense of membership by virtue

VADEC

of being Deaf. For a hearing person, entering the Deaf community is like being a foreigner in a small village or a newcomer to an extended family. It is not possible to casually drop in and out; nor is it possible to find a niche without learning the local language (a lengthy journey in itself), taking time to build some shared experiences and community knowledge, and appreciating that a common denominator for the experiences and attitudes that bond Deaf members is being marginalised by hearing people.

Most hearing people who regularly mix in the Deaf community have an accepted role or reason for being there: they are children of Deaf parents (CODAs), have Deaf siblings or a Deaf partner, are sign language interpreters, or, more occasionally, are parents or teachers of Deaf children. In general, CODAs and interpreters are more accepted in the Deaf world than other hearing people, because they tend to have more regular interaction in the adult Deaf world and more fluency in sign language, and are therefore seen as somewhat closer in perspective to Deaf people. Teachers and parents usually have more limited contact with Deaf adults in their own territory, and have historically expressed a medically influenced orientation to deafness that distances them from the values and self-perception of the Deaf community.

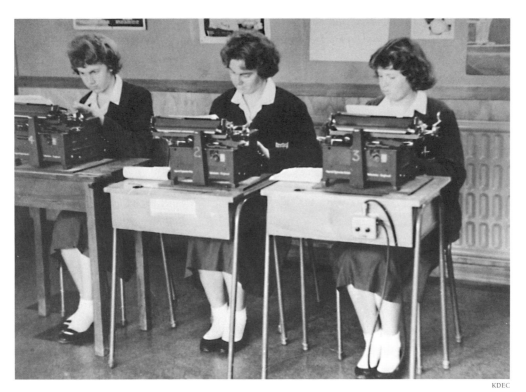

Typing class at Kelston, 1958. Secondary education for Deaf students had a strong vocational focus throughout most of the twentieth century.

Aspirations and opportunities

The personal aspirations of many Deaf adults in New Zealand have been dampened (or in some cases fuelled) by low expectations internalised during school years and by their actual experience of communication and attitudes in society. One little-understood hurdle for Deaf achievement is English literacy. A recent New Zealand study found that at least two-thirds of severely and profoundly deaf 16-year-olds could not read at age-appropriate levels.[28] Leaving school with a functional reading age of seven to eight years is not uncommon in New Zealand and elsewhere. Learning to read presents a challenge for most children who are Deaf from birth or infancy, because knowledge of spoken language cannot be assumed as a basis for learning to decode the written word. The majority of Deaf children from hearing families arrive at school without a coherent first language, and thus have a lot of basic language development and world knowledge to catch up on in the early years of schooling. Under the oral system that prevailed for the past century, schooling involved heavy doses of mechanistic speech training and rote learning, with students typically leaving school significantly under-educated. Secondary education tended to be vocationally focused, emphasising the acquisition of manual and home-making skills and work experience. Thus, in the current community of Deaf adults, those who have achieved academically are regarded as exceptional.[29]

Deaf people in New Zealand have traditionally worked in a limited range of jobs, from skilled manual trades (such as cabinet-making, welding, upholstery, draughting), to semi-skilled jobs (such as machinist, data-entry, gardening, mail-sorting), to unskilled labouring (cleaner, factory-hand). A disproportionate number are unemployed, and even more are underemployed in relation to their actual ability – which is often judged at first impression by the ability to speak rather than by skills or intelligence.[30]

With many avenues of education and career choice virtually closed, the current generation of Deaf adults usually find accomplishment and satisfaction in life by taking part in the activities of a Deaf community, in sporting achievements, through raising children and managing independently in all the everyday aspects of life that are more complicated by being Deaf. Some of the people in these stories are aware of their unrealised potential, and some have achieved more than they, or others, would have dreamed was possible. The storytellers express aspirations that range from the lofty to the non-existent; many have ambitions that seem quite straightforward but are exceptional in Deaf terms (such as being a teacher, a nurse, a zoo-keeper), while a few are highly ambitious in the New Zealand context (such as being an educational administrator).

Over the last decade, the ceiling on Deaf people's achievements has noticeably begun to break open, as signing has lost its stigma and self-advocacy skills have blossomed in Deaf community leadership. However, practical barriers that have been removed in other countries (through legislation and funding) remain in New Zealand. This country still lacks, for example, a telephone relay service, which would make many occupations accessible and give Deaf people more independence in everyday communications, and there is an insufficient supply of interpreters to make higher education and training opportunities available on the same basis to Deaf and hearing people.[31] Stories in this book tell of both admirable achievements and average contentment, but they also point to much wasted potential in previous Deaf generations. This was wrought largely by the 'deafness as deficit' mindset of hearing experts who did not take into account Deaf adults' own ideas about how to learn and live successfully, and thus failed to imagine, let alone provide, the resources that could have made higher goals attainable.

A theme recurring through many stories is the lack of power and control that Deaf people have felt over aspects of their lives. They tell of important decisions being taken on their behalf, and of not being able to predict or fully understand what was happening within the family or at crucial times of their lives, such as starting or leaving school, changing schools or finding work. In some cases, young Deaf people were taken advantage of as easy victims, unable to tell of the abuse at the time or even in adult life, because of communication difficulties and uncertainty about standards of acceptable behaviour.[32] In the videotaped narratives, anger and pain were written on signers' faces when recalling such powerless episodes, much more plainly than can be conveyed in the written word.

A few of the narrators mention seeking counselling in adult life to address emotional difficulties stemming from childhood experiences. For Deaf people in New Zealand, access to such mental health services in an appropriate form is still just emerging, and is often not altogether satisfactory since communication with a hearing counsellor generally takes place through an interpreter. Qualified and adequately skilled interpreters are hard to find. Even when available, the presence of a third person facilitating communication in such delicate situations is not ideal, and cannot compensate for a counsellor who lacks direct insight into the Deaf experience. There is one Deaf person in New Zealand trained and qualified (at Gallaudet University in the USA) as a mental health professional who is not currently practising full-time, partly due to the inevitable stress of being the only one. This leaves a serious void for Deaf people who need occasional support to deal with the usual life crises or ongoing therapy for more serious mental health concerns. Traditionally, Deaf people have turned to others within their own language community for informal advice and emotional support in coping with personal problems that others may have similarly experienced. Increasingly, they have the expectation of using professional avenues of support, but like other ethnic minorities, their experiences in doing so are often problematic due to a communication and culture gap. The Deaf community's needs in the area of mental health are still greater than can be met at the level of prevention or intervention, due to lack of appropriately skilled service providers.

Identity, diversity

The stories in this book reveal a rich diversity of Deaf experience, tiny though this group is. While being Deaf dominates the landscape for all these people, different personalities and family backgrounds shape each particular journey. The range of identities includes Deaf in combination with Maori or Pakeha, male or female, young or old, professional or blue-collar, rural or urban, gay or straight. Gay Deaf storytellers are included in the book but chose not to discuss this aspect of their identity in this public forum, perhaps indicating ambivalence about their double minority status in both Deaf and hearing worlds. One informant explained this choice, saying that being gay was a less defining identity factor than being Deaf.

This chapter has outlined some historical context and broad generalisations that underlie the various life stories. The narratives themselves present a collage rather than a uniform image, since being Deaf does not imply a homogeneous set of experiences. Indeed, a challenge in editing the book was to retain a sense of the strong consistencies through the stories, yet to highlight the variation as well, since both contribute to an understanding of this community. It is the consistencies in experiences and perspective that present a collective challenge to society's assumption that assimilation into the mainstream is the paramount goal for everyone. The phrase 'it's a hearing world after all' is routinely used to justify educational and other choices made on behalf of Deaf people. The cliché of course says something about where power and opportunity are located in society. But the formula is familiar: in place of 'hearing' insert 'man's' or 'Pakeha', and the phrase sounds anachronistic and unpalatable. The obvious rejoinder in each case is: 'through whose eyes?' There are many ways to construct the world, and 'Deaf' is simply another way of seeing and doing life in New Zealand.

Notes and References

1 George Veditz, 1910, cited in D. C. Baynton, *Forbidden Signs: American Culture and the Campaign against Sign Language*, University of Chicago Press, 1996, p. 10.

2 John's story, p. 216.

3 For discussion of aspects of Deaf Culture see C. Padden and T. Humphries, *Deaf in America: Voices from a Culture*, Harvard University Press, 1988; or H. Lane, R. Hoffmeister and B. Bahan, *A Journey into the Deaf World*, Dawn Sign Press, San Diego, 1996.

4 H. Lane, *The Mask of Benevolence*, Alfred A. Knopf, New York, 1992, provides a radical critique of the medicalisation of deafness.

5 H. Lane, *When the Mind Hears: A History of the Deaf*, Random House, New York, 1984.

6 See P. Dugdale, 'Being Deaf in New Zealand: A Case Study of the Wellington Deaf Community', PhD thesis, Victoria University of Wellington, 2000, for a detailed account of the transition from oralism to Australasian Signed English.

7 Cheryl Anton followed one other pioneering Deaf person, Bev Snook, who successfully challenged some major barriers to enter and complete teacher training in the late 1980s, which helped lay the path for others to follow. Bev, however, differs from Cheryl in that her hearing loss was of a progressive nature and thus spoken English was her first language. In contrast, Cheryl grew up within a Deaf social network, identifying primarily

with signing Deaf people despite an oral education; this linguistic identity was previously seen as an insurmountable disqualification to even contemplating teaching Deaf children. Bev has since become a signer and member of the Deaf community, and was a strong professional advocate in the establishment of bilingual education.

8 See Baynton, *Forbidden Signs*, for an analysis of social factors contributing to the rise of the oralist movement.

9 W. Forman, 'Towards a Critique of the Exclusive Use of the Oral Method in the Education of the Deaf in New Zealand 1880-1923', *New Zealand Journal of Disability Studies*, 7, pp. 40-56. This article provides an account of oralism in Deaf education in New Zealand.

10 Annual Reports of the Ministers of Education to Parliament, 1879-1906, cited in M. Collins-Ahlgren, 'Aspects of New Zealand Sign Language', PhD thesis, Victoria University of Wellington, 1989, p. 17.

11 D. McKee and G. Kennedy, 'A Lexical Comparison of Signs from American, Australian, and New Zealand Sign Languages', in K. Emmorey and H. Lane (eds), *The Signs of Language Revisited*, Lawrence Erlbaum, London, 2000.

12 For an account of the history of NZSL, see Chapter 2 in Collins-Ahlgren, 'Aspects of New Zealand Sign Language', p. 17.

13 This discrepancy of perception was demonstrated to me vividly from day one of my own signing career. In 1985, I was trained with the first group of sign language interpreters in a pioneering course under Dan Levitt, an American interpreter brought to New Zealand for the task. Without books, videos or documented resources to help us learn the language of the Deaf community, Levitt organised daily rosters of Deaf people to come to our class as our language models. Many of these wonderful visitors were older people who had retired and had free time during the day. On arrival at our classroom, faced with a group of nine hearing people, most of these folk began by lowering their hands to their laps and making a disclaimer in careful speech along the lines of: 'I don't really sign. I'm oral. It was all speech and lipreading at school in our day - I don't know many of the signs.' A cup of tea and a scone, and a story or two later, the hands had invariably started to help the stories get out, and we would be scribbling down descriptions of signs. From these older 'oral' people and some of the next, middle-aged generation, we recorded at least 1,200 signs over six months, which Levitt compiled and published in a photographic dictionary: *Introduction to New Zealand Sign Language*, National Foundation for the Deaf, Auckland, 1985. This modest but significant book became a source of affectionate pride - a concrete acknowledgement of Deaf people and their own language - as well as slight horror amongst the older people that they had been permanently caught in the act, as it were, of displaying publicly the thing they hadn't really believed they did. From some younger people, reaction to the book has included puzzlement to outright disapproval that these 'old' signs would have a place in a book on NZSL. They don't see it as representing them and their way of signing, according to their modern perception of NZSL and who uses it. It is true that older Deaf people in New Zealand use a more restricted set of signs than younger signers, and that they typically combine signing with the use of their voice - this is partly what they mean when they describe themselves as 'oral'. However, communication amongst themselves is generally more understandable as a version of sign language than as a version of spoken English. This is unsurprising since regardless of their own attitudes about one mode of communication against the other, in the end, communication between Deaf people must be visually meaningful.

14 Brian Hogue (a former teacher of the Deaf), personal written communication, 1999.

15 See Collins-Ahlgren, 'Aspects of New Zealand Sign Language', and Levitt, *Introduction to New Zealand Sign Language*.

16 G. Kennedy, R. Arnold, P. Dugdale, S. Fahey, and D. Moskovitz (eds), *A Dictionary of New Zealand Sign Language*, Auckland University Press with Bridget Williams Books, Auckland, 1997.

17 Personal communication, 2000.

18 Officially these institutions were called 'Schools for the Deaf', and now 'Deaf Education Centres', but they continue to be known in NZSL as 'Deaf school', possibly with the implication that despite their administration by non-Deaf people, they are places *of* Deaf people. I have used the translation 'Deaf school', which is closer to the idiom by which Deaf people refer to them, and easier to read.

19 For a description of the development and role of Deaf Clubs in the New Zealand Deaf community, see L. Monaghan, 'The Development of the New Zealand Deaf Community', in L. Monaghan, K. Nakamura and G. Turner (eds), *Many Ways to be Deaf: International Linguistic and Sociocultural Variation*, Signum Press, Hamburg, 1999.

20 A concept expounded in Lane, *When the Mind Hears*, and Padden and Humphries, *Deaf in America*.

21 Excerpted from an interview (1999) not included in this book.

22 Since the early 1990s, the two Deaf Education Centres have employed Deaf staff who have contact with some parents as sign language tutors, home visitors, or classroom teachers in some cases. Many parents report that this has given them relevant and positive perspectives on parenting a Deaf child. Another potential link to the Deaf community nowadays is through evening classes in NZSL, taught by Deaf tutors. These are valuable for developing communication skills in the family, and also for bringing hearing families into contact with Deaf adults; in previous generations this was generally frowned upon by professionals, for fear of frightening or discouraging parents with the reality that their child would remain Deaf (and all that implied) as an adult.

23 Della Buzzard's story, p. 162.

24 See Lane, Hoffmeister and Bahan, *A Journey into the Deaf World*, pp. 124–30.

25 'Turangawaewae' denotes membership of a particular community and its associated territory – i.e., a place where one has the right to stand or plant one's feet.

26 See D. Stewart, *Deaf Sport: The Impact of Sports within the Deaf Community*, Gallaudet University Press, Washington DC, 1991.

27 A more detailed overview of the development and structure of Deaf social and political organisations in New Zealand is included in Dugdale, 'Being Deaf in New Zealand'.

28 P. Pritchett, 'A Survey of the Reading Comprehension of a Sample of New Zealand Children with Prelingual Severe/Profound Hearing Loss', MA thesis, University of Melbourne, 1998.

29 For further evidence on this point see Dugdale, 'Being Deaf in New Zealand' and S. Townshend, 'The Hands Just Have to Move: Deaf Education in New Zealand – A Perspective from the Deaf Community', MA thesis, Massey University, 1993.

30 Dugdale's survey of 100 people in the Wellington Deaf community reports that while Deaf people have a higher rate of employment than people with disabilities in general, underemployment is prevalent in the Deaf community.

31 For a description of the current challenges facing Deaf people pursuing higher education in New Zealand, see S. Sameshima, 'Deaf Students in Mainstream Universities and Polytechnics: Deaf Student Perspectives',MA thesis, Victoria University of Wellington, 1999.

32 Townshend, 'The Hands Just Have to Move', documents recollections of childhood abuse in a study of Deaf people's school experiences.

Kelston Deaf Education Centre, Auckland

Lunch break, National Deaf Cricket Tournament, Christchurch

Clapping a team mate's 100 runs, National Deaf Cricket Tournament, Christchurch

Discussing text messaging, Hagley Park, Christchurch

Responding to a teacher's questions, Kelston Deaf Education Centre, Auckland

Story-telling, Kelston Deaf Education Centre, Auckland

OVER: *Playground conversation, Kelston Deaf Education Centre, Auckland*

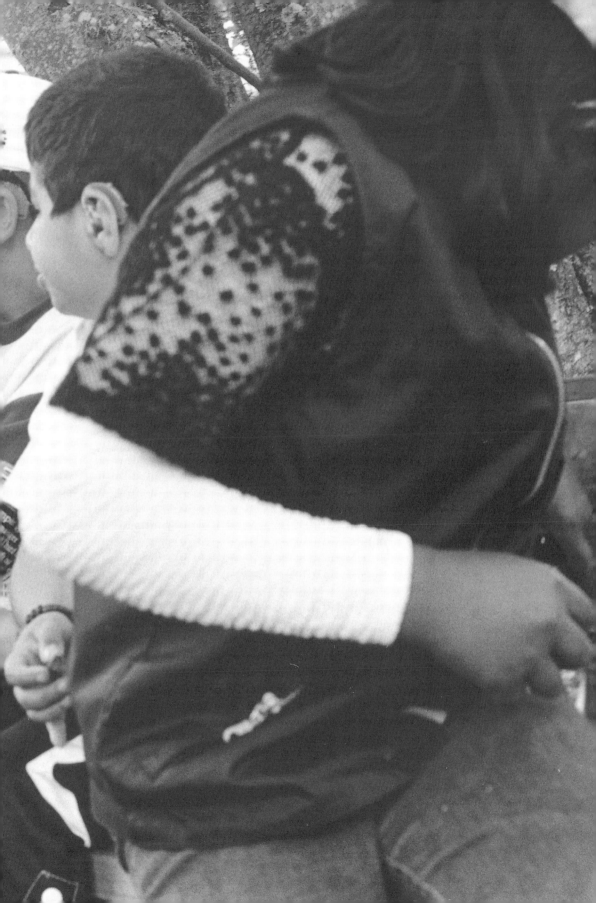

Educational video, Kelston Deaf Education Centre, Auckland

The Stories

Kathleen French

Born 1913

At the age of 86, Kathleen French remembers growing up in a provincial home town and at Sumner School for the Deaf in the 1920s. It is only in the latter part of her life that sign language has been accepted by both Deaf and hearing people, and she herself prefers to speak. A tailor and the mother of six hearing children, Kathleen tells some of the history of the Deaf community (or Deaf world as Deaf people traditionally call it) in New Zealand.

I was born in Eltham, Taranaki, 22nd of May 1913. My mother didn't know I was Deaf. I got whooping cough and that made me Deaf. But there's also another story: my mother thinks perhaps I was born Deaf, because one day my auntie was watching me play outside in the garden, and she knocked on the window and I never heard her. She said to Mum, 'I think Kathleen's Deaf.' My mother said 'No, no, she's not.' But later, when I was two, she took me to the doctor who said that I was Deaf. My mother and father heard through my grandfather that there was a school for Deaf in Sumner. My mother took me down to the Deaf school when I was four years and nine months old. They let me start then because I was going to turn five the following May. Mum told me years later that I clung on to her skirt when we got to school, not wanting her to leave me. Poor Mum. I was her first child. Before I went to school I remember going to the neighbour's to play with the girls, and going over the road to the convent school to play. The nuns would ring my mother – 'Kathleen's here!' – and she'd have to come and pick me up. I was lonely, I suppose. I didn't really communicate with the other girls because I was Deaf and I couldn't talk. We just played.

When we got to Sumner Deaf school, all I remember is standing at the bottom of the big stairs leading up to the front door. Soon after I started, I got influenza during the outbreak of 1918, and I was put upstairs all by myself in bed. One teacher looked after me. I had to eat all alone. I wasn't allowed to go downstairs with the others. It was a terrible time! There were tents outside for some of the Deaf children to sleep in, and classrooms outside.

We went home for the holidays twice a year – once in the May holidays, which my father had to pay for, and then at Christmas when the government paid for us to travel home. I was always so glad to go home. At school we had to work in the laundry, washing filthy handkerchiefs. Oh it was awful! We had to scrape them off first, and then put them in the boiler. Disgusting. We had to work hard at school, scrubbing the schoolrooms upstairs with hot water and a mop, all those dirty floors. We had to get up early and polish everything endlessly, and I hated the food – it was terrible, really dreadful food. Saturdays it was stew: horrible boiled stew with potatoes and everything thrown in it. Makes me sick to think about it. We never, ever had a roast dinner – only the teachers would have a roast on Saturday and then cold meat on Sunday. The children had to clean the silver, wash the dishes, do everything. The boys stayed in the boys' house, but they came in with us for meals and school. We played together at breaks. Lunch was in the dining room, and we had to line up outside and march in – the girls and boys separate. We had duties to ring the bell for coming in.

My first teacher was a good teacher. She taught us to talk, using a lot of different ways. I'll never forget when my father came down to see me at school, and the teacher told me to say 'Daddy'. I said 'Daddy' and my father cried. He couldn't believe I could talk. It was lovely. I was five. When my mother visited me, she would bring a box of figs because she knew I was very fond of them. I loved to eat those!

They taught us geography, composition, sums – we called it sums back then, not maths. Oh, I loved sums more than anything! Classes were alright, they didn't bother me. I picked things up easily. I was well educated and I had good teachers. They didn't change, so we had the same teachers for many years. That was good. One of them was very hard, but he was a good teacher – made us wake up! We used to go out to Christchurch sometimes to the zoo, or picnics, (or the dentist – I hated going to the dentist. No anaesthetic of course!) After school we did painting, drawing, played cards, basketball. We went swimming at the beach every day – it was a beautiful beach at Sumner then. There used to be sand dunes, where we'd play hide-and-seek.

I was going to leave school when I was 13, but the principal told me my speech was very bad, and so I had to stay until 1929. I had a lot of friends at school, and we had lots of fun, especially with sports. But I was glad to leave.

Whenever we came back to Sumner after the holidays, we took the ferry from Wellington to Lyttelton and then we had to walk four miles over the hill and down to Sumner. We hated that; we didn't like getting back to school. We'd get to the top of the hill, look down and see the school, and start thinking, yuck – the dinners, the awful porridge, the horrid potatoes, and we'd cry. But we got over it. When it was time to go home again, we'd walk back along that road. It was uphill, but we didn't mind at all. It didn't seem far.

KATHLEEN FRENCH

The matron was the same right through school, a big, tough woman, always telling us off for something. She was hard on us. If we got hurt or had a sore, she'd smack us hard. She had no time for us at all. One day we were running around in a circle, racing each other, and I fell over and sprained my ankle. The matron yelled at me, 'Oh you're so troublesome!' And gave me a good whack. My ankle had to be bandaged. Oh, we hated her. Not long after that, we were playing in the square near the school where they played sports, and I found a horseshoe. I got three friends to spit on it, then I spat on it myself, and threw it backwards over my shoulder. Next thing, I felt something running down my face. I touched it: blood. The horseshoe had caught in the hem of my dress as I lifted my arm to throw it and cut me on the forehead, but I hadn't felt anything. A teacher put a handkerchief around my head to stop the bleeding. I was caught out again! Ugh. The boys teased me that I was a returned soldier, with one bandage around my ankle and another round my head!

I was always looking out for mail from my mother and father. I wrote letters home to them. I could read and write well. My education was much better than the Deaf children have today, because now they don't use their voice or lip-read. I was at the Deaf Club one night a few years ago and a young Deaf girl about 17 or 18 was there. I went up to her and said 'Hello, what's your name?' She turned around and signed to her friend, 'Hey, what did she say?' I was disgusted. She didn't know what I was talking about, and all I was asking was her name! They would rather I sign to them, but I don't. Only a few things, that's all. At school we were mainly oral. Outside in the playground we used a few simple signs like *boat, fish, stupid, clever, bad, good*, but now they use it too much. Too many signs! I went to the Deaf school last year to help with the Deaf children, and they couldn't understand me. They kept looking at my hands, but I don't use them very much.

They have too many *Deaf* teachers at the Deaf school now. I think that's very bad, but what can I do about it. It's not right to have Deaf teaching Deaf children – too many Deaf everywhere! It's better to have hearing teachers because that's how it's always been for many, many years. In my time, all the teachers and staff were hearing, even the matron and cleaners. There was one

Deaf lady who worked in the laundry. The children talked to her, but she was very moody and quite old. I might be wrong, but it doesn't seem right to have Deaf people teaching Deaf children. The Deaf teachers can't hear the children's voices. How do they learn to talk? It's better to have hearing teachers who can hear their voices, and if their speech is bad they can help the children improve. I think it's harder for the children when they grow up if they use signing. I want the best for them when they grow up. When I'm with my friends at Deaf Club we sign a little bit in our old way, but not waving our hands around flat out like the young ones.

When I went home for the holidays to Eltham, I can't remember how I communicated with my family. Mum was a good mother, but she made us work. I had to scrub the floor - but my sister didn't. Why only me? But I'm grateful to my mother and father. My father was so upset when he heard I was Deaf. He arranged for me to have my tonsils out, but that did nothing. Then he took me to Auckland for some other treatment using needles; I don't know exactly what it was, but it didn't work. Poor Dad, he spent a lot of money on me. He couldn't accept that I was Deaf. Then when I left school, my father got hearing aids for me, and I couldn't stand them! They were terrible. They hurt, and I needed to start from scratch to understand sounds. I had no patience for that. I didn't want them. It was foolish. I'm very Deaf, I can only hear loud noises, like a bang.

It's a shame, but being Deaf didn't really bother me. The only thing is that all my family are hearing. When they get together at my place, they all talk, talk, talk, and I'm left out. I get wild. And I've told them 'I'm *not* a piece of furniture!! Talk to me!! I'm *normal* like you!' But they still do it. My family are good to me, they come and see me, but now they've got their own lives and their families, and I can't complain. When my children had young children and we got together for Christmas and so on, I was happy playing with my little grandchildren. I never felt left out then. But now some of my grandchildren don't talk to me at all when the family is together. They don't bother, and it's not fair. I blame the parents - they should tell them to talk to me, but they don't. When my own children visit me just by themselves, they talk to me. My children don't sign, of course, but when they were growing up I took them out to Deaf Club activities like picnics, sports, boat trips to Waiheke or Rangitoto Island. We took them everywhere and they'd have a lovely time. They knew Deaf people when they were growing up, but they don't really know how to talk to Deaf people now. The girls will talk to Deaf, but not the boys. I don't know why. Perhaps girls are more sensitive.

I didn't go to high school. I left in 1929 and at that time they didn't have the

proficiency exam. But I had no trouble getting a job in tailoring. I was so glad to leave school. I wanted to go home, because the food at school was so revolting. Mum got me a job sewing for a tailor. I remember making five-buttonhole flies on trousers, sewing by hand *all* day. It was tedious. Later on I made trousers, waistcoats, and the rest, using a machine. The buttonholes and buttons and topstitching of lapels were all done by hand – very fine work.

After a while I left Eltham and moved to Auckland because I wanted a change, a new life somewhere. I met my future husband there. I was a damn fool because I only knew him five months before I married him. Yes, I was young. My mother was right. She told me, 'You don't really know him', and I retorted, 'Oh yes I do!' I was a bit of a headstrong girl. My husband went Deaf when he was 12, from an abscess in the ear. He went to Sumner school to learn lipreading, but he was eight years older than me. He was good-looking, had a nice voice, so I fell in love with him. Never mind, we all make mistakes! I met him at the Auckland Deaf Club, which was in Grays Avenue in those days. I used to go to the Deaf Club to see my Deaf friends, because I'm in the Deaf world. You know what I mean: the Deaf world. I feel more comfortable and content with my Deaf friends. I'm happier with them than with my family and hearing people. My husband didn't enjoy the Deaf world as much as me. He was a bit reserved, stand-offish, and he wasn't really interested in having fun. But I loved him just the same. He died in 1961 from cancer – a terrible chain-smoker. The poor old man.

At the Deaf Club only a few of my Sumner friends are left now. We play cards, talk, and gossip. When I was younger I used to go to Deaf Club every weekend to play cards and table-tennis. Oh there was a lot going on, but now – I don't know what's happened. It was much stronger before. We used to have stalls to raise money for the club, and picnics, and all sorts of activities. It was wonderful, a lot of fun. But now all they think about is sport, sport, sport, and there's nothing much for us. We formed a Senior Citizens club, and I was secretary and treasurer for a long time, but I gave that up because of my health. Once, I won Grandmother of the Year at the Deaf Club. I didn't want to go in it, but people urged me to enter. There were 13 of us. I made my own frock. I was shocked that they picked me. It was lovely! But I was disappointed that my family couldn't come. Never mind.

When I first came to Auckland, my brother's wife heard of a tailoring job, and she helped me get it. I got along very well with my workmates. One of them lent me her wedding frock. It was all handmade, with handmade lace around the hem. I stopped work when I had my first child, but after a while I went back to work, because my husband didn't give me enough money. He was so mean, he only gave me enough money for food and nothing else. Then I got pregnant again, left work and never went back again until the children had grown. Six of them, three boys and three girls.

When I brought my first baby home from the hospital, I was worried about how I would know if the baby was crying. Somehow, God told me to move the cot under the edge of my bed, so when the baby woke she banged the cot and I could feel it and that woke me up. No one showed me that, I think God told me. And that was how I managed with the rest of them. My mother thought I was wonderful with my children. All her friends would say 'How on earth will Kathleen manage, being Deaf?' But my mother just told them I could manage fine. Mum and my husband's mother helped me with the first baby. With the younger ones, the older children would tell me if the baby was crying. My husband was completely hopeless, he left everything to me. It made me wild. If we were going out somewhere, he'd yell at me to hurry up and get all the children ready! I never helped the children with their homework because I didn't know how, but they did very well in school – they went through high school.

Nowadays I do a lot of crocheting. I can't be bothered going out as much as I used to. I used to like going to the pictures in town with some Deaf friends. We had a lot of fun. We couldn't follow the words, but we watched the body language and followed what was happening. I liked the funny ones best. Now I watch TV with subtitles, that's great. I got my first TTY in 1981 and it was marvellous. It was my lifeline. I used to ring all my Deaf friends on it. Now I use it very seldom because people mostly use the fax now. Really, I like the TTY better than the fax because you can have a conversation on it. And with the fax you have to pay for the fax paper all the time. In my house I've got light signals for the phone and the doorbell. When I was married, we had nothing at all like this. I only got a TV after my husband died. My family got a big surprise when they came home and saw it, and said 'How did you get the money for that?' But I paid it off myself. I worked as a machinist in Onehunga after my husband died.

My mother and father were Salvation Army people. My father joined when he married my mother and I'd have to go along to church and sit there squirming, bored. I couldn't hear anything so I just sat there looking around. But sometimes they'd have a social, and I enjoyed those. When I married I didn't go to church, but I sent my children to Sunday school. They gave up after a while – you can't push them. In 1971 a small group of Deaf people started up a church group that met in the Deaf Club with a minister once a month. It was good. After a while the first minister, Mr Fear, couldn't do it any more, and the

Revd Edna Garner took over and we moved to the Aotea chapel (the Methodist Mission) in town. It's held twice a month, and I enjoy going along to see my Deaf friends and talk, have a cup of tea, and think about God. There's an interpreter there, or the minister signs. One of the chaplains is hearing impaired. She's very good. I've tried to get more Deaf people to come along, but they're not interested. It's a shame. I go to church regularly, and I look forward to it – to see my friends and think about God.

KATHLEEN
FRENCH

Patty Still

Born 1932

Patty (Noeline) Still has kept a foot in two cultures, being bilingual in spoken English and NZSL. But she is firmly anchored in the Deaf world for the central parts of her life. Born in Wellington, she attended Sumner School for the Deaf during the war years. Patty was a grandmother in her sixties when she attended university for the first time to gain the qualification Certificate in Deaf Studies: Teaching NZSL. She has had long involvement in running the Christchurch Deaf Society, and more recently the NZSL Tutors Association since she has been teaching NZSL in Christchurch.

I was born Deaf, an only child – perhaps a bit spoilt! I don't know the cause of deafness, and no one else in my family was Deaf. I started at a hearing school when I was five. From the teacher's point of view I was just a naughty child, and the school said they couldn't deal with me. So I moved to a Catholic school. The nuns were very sweet and patient, and gave me a corner to sit where I played and drew pictures. When it came to lessons, I sat and watched the teacher along with the other children. I couldn't understand a single thing, but I was happy enough. I don't remember much from that time.

Then one day Mum said to me, 'We're going on a boat to a bigger place.' I didn't know what she meant, but off we went on a journey that led to the School for the Deaf at Sumner. We arrived at the old school building, which seemed gigantic to me. The front entrance was very imposing and the steps so high for my little legs to climb up. I was seven. Mum came in with me and we

had dinner with the other children. It was a long time ago now, but I remember the scene very clearly. I looked around at all the other children at the dinner tables, feeling half excited and half scared. After dinner all the small children trooped off to have their baths, and I went along too. Then it was bed-time, and I followed along with the others. A big girl gave me a doll that was all my own. Each little girl had her own doll and I remember mine had a green dress. Mum came and said goodnight and tucked me in, and I went off to sleep. The next morning, Mum had gone. I was a bit thrown by that, but had to accept it. One of the staff helped me get dressed and do my hair in the morning. She was pretty rough, brushing my hair, yanking away at it and trying to put the bows in. I had long curly hair, and they decided it was going to be too much trouble at school, so it was cut short to make it easier to comb. I was rather upset to see my curls gone just like that.

I soon joined in quite happily with the other girls. I saw the other children using sign language and I suppose it was just natural for me to copy them and pick it up. I remember one older girl, Kath, who took me under her wing from the start. She was a really dear friend. At school there was a routine of class, play times, drill and sports. I wasn't that athletic – always straggling in the rear – but I loved sports. There was sewing, woodwork, and of course on Sundays we traipsed off to church in our navy-blue gym frocks and polished shoes. We didn't understand a thing that was said at church, but it was fun to get out of the school grounds.

Mr Chambers, the headmaster in my time, was lovely – like a father to us. He used to take us over to the beach and let us go swimming. They didn't worry so much about safety in those days: we all just jumped in the water and amazingly, nobody was ever drowned! We also used to walk over the hill to Taylor's Mistake for picnics, always exhausted by the time we got back. We were fascinated with the cows and the draught horses in the farm paddocks around the school. We spent a lot of time making our own playthings from whatever we could find – sticks, a ball, and one Deaf boy even made his own roller skates from old cotton reels. Every June or July all 120 of us children were taken to the fancy dress ball in the Sumner Town Hall, and the matron of the school, Mrs Gray, would make all our costumes. One year, I went as a rabbit in a one-piece costume with domes up the back. Half way through the ball I needed to go to the toilet, but I couldn't get the costume off and so I wet my pants!

The war started while I was at school. The older children used to tell us little ones, 'The Germans are coming! The Japs are coming to get you!', until we were really frightened. So at dinner time, we'd sneak a knife or fork, anything sharp, from the table, hide it in a pocket and take it to bed with us, ready to fend off the invaders. Another fear I had was that perhaps I would never see my mother again, but that didn't last long because later she moved to Christchurch and I could go home every weekend. During the war the school had to move to 25 Fendalton Road in town (now 'Monavale'), because the army needed the school for barracks. During that period I rode my bike to school as a day pupil. Two years later, when the army moved out, the school returned to Sumner and I became a boarder again.

When I was 14, Mum bought me a piano and I started practising every day. Because there was no piano at school, I became a day pupil again, using the new school bus service to get back and forth. I learned the piano for about four years, but I'm afraid the piano lessons went by the wayside as flirting with boys began to take up more of my attention. I can still read music, but I've long forgotten how to play. At the time, I passed the theory exams, but I was pretty hopeless at actually playing. Not surprising, but I did enjoy the experience. I think my mother had her hopes a bit high in thinking I'd succeed at the piano!

The good thing about Deaf school was the company of other Deaf children. I really enjoyed having Deaf friends, all being the same. They signed, and we could understand each other easily. That's where I learned sign language, from the other children. What wasn't so good about Deaf school was the actual education, the limited subjects they taught. I was always hungry for more knowledge. I wanted to excel. I wanted to know more about everything. What I most enjoy learning is language. I learned English at school, picked up NZSL outside class, and recently I've studied more about NZSL. I also enjoyed picking up bits of foreign languages like German, Dutch, and Italian when I was travelling in those countries; it was fun trying out different words and seeing if I could make myself understood in another language.

I married a Deaf man. In fact I married the boy I fell in love with on his first day at school! He arrived at Sumner a year after me, and we clicked straight away. Later on I had other boyfriends, but he was the one I always came back to. He had to leave school at 14, because his father and older brother died and he had to help the family earn money. So I lost touch with him for a few years, until one day when I was 19, I met him again at the Deaf Club. Another Deaf girl had run into him in the Christchurch Square, where he was just hanging around, bored, with nothing to do. She took him in tow to the Deaf Club where we met again, and have been together ever since. We married and had two children, both hearing, and now we have four grandchildren and two great-grandsons who are all hearing. The third grandchild is my favourite – she's my best friend because she signs.

I always worked in the wool industry, making carpets, spinning, and making

woollen garments through all the stages of knitting, cutting, and sewing. Some of the places I worked used to also get me to model the garments. I guess I was a cheap model! When a new carpet factory set up round the corner from our home paying good money, my husband and I ditched our former jobs and went to work there. My husband left, but I stayed on for 30 years. I really enjoyed working there, it was so interesting doing a bit of everything: spinning the wool, working with the chemicals for dyeing and so on. I wasn't an expert sewer but I got very fast. I loved my job there, but I had to give up work on the machines when I got cancer of the breast and had a mastectomy. They asked me to come back from retirement and re-train to work in the lab because I was a valuable employee to them.

I was always very lucky with my workmates. They knew it was hard for me to join in group conversations, so someone would always make the effort to talk to me one-to-one. My boss always came up to tell me things I needed to know. My workmates and I used to go out together and I still keep in touch with a lot of them. I think my employers treated me very fairly, and I was given promotions because they knew I had skills. I used to train new staff how to use the great big machines, so I'm proud of that. I had very good experiences at work. Of course there were always one or two people who mocked me, but I ignored them and didn't let it bother me. When I've seen those people since I left work, I always stop and say hello as if nothing had happened, and they do the same. I think actually they were jealous because I was a fast worker and kept my mind on the job, so I always made bonus money. Possibly they resented the fact that a Deaf person could do better work and earn more money than them.

Times have changed. I think young Deaf people today have more opportunities than we had. On the other hand, there are fewer jobs for them, so it goes both ways. When I was young, employers wanted Deaf staff because they were regarded as diligent workers. Now that technology has changed so much, and computers are a big thing, the situation has changed a lot for Deaf workers. I would have liked to have been a teacher, but in my day, the schools for Deaf would not accept Deaf teachers, and I accepted it. Now there are Deaf teachers, which is a sign of the community changing.

To me, Deaf and hearing are different worlds. I think hearing and Deaf people basically look at each other as foreigners – they have different tastes and ways. It's impossible for them ever to be the same, because Deaf people live in the world of silence and hearing people live in a noisy world – each world is different. Even within the family, a Deaf person may have to live in two worlds. If everyone in the family signs, it's fine, but my family don't sign much to me. Sometimes when my children were growing up they'd say to my husband, 'tell

Mum ...', 'ask Mum ...', because Tom, who is half-Deaf, can talk to them more easily than me. It was too much effort for the children. But now they've grown up I think they have more understanding: they talk more slowly and move their lips so I can lipread them. We're closer now than when they were young.

When my children were babies, I talked to them and they were used to my voice. Even when they were still in the cot, they knew to bang hard on the wall to call me if I was in the next room. Then they learned to tug on my clothes if they wanted to talk to me. But once they got to school age, they started talking too fast for me to follow. Tom would help by relaying to me what the kids were saying. It was hard at times. If I could go back in time, with what I know now about how children acquire language, I would do things quite differently. I think maybe I would have taught them to sign from the start, and made them more aware that sign language is an easier way for me to communicate.

I picked up signing at school, and in those days it was 'old' signing. For instance, the old signs for days of the week related to what we did on the different days: Monday, Thursday and Friday are the same as the sign for *school* because they were just normal school days; Tuesday and Wednesday were signed as *sewing*, because the routine was sewing on those days. Saturday was named for being a cleaning day, when we cleaned the house, polished, washed our hair and everything. The sign for Sunday is *church*, which is what we did on Sundays. Nowadays, the days of the week have changed to fingerspelling signs, just *M, T, W, TH, F* for Monday to Friday; only the old signs for Saturday and Sunday have been kept. My older friends and I still use the old signs when we talk to each other. Another example of an older way of signing is how we signed colours. There was one general sign that meant *colour*, and the name of each colour was shown by mouthing the word on the lips. It seems a bit funny, but really that was an appropriate sign for the concept of colour, because that sign also means the surface or appearance of something, or a shadow, or shade. Now there are new signs for each different colour.

I accept new signs because they go with each generation. There are signs that my age group have; then the next generation of Deaf children comes along and has theirs; and so each generation develops some new signs because life changes and the language grows. When I was small, there were no videos, and no TV, and even the telephones were old-fashioned. So we had an old sign for telephone that mimicked the way people held the earpiece and mouthpiece, and cranked the handle. When phones changed, a new sign came along to reflect that. So as life changes, sign language changes and grows too. I like to think that I've kept up and changed along with the times, adding the new to my old sign language.

I remember around 1980 I became aware that this new Signed English had appeared in schools. I thought it was some kind of new language, and I wasn't too sure about it. But I could see that a lot of the younger people were good at it, and thought it would be useful to learn a wee bit so I could communicate with them. I like to be able to talk with younger Deaf people. So I did go along and learn the new signing. To tell the truth, I wasn't comfortable with it – it was actually quite boring, but I thought I had to learn it for the sake of the future generations. But do you know what I noticed after a while? When those Deaf children grew up and joined the Deaf Club, they were using fluent, normal Deaf sign language anyway, not the new Signed English at all! But nevertheless, I gained a new skill – not a very useful one – but something to file away in case I meet someone using signed English. You see, I love to be able to adapt and talk with a whole range of Deaf people, whether they use NZSL, Signed English, speech, or even Deaf people from overseas who don't know NZSL and communicate with me through gestures, which works just fine!

I really do love sign language. I don't know why, but I feel quite passionate about it. To me it's a beautiful language. I've never been embarrassed or ashamed of it. If a hearing person tries to put me down for signing in public, I just ignore them and carry on. I don't care what they think. Well, maybe there were times in the past when I would turn away and sign a bit smaller, to be less conspicuous in public. But I shouldn't have done that. I should have just gone ahead and felt proud of my language and to heck with them. But I didn't always.

A Deaf person first took me along to the Deaf Club in 1945 when I was 13. Someone else took me to a Deaf Sunday school, and I liked that, because there were plenty of Deaf people there to talk to. When I left school, my mother encouraged me to go to Deaf Club as I pleased, but some other parents used to restrict their children and try to keep them away from other Deaf people. They didn't want them to go to the club and pick up habits like signing or drinking. They thought Deaf people were a bad influence. But my mother wasn't like that. She welcomed Deaf people into our home and there were always loads of Deaf people coming over. They loved my mother; they saw her as a mother figure and used to ask her for advice over a cup of tea and a smoke. I remember two Deaf refugees who arrived in 1948 from Latvia. They had no home, no English, nothing – but my Mum could sit down and talk with these men, no problem. They were very valuable to the Deaf community here, because they introduced new ideas, like starting Deaf basketball and other Deaf sports. That was our first exposure to Deaf life overseas. It was a boost for us.

In the early days of the Christchurch Deaf Club, we worked at constantly selling raffles and raising funds to get established. We were the first Deaf

Society in New Zealand to be formed (in 1920) and to have our very own club-rooms. The government gave us a pound-for-pound subsidy to build them. Even before the first clubrooms were rented, folk used to meet regularly in each other's homes. The Deaf Club gradually became more formalised and was incorporated in 1951. I'm very proud to be part of the Christchurch tradition.

One big event that affected the New Zealand Deaf community was the World Games for the Deaf [WGD] held in Christchurch in 1989. Four years earlier, our Deaf international sports delegates, Margaret Coutts and John McCrae, announced to the Christchurch Deaf community that New Zealand had won the bid to host the next WGD. We were aghast at first. Could we cope with that? It was a huge responsibility to raise the money and do all the organising on such a big scale –we were very nervous about the whole prospect. But Margaret and John assured us that it would go all right. 'Deaf people *can* do it', they said. They seemed confident, so we followed their lead, and it was amazing how well we did in raising the funds needed. The Deaf community completely mobilised and worked together. One year before the Games we had to start teaching NZSL to 100 hearing volunteers in 10 classes around Christchurch. There were two Deaf tutors assigned to each class, and honestly, we knew absolutely nothing about teaching sign language! But we did pretty well, considering. The Games were a great success. I believe it was the only WGD that has broken even financially: it actually made a small profit. So once again, Christchurch Deaf did well!

The WGD had a big impact on Deaf people's consciousness. First of all we got more seriously sports-minded, and we also got a lot of administrative experience quickly. It pushed us to become a lot more independent, because we wanted to prove ourselves, show that we could pull it off. For three weeks during the Games we were in the constant, exciting buzz of a big international Deaf community. Everyone was on a kind of high. After the Deaf teams had all packed up and gone home, it was a very flat, depressing feeling for us. I remember sitting around with some Deaf friends later all asking each other miserably, 'what's the matter with you?' But as a result of the Games, membership of the Christchurch Deaf Club increased – it really brought people together.

Studying Deaf culture and NZSL at Victoria University has changed my thinking and my understanding in a big way. I used to think that Deaf culture meant things like Deaf artists, and I was never very good at art myself. But now I understand that Deaf culture means everything that's inside me – my language, the way I live, my habits, my beliefs, the way Deaf people are together. I realise now there is so much more to it than I was ever aware of. I found it fascinating to learn about Deaf history around the world. It's given me a real sense of pride in being Deaf.

Daniel Beech & Beth Titter

Born 1942   *Born 1950*

The Catholic School Experience

Danny Beech and Beth Titter have known each other since
their years at St Dominic's Catholic School for the Deaf in
Feilding, a smaller residential school in a country area.
Here they recall together some of the school's history, and

its strict routines (including a staunch adherence to oralist
teaching). Danny and Beth have both become leaders in the
Auckland Deaf community: Danny is a long-serving board
member of the Auckland Deaf Society, while Beth was elected

as the first woman president in 1998 and is a familiar face as
bar manager at the clubrooms on Friday nights.

Beth: I started school at St Dominic's in 1955, when I was almost five. The first
thing they did was give me a hearing test, and then fit me with some hearing
aids. When they put them on, I was surprised to find I could hear sounds. I
loved my new hearing aids. Even when I went to bed at night I hated the nuns
taking them off, and I'd have a tantrum. I liked hearing the noises around me
– the thuds and bangs and people's voices.

Danny: I wasn't discovered to be Deaf until the age of five. We lived on a farm
in Pahiatua, which is half way between Masterton and Palmerston North.
There was rationing due to the war, so we couldn't go into Palmerston North
all that often. My mother was concerned that I was not talking at five years of
age, so she took me to the family doctor, who recommended that we take a trip
down to Wellington to see a specialist, who confirmed that I was Deaf. So my

parents started to look for a school for me. They found a Catholic Deaf school in Wellington – St Dominic's – and I started there in 1947 as a boarder.

Before World War II, there was just the one Deaf school in Christchurch, where all the children went from both the North and South Island. Once war broke out, crossing the Cook Strait was considered very risky. Then Sumner school was taken over as army barracks, and all the North Island children had to go to Auckland where they established another school for the Deaf at Titirangi. It was also decided at that time that Catholic Deaf children should be able to have a Catholic education, so nuns were brought in to provide this at St Dominic's. Before the school was established, the Bishop of New Zealand would raise money to send children one at a time to Australia to be educated. Later, an Australian priest who had two Deaf sisters happened to come over to New Zealand to train young priests. He was astonished to find that there were no Catholic Deaf schools here, so he told the church that they had to have one. The school was quite small until 1951–1952, when there was a huge influx of Deaf children, forcing the school to move to a larger site in Feilding. The largest number that they reached was around 60 children. I stayed there until I was 17 years old.

A year before the school started in 1944, two nuns were sent over to the Dominican Deaf school in Warratah, Australia. They actually went over to learn the methods of teaching through Irish signs and one-handed finger-spelling. When they returned to New Zealand they were all ready to teach this signing they had just learnt. But a month after they arrived, the Department of Education paid a visit and advised them that they could not be registered as a school if they continued with these methods of teaching. So they started teaching through speech only. A teacher from Sumner School for the Deaf came up to St Dominic's to instruct the nuns on the oral teaching. Initially, they tried to reinforce it with punishment, but then they realised that kids were signing anyway, so they barred signing just in the classroom instead. We had a lot of different signs from Deaf children at Sumner and Kelston. In fact some of the signs that we used were Irish – they'd been introduced by nuns in the very short time before oralism was brought in. One of the nuns recently told me that she had learned signing during her training. An ex-teacher told me that she personally felt that the children would have been much better off with signing but she had to follow the rules of the authorities. The school is closed down now; the children were shifted to a Deaf unit in a hearing school where they used Signed English, and later they were main-streamed.

Beth: I stayed at St Dominic's for 14 years. I liked school, except for the fact that the nuns didn't like us signing. If we didn't pronounce a word right, one nun would twist and tweak our noses and ears. They were constantly teaching us how to speak – which I appreciate now, because prior to that all I did was make unintelligible noises. I couldn't talk when I first started school, so I'm pleased that I was taught to speak. At home, my mother and grandmother always encouraged me to keep up and practise my speech, and I talked and signed with my brothers and sisters when we played.

My favourite times at school were Friday nights and Saturdays. On Fridays we'd have a film at school and on Saturday we could sleep in for an hour and wear mufti, which I loved. But we still had to do our chores: mowing the lawns, doing the gardening, polishing our shoes! We had line-ups to check our shoes, and if they weren't done properly we had to go off and do them again.

Sunday to Friday we were up at 6.30 a.m. for mass at 7.00, then breakfast at 7.30 a.m. Every morning it was porridge, bread, butter and cocoa. We were well fed, with three hot meals a day – lunch was as big as dinner. After breakfast we made our beds and then did the chores we were rostered for. I remember polishing the floors first with a waxed cloth and then a sweeper. After that I'd go over it with a polisher. It did look nice and shiny! Another part of that chore was to polish the brass candleholders in the church. I'd be rubbing and polishing, but if they weren't up to scratch, I'd have to do it over again. Most Sunday afternoons we had to go for a long and boring walk.

After our duties we went to class. In each class there were about 12 students. We sat in a semi-circle instead of the traditional rows. Sitting in rows wasn't suitable for Deaf people, because we needed to be able to see each other.

Danny: Our subjects were speech, lipreading, English, geography, spelling, writing, and arithmetic.

Beth: All boring!

Danny: The boys would go off and learn woodwork while the girls learned how to cook and sew. Not until my last two years there was I taught maths. I hated it and didn't understand it at all – hopeless!

We didn't go out to the pictures, but on Sunday mornings the priest from St Paul's Maori boys' college [Hato Paora] would come over to say Mass and bring films to swap with ours. He brought Westerns, which were great compared to the boring movies that the nuns picked.

Beth: If there were any romantic scenes with smooching, the teachers would put their hand over the projector or sometimes they'd blur the focus. Honestly! It was really unfair because the nuns could still hear what was going on while we only had our eyes. I'd be cursing to myself. Sometimes I could hear the nuns laughing while we didn't know what the joke was about.

We would only leave school to go home for the holidays, and when we got older the Lions and Rotary clubs would sometimes take us out for the day, to visit farms or go for picnics. Families from the clubs would also take one or two of us out at a time. I'll never forget one family I liked, they were so funny. When I arrived they looked at me and the uniform I was wearing and decided it wasn't on. They would let me wear their daughter's clothes for the day. I felt free!

Danny: From 1944 to 1948 we were only allowed to go home once a year at Christmas. Then the nuns decided that this wasn't enough for us, and they needed a break too, so they changed it to twice a year. Soon after that we could go home three times a year.

When the school was in Wellington, when it was first opened, I felt that we were extremely cut off from hearing people. We went out maybe once a month – to the zoo, or the museum or beach, or for tram rides. Otherwise, we weren't allowed outside the enclosed area of the school. We just didn't know what was going on in the outside world and we only got a glimpse of it once a month. I used to be responsible for getting the milk and paper, and every time I got it I'd scan the pages, keen to know about what was going on in the world. What I learned at school did not satisfy me at all. The focus there was very narrow, and once you left, getting a job was your own responsibility. It was actually good training to have done all those chores while we were at school. I'm pleased to have learnt all of those things, but it didn't prepare me for work in the outside world.

Beth: I think it's better now that Deaf children aren't kept in one place like we were. They're out in ordinary schools. The reason I say it's better is because our education was pretty poor. If I had finished my exercises from one book before the other kids, I'd have to repeat the same book. It was boring and completely unmotivating. I would hassle other kids and tell them to hurry it up because I was so frustrated. They couldn't help it, I know, that they were slow. Everyone was at different levels, even though we were all the same age. It wasn't the nuns' fault either really – it was the education system at the time.

Danny: On Sunday mornings we had to write letters home. One girl's English was so bad that the teachers didn't even understand her, and they had to ask me to help her out. If those children had been allowed to use fingerspelling and signs, it would have been extremely helpful for their English. Oralism was a failure for some of those children. I used to visit one of our old teachers, who died last year. Every time I paid a visit to her and the other nuns she would always say, 'Danny, I told you before not to sign!' I'd just look at her and carry on signing while she sat there seething.

Every day we had catechism in the morning. I actually learnt more about religion as an adult doing a lay leadership training programme than I did the whole time I was at school. As an adult, I was free to think about what was right and wrong, whereas at school there was no encouragement to think for ourselves. We were told that if we were naughty we would go to hell and so on. This is the reason so many Deaf people are put off religion. Deaf people also say that church is boring: they don't bother going because they can't understand what is being said anyway. I think if there was a priest who could sign you would have more people attending.

Beth: When the nuns were teaching us in those classes they would spiel off all this information that I never understood. They just laid down the law, black and white. We learnt nothing from that. One of the nuns, who has since married, was telling me how they were instructed to teach in a regimented way. In question-and-answer times, if the answers weren't exactly right, then they were considered wrong. It would have been so much better if we could have discussed things.

When I left school, I lived in Wanganui where there weren't many Deaf people and I had several hearing friends. I was quite involved in one of the marching teams, a swimming team and a few other sports as well. I didn't encounter many difficulties in the hearing world. There was even a job ready for me when I left school that my mother had organised. I never had a problem finding job but I know other Deaf people have had difficulties finding jobs. There was a lot of work around at that time though. Back then they used to think that Deaf people should be working in factories. I think that if a Deaf person wants to work in an office – for example, with computers – then they should be given a chance. They're just as capable or possibly more so than a hearing person is, and more efficient because they don't get distracted.

Danny: There was a job waiting for me on a farm once I'd left school. There were no problems with the farming life, but I felt very cut off in the country, so

I moved to Palmerston North and started work in a nursery. It was a lot better for me having Deaf friends nearby that I could socialise with. I was quite involved in the Deaf community, serving as the Manawatu Deaf Club secretary for many years. Later I went on to be chairman of the Auckland Deaf Society Board of Management, and I was involved at the beginning of the New Zealand Association of the Deaf.

One time I was with a group of Deaf people in a pub. We were sitting in a circle signing to each other and some people were staring at us. I just ignored them, I didn't give two hoots – I knew they were probably intrigued by us signing. But one guy from our group was getting annoyed with them gawking, and he turned around and asked them if they thought they were watching a TV or something.

I remember back then thinking that there was something different about being Deaf, and it wasn't until I heard Nancy Lewis* talk about Deaf culture that it hit me. It was the first time I had heard the term Deaf culture. She talked about the language we use and how we point in signing, and stare at faces. Hearing people view this as rude, but she was saying that it was normal for Deaf to do these things. She talked about our reliance on visual things, the way we live, the difference between hearing people and us. That made a big impact on the way I viewed being Deaf. I was able to accept that there was nothing wrong with being Deaf, and now I knew why. It was a relief to see her explain these things.

Beth: I married a hearing man and had two hearing children. I had no hassles communicating with him. With my children I would talk and sometimes sign, and we communicated easily enough. When we went out shopping they would never worry if people saw that their mother was Deaf. When my son, Bruce, was about six years old he came home quite upset one day, and told me that some kids had been teasing him because of me being Deaf. Even one of the teachers had said that I was 'Deaf and dumb', which he didn't like at all. The next day I went to see the principal and he said he would sort it out, telling me, 'Come back tomorrow morning'. So I did, and found the whole school gathered for assembly. The principal stood up, talked about Deaf people and told the children never to tease Bruce again or call Deaf people dumb. He even reprimanded that teacher right there in front of us all. I was blown away! Bruce felt

* Dr Nancy Lewis is a Deaf American mental health professional who visited New Zealand in the late 1980s and gave workshops to Deaf people on Deaf identity and culture. Her visit had a great impact on the self-esteem of many Deaf people who saw their identity defined in a positive way for the first time.

better, I felt better. If Deaf people are dumb, you have to wonder how they bring their children up!

Danny: Some people get really angry about being called 'Deaf and dumb', but I just correct people when they say that. I prefer to be called Deaf and that's it – none of these other terms that are a bit of a mouthful, like 'hearing impaired' and 'hard of hearing'.

Beth: Those terms are for the elderly and people who have lost their hearing. I'm Deaf.

Danny: I've been called Deaf all my life, and I still use that term. When people talk about having my hearing 'fixed', I'm not even interested! I'm Deaf and that's who I am; that's me and I've accepted that. At work, I wear hearing aids to help me understand people's lip patterns, but not when I'm at the Deaf Club and places like that. I'm really Deaf then.

Beth: Pupils from St Dominic's always keep in touch; we're quite a close-knit group. Whenever I go on holiday, I'll go and stay or drop in on school friends. We don't really write – you just pay a visit. Like the Labour Weekend Deaf Games – people enjoy catching up there. It's good fun. There used to be quite large gatherings at the Games, but now a lot of the younger people aren't that interested in sports. There are also young Deaf people who don't want to iden-tify themselves as Deaf, so they join the hearing world and they call themselves hearing, not Deaf. They think they're fine out there but they're really quite lonely in their lives. It's impossible for a Deaf person to fully mix in a world of hearing people. It's okay only if they're completely oral.

Danny: But later on down the road, maybe five or 10 years later they still come back to the Deaf community. They go off and marry hearing people and disap-pear from the community for a while, but they come back.

Mel

Born 1954

Mel was born in a provincial North Island town, and now

lives in a large city. Like most Deaf children at that time,

he was sent to board at Sumner School for the Deaf, of which

he has mixed memories. Mel had an unhappy home life, and

the companionship at school provided a sense of community.

But his experiences at the school in the 1960s are amongst

the most bleak recorded. Mel's adult life has included

struggles with alcohol and with violence. His willingness to

tell his story here (with the names changed) is part of a

process of reflection and change.

I was born hearing and became Deaf when I was two. It was sad. My father was abusive. The rumour in the family is that when I was a baby he threw me down and I hit my head really hard, and I lost my hearing from that. That's what they told me, but I don't know for sure. I was sent to the Deaf school at Sumner in 1960 when I was five. I was pretty shy when I first got there – the older children were signing fast, I didn't know what was going on. I also had a problem with my hands: my wrists were bent and my hands were hard to co-ordinate.

I didn't know I was going to school. My parents didn't explain anything about it, in fact they didn't actually take me – a teacher of the Deaf took me down to Christchurch. I didn't know where we were going or what to expect. I cried a lot after I got there. I wanted Mum.

I had a wetting problem at school. The staff got fed up because I wet myself so often. They came up with this idea of putting a cover over the mattress on the bed so it wouldn't get wet all the time. I wasn't very comfortable with that.

When I was eleven, one of the staff had another idea: one Saturday morning after breakfast, they took me to the laundry and told me to wash the things I had wet before. They made me put on a nappy. I had to stand there wearing nappies while all the other kids laughed at me. It was so humiliating. One boy helped me because the nappies were loose and slipping down. That was nice of him.

Then later on I remember one Deaf boy, Tom, used to taunt me all the time. He used to call me 'wee-wee' (in sign language). It really got to me, made me wild because he went on and on with it. So I had an idea for revenge. I got a jar with a lid from the kitchen, emptied the stuff out of it, and then I peed into it. Then the next time Tom teased me, I waited until bedtime, hid the jar of pee in my bedside drawers, and pretended to be asleep. When Tom got up to go the toilet, I sneaked over to his bed and poured the urine all over his mattress, chucked the jar out the window, jumped back into bed and shut my eyes. Tom was furious when he found it! He came over to my bed, and I just lay there snoring, but inside I was cracking up because I knew the staff would be angry with him in the morning. Tom was really scared. Sure enough, one of the staff came over and held up his sheets and gave him a real telling off. Tom wanted to know who'd wet his bed, and I kept quiet, but later we had a big fight about it. It was pretty serious and we were sent to the headmaster. The headmaster came in and paced up and down, with his hands behind his back. Tom and I had our hands in our pockets and he came over and yelled at us to get our hands out of our pockets. We straightened up quick-smart. The headmaster kept pacing up and down while we had to stand there. Then finally he looked at me and started telling us off. I could understand him, but Tom couldn't understand a word. Afterwards, the hostel staff told us that our punishment was to go straight to bed after tea every night for a week. No going to the shop or playing hockey – just dinner, bath and straight to bed. After that, Tom stopped calling me wee-wee and he was nice to me from then on.

In class I mainly remember doing speech practice – blowing on bits of paper, and wearing great big headphones and taking turns talking into a microphone. I don't really remember learning much else – well, we always copied a lot of writing off the board. Every Sunday the hostel staff wrote a letter on the board and we all copied it out to send home to our parents. We practised handwriting in class. I hated that; it was hard for me because of my weak hands. Only one of the teachers, the vice-principal, could sign, but none of the others.

When I was little at school I was frightened for a while, but later I enjoyed having Deaf friends and using sign language to talk to each other. What I really liked was sports – we played a lot of sport. The bad things were being punished with the strap, or writing out 100 lines when I forgot to put my hearing aid on after games at lunchtime. There was a rule that you had to leave your hearing aid on all the time in class. I remember having to stand in line a lot, and the prefects –the older Deaf kids – were hard on us. They'd make us younger ones give them our lollies. But I have to admit, when I got older, I was a prefect and we did the same to the younger kids. All the mean things the prefects did to us – like punching us or making us go to bed early – we did exactly the same to the next lot of kids, and then they did the same, and so it went on! That was the system.

I liked going home for the holidays only because I missed my younger brother. We used to play together a lot. He was a year younger than me and I hung around with him, even though we couldn't communicate that much. It was different when we were older; we went our own ways after we grew up. It was actually lonely for me at home with the family because they would talk and I was always left out. It was a bit miserable really, because my stepfather, who married my mother when I was nine, would often take me and my brother out on business, and he would talk endlessly at some hearing person's place, and I always wanted to go home because it was so boring and frustrating for me. My stepfather always favoured my brother and had no time for me – he thought I was stupid. I was glad to get away from home when I left.

At high school age, I was sent to Linwood High Deaf unit for a year, and then I was sent back to the Deaf school. I don't know why, they never explained it to me. At 15 I left school. My mother practically took me by the hand along to a job interview at a furniture-making firm. She did all the talking for me while I just sat there feeling stupid. They gave me a job. I was happy to have left school at 15, but after that I was a bit lost and confused. I didn't like going to work with all those people I couldn't really communicate with. They didn't seem to like me, and when they all talked at lunch-time they didn't try to include me so I just kept my head down and ate my lunch. I felt lonely. There was an older Deaf man working there but he didn't sign at all and he kept to himself. He sat with all the others but he was left out of the conversation too. So I ended up going home for lunch every day instead of sitting there by myself.

One day I got a letter from a Deaf friend in Wellington inviting me to go there for a holiday. They took me to the Deaf Club and I really liked it there, and so I decided to leave my family and stay there. The next job I had was at the zoo as a cleaner, cleaning the paths and drains and toilets. After two years there, in 1972, the head zoo-keeper asked me if I'd be interested in working with the animals, as a zoo-keeper. I was really keen on that because I'd always watched the zoo-keepers feeding the animals and thought it looked like a good job. Cleaning was lousy. So the head zoo-keeper went to see the boss at the City Council. He told him that there was a Deaf man who wanted to become a zoo-keeper and the boss replied, 'Oh no way, a Deaf person can't do that, it's too dangerous for a Deaf person.' The zoo-keeper had to come and tell me I couldn't have the job. I was really disappointed; I didn't see why he thought I couldn't do it just because I was Deaf. I threw in the cleaning job because two years of that was plenty. Years later, I went back to visit and two of the same guys were still working there and they asked me if I wanted to come back to work, but I was so angry and hurt about not getting the zoo-keeper job that I wasn't interested in going back. You see, at the time I just took it, because I didn't know much – I was young and I didn't have older Deaf people around to support me. Later, I got involved in the Deaf Club and started to learn from other Deaf people about being assertive and standing up for yourself. I learned heaps when I was older, but I didn't know what to do at the time. I would have loved to become a zoo-keeper.

I've had a hard time in many jobs where other workers have picked on me. In my last job I had sole charge as a cleaner – cleaning by myself and locking up afterwards. That was good. I like working on my own much better.

I married a Deaf woman, and broke up with her. I've never had a hearing partner, only Deaf girlfriends. Maybe one reason is because I snore so badly – hearing people have told me my snoring is absolutely terrible! At the moment I'm staying in the night shelter because I haven't got my own place, and people there have thumped me in the night to wake me up because my snoring wakes everyone up. They told me not to sleep there. What can I do?! I think I'll have to get my own flat. In the last 25 years none of my partners has complained, but it's a big problem around hearing people because I can't relax and go to sleep.

I have some bad memories from the past. When I was at the Deaf school, a staff member sodomised me and another Deaf boy. It happened in a weekend when he invited us to come and watch him building a boat. I was 13 or 14 at the time. It happened again on a school camp. The same man came up to me all friendly, and told me to follow him. I knew what he wanted and I was scared, but I felt I had to obey him and he did it to me again. I was also sodomised by an older Deaf boy in the school hostel. Afterwards I asked him, 'Please don't do that again', and he didn't ever bother me again. But I was scared of the hearing staff member; I couldn't stand up to him. When I went home, I was very quiet and I didn't say anything about it. I didn't know that I could tell someone or ask for help, and I bottled it up. My mother wasn't there when it happened. It was very painful holding it in like that. Later I started drinking heavily, and for years and years I never told a soul about what happened.

Last year I was having some problems after my children were taken away and my partner left me. I was really upset. I went to a violence counsellor and let the whole story out for the first time. I felt so good to get it off my chest. All through those years I hadn't been able to tell anyone. Now that I've finally let it out, I realise how much that experience damaged me; that person messed me up. That's why I was drinking heavily for a long time. I tried to stop drinking in 1980. I met a Deaf social worker and asked her to help me so she arranged for me to go to the Salvation Army programme. But there were no interpreters back then. I went along, but I didn't say anything and I couldn't hear what the others were talking about. It wasn't much good. Recently I've been going to another counsellor and talking about what happened. I've been changing a bit since then. Last year I went on a Deaf Life Skills course, and my confidence increased a lot. I learned more about sexual behaviour, which helped me be more aware of some of my own past behaviour. I have to change some things about myself.

As for my goals or dreams, I'd really like to see the Deaf Club improve, with better facilities like a nice bar where you can go to talk with friends and have a drink. When I drink at the pub with hearing people, I end up drinking too much and wasting all my money on shouts because you have to keep up with the others. It's pointless. So I'd like the Deaf Club to offer their own place to go for a drink and socialise - I've been waiting a long time for it to develop. I used to go the Deaf Club regularly and to Deaf sports in the weekends. Lately, it's only special events like New Year's parties and I've been less involved. The younger Deaf only seem to think about organising sports, and they don't bother to think about the older age group like me. I've pulled out a bit.

I enjoy talking with new people and seeing their different ideas and experiences - they're all different, and you can learn from that. Of course there are a lot more Deaf people to meet in Auckland - it can be a bit quiet here in Wellington with a smaller Deaf community. My personal goals are to clean up my lifestyle - my life is not healthy at the moment. I'd like to learn more about respecting people and about life skills, like the course I went on. Oh, and in my dreams I'd like to be the Prime Minister next year!

Susan Hamilton

Born 1953

Susan Hamilton is known in the Deaf community as a
keen sportsperson, and as a former president of the Deaf
Association of New Zealand (1994–1998). Susan is now
working as the archivist at Kelston Deaf Education Centre,
where she is collecting documentary evidence of Deaf
history. A keen traveller, she has broadened her own
horizons and raised her goals for the Deaf community
through her knowledge of the Deaf world overseas. Her
childhood memories are full of the frustrations of a bright
child struggling with the expectations and teaching
methods of the time, both in the Deaf schools and in the
mainstream. Immersed in the Deaf world from the age of
three, Susan says that being Deaf is not a subject that has
ever prompted much conscious reflection on her part: it's
just who she is.

My poor mother had to wait 10 months for me to be born: such a long
pregnancy! I was 27 inches long when they first measured me and
the doctor said that he had never seen feet as big as mine. I was born
without one ear, so my mother knew that I was partly Deaf straight away.

When I was about 18 months old I was in the kitchen playing with all the
pots and pans, making a real racket. Mum kept saying, 'Stop it Susan, stop it!'

but I carried on, oblivious. So she went up behind me and clapped her hands loudly a few times. No response. That's when she realised that I was completely Deaf. She was very disappointed. She took me to the doctor and asked him to do some tests on me. He did the tests and said that there was nothing wrong with my ears, but that I was mentally retarded. He advised my mother to take me to the IHC. She was upset. She didn't believe what this doctor was saying; she felt sure I was Deaf. So Mum contacted her father in Australia and arranged for me to be tested at a hospital over there, where a doctor diagnosed me as profoundly Deaf and mentally normal. I was just Deaf. In later years a German ear, nose and throat specialist was visiting New Zealand, and my doctors asked him to try and find out how I became Deaf in the first place. He asked my father a lot of questions and finally discovered that the umbilical chord had been wrapped around my neck at birth and oxygen was cut off from my brain. The most affected part of my brain was the hearing area. So it was brain damage that caused it, apparently.

Until I was about three, I wasn't a very strong baby. I couldn't sit up and I couldn't walk properly. I had spastic problems in my legs so I had to do exercises. I think that was when frustration started for me. I would yell and jump; I couldn't sit still for long periods. It was tough for my mother. I wanted to get up, play, and run around every two hours during the night. My mother would try and explain that it was night time and I should be asleep. But I wonder how she communicated this? I was only about two and a half years old. After a while, she couldn't take it any more, so she asked the doctor to give me tranquillisers to calm me down, and stop me screaming. I think I screamed because of lack of communication; I was frustrated at not being able to get through to anyone.

Soon after that, I started to run off all the time. I got so frustrated it was easier for my mother just to open the door of our house and let me take off, rather than keeping me penned up and trying to protect me. We lived in Whenuapai Air Base, which was enclosed, so it was safe to let me go, and she could trust that I'd come back. But it was hard on Mum, because I used to always go into the hangars and other out-of-bounds places where people would find me and ring her to come and get me. One time, Mum was looking for me to take me to hospital for some eye surgery. I was out on my little bike when she finally found me and told me to come home. I started following her but veered off in a different direction. She had to turn the car around to chase me. It took her two hours to catch me before we could go off to the hospital! That was just one of many incidents.

Eventually, Mum needed a break. She asked if Sumner School for the Deaf would let me enrol there. It was actually against the law at my age - I was only

two – but the principal saw my mother's need and he kindly let me come to school two or three times a week. I would be in the classroom and keep as quiet as possible. Then when I was two and a half we moved to Auckland and I started going to the Titirangi School for Deaf three times a week. The drive took over an hour each way, on the old roads before the motorway.

In my first class I remember there were only three of us, all aged three; the rest of the kids at school were older. Because of my father's job in the air force, he later had to transfer to Fiji, so I started boarding at Titirangi a month before I turned five. I only saw my brother in the school holidays and we didn't talk much. With my parents there would be a bit of mime and speaking and lip-reading between us to communicate. My mother wanted to teach me to finger-spell (which she'd learned in high school in Australia) but it was not allowed at school, so she contacted the John Tracy Clinic in America for advice. She obviously heard back, because from then on she sent me letters every week from Fiji. Those letters always had a piece of paper with four pictures on it. Under each of the pictures there were simple words, and the teachers would tell me what they meant.

I remember vividly the evening when I became a boarder at school. You know, most Deaf children had no idea what was happening when they were dropped off at the residential Deaf schools. I didn't realise I was going to be staying at this place either, I was just dropped off. It was evening and the kids were asleep. Where were my parents going? I knew that they were leaving and I was going to be left behind. I clutched my parents desperately and cried. After they left, I felt completely abandoned. I cried a lot, while the matron tried to comfort me before putting me to bed. It was a small bed in a room with older kids. I didn't have a friend the same age as me until a year later. That was when I got into mischief! I don't remember much about Titirangi, not as much as I do about Kelston.

In 1958 Kelston School for Deaf was built brand new, to replace Titirangi. I was the first boarder to arrive at the new school, because after the holidays, I was flown back from Fiji a day before term started. I used to fly back and forth to Fiji for the school holidays and every time I went to Fiji I'd have a new word that would drive my mother up the wall. The first one was, 'why?' The next time I came home it was, 'what for?' When Mum would say, 'let's go to the swimming pool', I would say, 'what for?' She would reply, 'to swim and keep cool'. I would say again, 'what for?' And it would go on. The last time I went over my new word was 'because'. It drove my mother crazy! 'Why? Why? What for? Because.'

At school we had speech therapy where we did repetitive and tedious exercises like pronouncing *p*. We knew we'd got it right if the wee strip of paper in front of our mouth blew away from us. I remember practising *the* and *mm*, closing off one nostril to pronounce it. It was pretty difficult at first and I only improved a bit. It was a relief to be able to sign out in the playground, and once you were back in the classroom it was a struggle not to sign. I don't remember being punished if we did happen to sign in class. Maybe only a few teachers did if there was cheating, but then it was only a slight telling off.

When I was about nine, we had a male teacher for just six months, who was fabulous at story telling because he used mime. The children got so much out of that. He loved telling myths about men with three eyes. In every story he would use gestures and mime to convey the meaning. When I saw these stories told in a visual way that I could understand, I felt so good. From that point on I decided that signing was the most effective way to communicate with Deaf children. When I think of all that oral business we had all the time, I really wonder what was the point of it.

I was mainstreamed when I was 12. I'd just come back from a school in Singapore, an oral Deaf school. At that school there were two separate groups of children: one group taught in oral English and the other group taught in oral Chinese. If you signed, you were strapped. I was lucky to have this one teacher there who spoke very clearly to us and made sure that we could understand. When I got her as a teacher, I made a dramatic improvement in my English as I started to read. She would explain to us what the story was about and guide us through the book; she would make us read some and then talk, all of us wearing those clunky old headphones to amplify the sound. We read the story, then she'd ask us questions about what we had read, once a week for an hour. My level of English improved tenfold.

When I came back to Kelston I was pleased to be back with my friends, but shocked at how low the level was there. The teacher I got was the same one who had made me fall asleep when I was there before, she was so boring. The work she gave the children to do was baby stuff. I wanted more of a challenge, so I had a lot of clashes with this teacher, getting strapped quite a few times for answering back. I was so frustrated, I kicked the doors in anger. They wanted to know then what I could do, so I wrote on the blackboard and they were surprised at the level of my writing. Actually I had learned this trick in Singapore about how to write the answer from the way the question was written: I just changed and added a few words to complete a nice sentence.

One day my teacher got fed up and sent me to the vice-principal, who asked me what the trouble was. I told him how bored I was, and so he gave me a story with questions to answer. I loved it. I was happy doing the work, and the vice-principal saw that I was capable. From then on I deliberately got

into trouble so I could go and do this other work that I really wanted to do. This carried on until one day I was asked if I had any hearing friends at a hearing school. I did have one, and told them her name: Carol. They went away and did some planning, unbeknownst to me. One day a teacher came to assess me to see if I could fit into the mainstream. They mentioned an intermediate school. A week later I was accepted into a hearing intermediate school.

I was a bit unsure about it at first. What were the teachers going to be like? Was I going to understand them or not? I must say I was fortunate to have my friend there when I first started. We didn't actually remain close, but I had grown up with her and she could use some basic signs. I was put at the front of the class so I could lipread better, and it turned out that my teacher was easy to lipread. She would always make sure that she didn't talk at the same time her back was turned to write on the board. But in science, I found I couldn't understand a thing the teacher was saying. I loved science but it was a waste of my time being there, so the teacher gave up her free time for some one-to-one tuition to help me catch up. It also helped my English. It was frustrating for me in science when I couldn't follow, because I had enjoyed it in Singapore and really wanted to do that subject.

I fitted in well at school, really well. The other kids were a bit uncertain at first, but this disappeared quickly and I was accepted. I was used to playing with hearing kids in my neighbourhood as well as my Deaf friends at school. I'm sure it would have been a different story if I had only ever mixed with Deaf children. An interesting thing I've noticed is that people who are profoundly Deaf manage better with hearing people than Deaf people who have a little bit of hearing. They can't seem to get along as well.

I went back to the Deaf school twice a week for the first few months, for help with maths and English. I improved tremendously from going back. It was really good to see my friends there too. By December, after starting in September, the teacher thought that I would be able to cope going directly to Form Three at Kelston with other students who were two or three years older than me, but I was in Form One at this stage, and I felt it would have been too big a leap. I insisted on going to Henderson Intermediate to do Form Two instead. In Form Two I said I no longer even wanted to go back to Deaf school twice a week. For Form Three I went to Kelston, which was a bad move; I should have gone straight on to Henderson High School. The quality of teachers we had wasn't good and they changed often. I became a bit lazy with my study. I wish that I had stayed in Singapore and finished my schooling there. I could have gone on to university. I definitely could have.

I left school when I was almost 17 years old. I was dux when I was in Form One. My scores were almost perfect. A teacher told me once that I had a photographic memory. I would read things once and remember what I needed to answer. But I wasn't happy at school and for a while I got hooked on the idea of farming. But someone at school saw me drawing things, copying a drawing. That gave them an idea and they spoke to a welfare person, a field officer for the Deaf. He suggested to Mum that I take a tracer course at AIT [Auckland Institute of Technology]. Next thing I was at AIT, thinking, 'what is a tracer course about anyway?'

What a small world it turned out to be. I found this other Deaf guy doing the same course, and it was much better than doing it alone. The practical aspects of the course were easy enough, because it was quite visual, but the theory I couldn't follow at all. There were no interpreters, no support services for Deaf students – nothing! This was in 1970. At the end of the three-month draughting course we sat the exams with the others and failed them, but the teacher decided to pass us anyway and asked the other students to decide how much to pass us with! I failed the technical drawing aspect by just one point. It was a bit of a puzzle for the tutor because I failed the simple things and succeeded at the difficult tasks, like the hardest drawing assignment during the year which all the other students had failed. We were passed in the end and got our certificates.

After the course I had a break and later on met up with my Deaf classmate who told me that he had got a job. He didn't tell me where it was. A month later I got a job at the Auckland Regional Council. My father went with me to the job interview – it still makes me frustrated thinking about it. There were no inter-preters then, and I suppose he didn't know what was right or wrong for him to be doing. I sat there twiddling my thumbs while they had this conversation between themselves. It should have been *me* they were talking to, not my father. Anyhow, this employer actually had the courage to take me on. Others had said that it would be too hard with a Deaf person, but he wanted to give me a chance. I was given a one-month probationary period. So there I was at my new job, a bit uneasy at first, but I got used to the people as I went on. I was taught how to do some of the drawing and I gradually picked it up. Morning tea came around on the first day and I went downstairs to the cafeteria and lined up with everyone else. I looked around and to my surprise saw the Deaf guy who I had been on the course with. He teased me about following him! It turned out he was working on the second floor in a different department. What a small world! I worked as a draughtsman at the Auckland Regional Council for 23 years – with one year off for a working holiday in England – until I was made redundant.

SUSAN
HAMILTON

I think having experienced a hearing school, and AIT, and having some hearing friends when I was growing up, helped me to survive with hearing people at work. I communicated with my workmates by writing things down, lipreading, and gesturing. It was always a matter of adapting to what would work between me and others. I didn't teach the people at work to sign: I'm not sure why. I guess I saw it as meeting people half-way. I met them half-way, and vice versa.

When I'm in the hearing world I leave my Deaf world at the doorstep, so to speak, and adapt to their way of communicating. But when I'm in the Deaf world I only sign – that's my real language. I remember my brother complaining about that once. I was talking to him and signing with him in the 'pidgin' way I normally did; then I turned to talk to my Deaf friend, switching into fluent sign language. My brother didn't get one word and asked me why I signed differently with others. It had never occurred to me before. I realised then that I was using a different language to communicate with hearing people.

In 1976 when I went to the Trans-Tasman Games for the Deaf in Brisbane with the first New Zealand team, I encountered fingerspelling. I knew a bit of fingerspelling through an Australian Deaf flatmate I'd had: I'll never forget that experience. My flatmate would try to catch me out with long fingerspelled words, which turned out to be sentences and not one word. No wonder I was stuck! It was a slow process for me to learn to read fingerspelling. To communicate in Brisbane we had to use gestures and a bit of mime. The New Zealanders all had problems. The Australians all fingerspelled flat out, and they seemed to use fingerspelling as much as signs. We would keep having to ask them to slow down but they didn't really. In the end we gave up and just watched their facial expressions for clues and tried to laugh at the right places. It was too fast for us Kiwis.

When I travelled to England, I found that the sign language over there was a little different, but fairly similar to New Zealand. I could generally understand people, no problem. The older Deaf people fingerspelled a bit more, whereas the younger ones tended to sign more. When we were coming out of the oral era in New Zealand, Deaf people were signing in NZSL but there weren't signs for many concepts, like 'system' and 'structure', so we borrowed signs from other countries that had them. We retained our basic language of NZSL, but there has been a lot of borrowing of signs for more sophisticated concepts. It's interesting. Things are changing in the Deaf community, and people are learning more, signing more. Children are allowed to sign in class now, and that's helping them learn. The younger ones are developing lots of new vocabulary in sign language. Being involved in the Deaf Association has helped me, because of having to read and use a lot of new words. There are also workshops and leadership training where ideas are picked up. Deaf people from overseas have also influenced NZSL. We see their signs and borrow them if we don't have our own - for example, the signs for *system*, *programme* and *project* are all borrowed from overseas sign languages. Ten years ago, most Deaf people in the community would never have known the meaning of *project*. Now they know what it means and we have a sign for the concept.

Things are getting better all the time for the Deaf community. I've noticed that the 'Friends of the Young Deaf' programme has increased Deaf people's confidence. I've met many Deaf people who have become aware of their lack of English and what they don't know. When the literacy tutors ask what problems most affect them, they've realised that it is English, and so they go out and do something about it. The English literacy classes are really growing now. All this change started with the training of those few interpreters in 1985, and from there it has gradually grown. Now there are workshops in the community, and sign language tutors' workshops where people have the opportunity to discuss NZSL with each other. From the increased contact we've had with overseas Deaf since the 1970s, we began to realise that Deaf people from other countries signed differently and that made us aware of our own sign language.

On the issue of Deaf identity, I think those who have difficulties with their Deaf identity are probably those who have some hearing, who aren't profoundly Deaf, and who are maybe in between two worlds. People's interest in the Deaf identity topic has certainly perplexed me. I know I'm Deaf, and that's that, from my point of view. When I used to work in a hearing environment, that's when I was always aware that I'm Deaf. To be honest, sometimes I feel really annoyed with hearing people - like when I'm trying to talk with someone, and someone else interrupts and disrupts the communication. I'm left out and end up feeling peeved. When that happened at work, I'd hate hearing people all day. I would not speak to them and I'd put up a sign that says 'I hate hearing people. Please leave me alone.' That startled them a bit, but I got so frustrated I just didn't care. I hated them! The next day it's forgotten, and I go back to thinking: that's normal when you're in the hearing world - communication not happening. I'd explain to them how I felt when those things happen and they'd understand, but in a few months it would happen again. I have to remind myself that most people in the world are hearing, and I'm a minority of one in that situation. How can they please me? It is difficult. If Deaf want to be able to talk to people comfortably, they have to go to other Deaf people.

It's like with my parents. I love them, but communication at the dinner

table is pretty hopeless. It's been like that for so many years and I've put up with it. A few years ago my parents were talking at the dinner table as usual and I decided I wanted to join in. I asked what they were talking about. My father replied that he was talking to my mother privately. I said, 'If you want to talk privately, talk somewhere else. *I'm here*! What are you talking about? I think you're rude!' My father was furious at that outburst and walked off. They stopped doing it after that, and my father saw the frustration I felt. But nothing much changed. I wish there were a course that taught families how to communicate with their Deaf family members. I have friends come over and they are shocked at the way my parents talk in front of me. For them it's just normal. When my whole family gets together, uncles, cousins and so on, it's still the same except for my aunt and uncle. They understand and try and include me by summarising what different people are talking about. My parents never said, '*So and so is talking about this ...*' Never. My aunt and uncle didn't always do that either: it was only after they noticed me being left out after they had been to stay with me once while my parents went to England. During that time we started to get to know each other a lot better. They saw me using a sign language interpreter to phone my parents in England, and that was a real eye-opener for them to see me communicating fully.

Sports have been an important part of my life – mostly, but not always with other Deaf. I've been involved in athletics, swimming, hockey, softball, netball, indoor basketball, squash, table tennis, badminton, and golf now. I'm a natural at sports, and I just have a passion for understanding how the games work, everything about them. I competed in shooting in the World Games for the Deaf in Christchurch. I didn't win any medals by a long stretch, but I was quite chuffed to be a competitor. I learned a great deal from that experience, because people gave me all this advice which was really helpful. A while after the Deaf Games, the school hall where I practised shooting burned down and that's when I stopped shooting and took up golf instead. I play golf now for my own exercise. I have arthritis and it's a bit painful, but it's important for me to keep my joints moving. I play with a handicap of 13.

I drifted into being the president of the Deaf Association after several years of being involved in a small way. I think the basic reason I was elected is that I'm good at signing clearly and explaining what things mean in a Deaf way, so Deaf people can understand me! Previous presidents of the Deaf Association were not really fluent signers and not everyone could easily understand them. As a leader I'm not sure how I fare, but I have done some leadership training through the Friends of the Young Deaf (FYD) programme and I've learned a lot through this, especially from observing how groups work. I have to say that my number one weakness is my temper. If things aren't right I lose it – but I'm quick to say sorry and I accept that I'm wrong.

I think a big achievement was to lead the council, which was difficult for me. When I was young, I was very nervous about speaking in front of others. Now I've been taught how to be a good leader and to present to a group without that nervousness. That was a big achievement for me. One very formal presentation I made was at the launch of the *Dictionary of New Zealand Sign Language* in Wellington, to an unfamiliar crowd. The occasion was very formal, lots of people. I really had to think about how and what I was signing, making sure that people on all sides could see me clearly. This was a big event, but when I got up to speak I felt fine. That's a big difference compared to the 17-year-old me!

Cheryl Anton

Born 1953

Cheryl Anton is one of the first qualified Deaf teachers in

New Zealand - a goal she did not even dream of until

encountering Deaf teachers in America. She attended Sumner

School for the Deaf in the 1960s, and went to a mainstream

high school. Her account of gaining a teaching qualification

in 1992 shows how recently perceptions about the capabilities

of Deaf people have begun to change in New Zealand: Deaf

education started here in 1880, yet it is only in the 1990s that

Deaf people have been able to train and work as teachers of

Deaf children. While Cheryl had Deaf grandparents and a

mother who was familiar with Deaf ways, she nevertheless

had her own struggle finding a comfortable identity between

the Deaf and hearing worlds, while striving also for academic

achievement.

I was born in Wellington in 1953. When I was 15 months old, my mother told my father she thought I might be Deaf. My father disagreed, as he couldn't see anything wrong with me. But my mother took me off to the doctor, who concluded that I wasn't Deaf because I seemed so responsive. Three months later, my mother was still convinced that I was Deaf and took me to another doctor. This time my deafness was confirmed by using different testing methods. The first doctor had tested me by setting an alarm clock behind me. When it went off, I felt the vibrations and turned to look at it.

Mum had had a rash during pregnancy and thought the cause may have been German measles, since my sister had had the measles. But my grandparents on my mother's side were both profoundly Deaf, so that's probably why I'm Deaf. My parents were upset about me being Deaf, but my grandparents said to them, 'Look at me – I'm Deaf and I'm fine.' Both of them grew up at Sumner School for the Deaf. I loved talking to them. Both my grandparents were oral, but they also used gestures and signs a lot. They used a mixture of signs from Australia, where my grandfather originally came from, and New Zealand. He was one of 12 children and five of them were Deaf. Sumner school used to include a farm where the boys would work, milking the cows and so on. My grandmother lived opposite the school on a farm and she became the first day pupil in the school. When my grandmother left school, she worked there in the hostels as a house mistress. Illingworth Drive, which is now in front of the school, is named after her because she was the first day pupil. My grandfather was there under the first principal, Mr van Asch, and he told me about something that happened in his class. Mr van Asch had a long bushy beard and my grandfather got a bit cheeky and signed to him that he should shave it off.* Van Asch gave him the cane for that.

So my mother grew up in the Deaf world, often going along to the Deaf Club with my grandparents. They also had a lot of Deaf people visiting their home. My mother enjoyed being around Deaf people; in fact she seemed to be more comfortable with Deaf than with hearing people. I suppose that was a cultural thing.

I was mainstreamed in a hearing school when I turned five, as there were no schools for the Deaf in Wellington. There was one in Feilding, but my parents weren't keen on me being in a Catholic school, and didn't want me living away from home as a boarder. They didn't like the idea of sending me away to a Deaf school at all. But after a year the teacher informed my parents that I wasn't learning anything and I needed to be at Sumner Deaf school. So my parents decided to shift down to Christchurch, and my father transferred with his job. They had both been in Wellington all their lives, and they would miss their friends, but nonetheless they moved so I could attend Deaf school as a day pupil. At Deaf school there were three of us together who were bright,

---

* Gerrit van Asch is famous (infamous from a Deaf perspective) for being the father of 'the pure oral method' in New Zealand. Yet the irony is that every photograph of him shows that the lower half of his face was covered with a bushy moustache and beard. Combined with pronunciation that would surely have been Dutch-accented, this must have made lipreading an impossible mystery. Cheryl's grandfather was probably not the first or last Deaf child to venture such a reasonable suggestion!

and we were quite competitive, always working hard to keep up and beat one another. During Form One I became extremely bored as the work wasn't stimulating enough and I was hardly learning anything. The same school work was repeated over and over again. I did have two good teachers though, who had university degrees. I was quite lucky to get them.

In school I was oral, since we weren't allowed to sign. I recall a time when I was signing to my friend in class. The teacher saw me and told me off. In front of all the boys and girls I was put over the teacher's lap, my dress was pulled up and I was spanked several times on my backside. I was so humiliated. I still hurt to this day when I think of it. I was just signing! My speech wasn't as good as some others in the class – what was I supposed to do? Other kids would boast about the good marks they got for speech but I couldn't. I got F's, 'fair', and 'very poor'. I tried my best to speak better but I just couldn't produce what they wanted. I thought the other children were more fortunate because they could speak better. At home with my parents we would talk and lipread, but with my grandparents I would sign. My mother signed with her parents, and she was easy to lipread too. My friends would always say how lucky I was that my mother was so easy to lipread. They wanted to have her for their mother! So I communicated with a mixture of sign and speaking and lipreading. When my Deaf friends came over Mum would watch us as we talked. She didn't mind us signing at all.

When it was time for us three girls to go on to high school, the principal of the Deaf school didn't want to let us go. He wanted to keep us there as the school's prize specimens. Our mothers weren't at all happy about that decision, and spoke to the deputy principal who arranged for us to go to a hearing high school. We won that one.

At high school we were in a Deaf unit with a teacher of the Deaf who had a BA. There were six girls in that unit with no boys at all. I asked my mother why there were no boys and she said that there were difficulties with the boys' behaviour. If they had behaviour problems, they were not accepted into high school. They had very low expectations of us at the school, and the Deaf unit was there on a trial basis – not for academic reasons, but to see if we could 'fit in'. They didn't expect it was going to work at all, of course. The teacher of the Deaf was responsible for teaching us English and social studies. We were mainstreamed into cooking classes and sewing classes. In the fourth form another girl and I were selected to do science in the mainstream class. In the mainstream we didn't understand anything the teacher was rattling off while she wrote things all over the board. So we'd just sit there and chat to each other, ignoring the teacher, who let us get away with it. It turned out that we came top of the class. We worked pretty hard; we didn't learn through the teacher but by doing a lot of reading.

In the fifth form we were mainstreamed for even more subjects, only going back to the Deaf unit for English. Out of six girls, four of us got School Certificate in certain subjects. One got it in art, one in typing and art, and Rachel and I got four subjects each. We couldn't take five subjects because they thought five was too much for us. I got an A for art, but 50 per cent for English, 50 per cent for geography, and biology 65 per cent. Rachel was intelligent, more so than me probably, but after the fifth form she'd had enough of the pressure and left. She couldn't take any more. I was lucky to be able to mingle with both Deaf and hearing people. At lunchtime I was comfortable with my Deaf friends, but I would often go to my hearing friends' houses at the weekends.

By the sixth form, all the Deaf students had left school except me. But I wasn't focused on school at all. I was really just filling time until I got a job. It was easy to get jobs then, doing typing, or insurance work. Rachel had a job at a private lab, which is what I wanted to do, and my sister worked in a lab too. For a long time I did nothing, just fluffing around, thinking that University Entrance [UE] was something I couldn't do. I just wanted to go out and work. The teacher wasn't impressed and halfway through the year she gave me a good telling off and urged me to get on with it, and catch up. I was fortunate to have hearing friends who took notes for me in the mainstream classes. That made a big difference to my coping. What I felt awful about was that the girl who took the notes for me failed UE while I passed. I was accredited, but she had to sit the actual exam.

Looking back at the reasons why I was more successful at school than many other Deaf children, I remember that I was quite a competitive person. I would see what my sister was doing and try to equal if not better it. Also, I was always encouraged to achieve what I aimed for. I felt equal to other people and comfortable with who I was. My parents were very supportive. They were always involved in parents' meetings and had an interest in Deaf people. Every night they read me fairy-tale stories. I loved it. There were no pictures, but I would look at Mum while she was reading. I was a good lipreader. I also used to read comics and copy them out all the time. I loved to read, and maybe that's why my English really improved when I got to high school – I didn't learn it from Deaf school. High school was so much more stimulating; I was starving for more information and knowledge. At Deaf school I felt so deprived; I was bored stiff and unchallenged. I was there for too long – from age six to 13. But what I did gain from Deaf school was Deaf culture and a link to the Deaf community. It's important to have both aspects.

I left school and got a job in the Christchurch Public Hospital working in the histology lab. My job was to prepare various body tissue samples ready for the pathologist to analyse under the microscope. That was an interesting job. I had to do training to qualify for a basic certificate that got me a pay rise. After a while there I wanted a change, I wanted to have more fun. A lot of my Deaf friends had boyfriends or were married, so for me the social life was pretty dull. I wasn't interested in any of the guys in Christchurch either, so I decided to move to Auckland where I got a job doing hospital lab work again. I was quite depressed in that job. The boss didn't want to have a Deaf overseer working there, and when he was having a go at me he'd grab me by the neck. I wasn't happy, and I wanted to find some Deaf people. I had moved to Auckland and gone flatting with hearing friends, not bothering to go and meet some Deaf people. I guess I had snubbed them. At this stage I hadn't really accepted being a Deaf person and I spent a lot of time with hearing people trying to fit in by speaking and lipreading. I had been going out with a Deaf guy (my future husband), but we split up and then I had a hearing boyfriend for a while. I was still trying to work out where I really fitted – in the Deaf world or hearing world.

CHERYL
ANTON

My flatmate and I went over to America for a five-week holiday. We'd go our own ways and then meet up again. When I was in Minneapolis I met a Deaf lecturer in Deaf education, Dr Winifred Northcott, whom I stayed with for a bit. She took me along to a place called Camp Courage. It was a Deaf camp, and there were all these Deaf children. Wow! I saw some Deaf adults signing and discovered that they were teachers of the Deaf. I was in awe. I couldn't stop staring – I was truly fascinated. This is what I wanted to do! I was 21 at the time. I had never imagined it was possible to have Deaf teachers of the Deaf. I thought at the time it was an impossibility, that it was a job that only hearing people did.

Two years after I went to America, I applied for and got a job as a residential social worker in the hostel at Kelston School for the Deaf in Auckland. While I was working there, I was enthusiastic about becoming a teacher, and I went and saw the principal of the school, the late Mr Young. I spoke to him about what I wanted to do. He replied, 'No, it's not possible, you can't do it. They wouldn't open the doors for you.' I told him, 'But they have them in America, they do it there.' He just said 'No, sorry, but I don't think so.' I was quite deflated and gave up on that ambition.

When I was 24, I went overseas again for a year to England. I went with a good Deaf friend of mine and stayed with three other Deaf girlfriends in a hostel in London. We had such a great time, we were never lonely. For three months my friend and I went on tours to places like Norway and Russia – all over the place, really. I came back to my old job at the hostel, but this time I was promoted to senior residential social worker. That's when I got back together with my old boyfriend. I first met him when I had moved to Auckland before, and went to the Deaf Club to have a look around. I went out with him for a while, but he would accuse me of being hearing because I was oral. I told him I was Deaf, but he didn't believe me because I talked. We split up after a bit and I hung around with hearing people, but I felt lonely with them and communication was always a struggle. I was really frustrated and depressed, although I did meet more Deaf people through working at the hostel.

My grandmother died when I was 14, but I remember a conversation I had with her when I told her that I intended to marry a hearing man. 'No,' she said, 'you're to marry a Deaf man.' 'No, I'm not going to,' I said. We debated back and forth on this. In the end, she said, 'We'll see, we'll just see.' And she was right! My old boyfriend and I got back together, and got engaged. When I introduced him to my mother, she liked him straight away and said to me, 'It's about time you learned.' She felt it was right for me to marry a Deaf man, and that it was a sign I had accepted my own Deaf identity.

We got married, and I worked until I became pregnant. From then on I really expected to be a housewife, never thinking I would return to work. I was solely focused on my two hearing daughters. With them, I speak or sign. My husband signs, but he has a habit of using his voice as well. The children understand us with no problems; they're used to our voices. My husband and I sign to each other, and the children can sign fluently.

When the children were five and seven, I was working as a reliever in the hostels at Kelston when someone suggested I apply to train as a teacher of the Deaf. My reaction was 'What are you talking about? It's impossible, I tried before and I was told I couldn't – no way!' This person encouraged me, so I thought about it and talked with my husband, decided to apply and I got in. And here I am today, a teacher.

There were two of us Deaf students at college, myself and David. Before us, there had only been one other Deaf teacher, who I had flatted with, so knew she'd been turned down for the course several times. Because of the problems she'd had, I felt negative about it all. She even had better speech than me because she wasn't born Deaf – her hearing had gone gradually. So I wondered how I could possibly succeed if it had been so difficult for her. Years before, I had tried to study extramurally and found it very difficult with no extra support. The first time I had just dropped out, and so did many other Deaf people who tried to study in those days. It *was* hard at training college; I felt

like a guinea pig. We had notetakers in lectures, but there were no sign language interpreters available at that stage. They were still going through training, which had just started in 1992. By the second year, some interpreters were available.

So it was tough at college with just the two of us Deaf students. We had few friends because we were always with the notetaker. It was deadly boring and took a lot of patience to sit through lectures while the notes were being taken for us. By the end, I'd had enough. My mother says that I have a lot of perseverance, more so than other Deaf people. I pushed myself hard because I really wanted to succeed.

After my teacher training I went directly to Kelston to teach Deaf children. I didn't get my Teacher of the Deaf Diploma first, like other teachers at the school had done. Nor had I been teaching in regular schools like the hearing teachers had before studying for their diploma.* This was a new experience for Kelston to have brand new teachers like us, who were still unregistered – in other words, not fully trained. I think we presented a bit of a challenge, because they had never had any kind of programme for beginning teachers like me and David. For the first year, I felt as if I was being watched like a hawk. It was very frustrating. I just wanted my own space. My training and outlook were different from the older teachers', but I felt that I knew what to do, and had a more modern approach.

When I first arrived in 1993 I had to teach in Signed English, which I loathed. In reality, I used NZSL when no one was watching, and after four months I used it openly. I had had enough; I hated being locked into Signed English. Towards the end of that year I knew that a bilingual (NZSL and English) class was on the cards for the following year, and that they wanted to appoint a permanent staff member for the position. Of course I wasn't a permanent staff member at this stage. To tell you the truth, some people had

---

* In New Zealand the standard path to qualifying as a teacher of the Deaf is to complete a regular primary teacher training course, then teach at least two years in regular schools to become registered before studying for the one-year Diploma in Teaching Deaf and Hearing Impaired. Trainees accepted and sponsored on the Teacher of the Deaf course are recruited from permanent teaching positions. This system has effectively been a barrier to Deaf people training as teachers of the Deaf. It is difficult if not impossible for most of them to fulfil the two-year mainstream teaching requirement with hearing children, yet if they work initially at a Deaf school without being fully qualified as teachers of the Deaf, they cannot normally be appointed to permanent positions; this then precludes them from meeting the criteria for the diploma course. This set of policies has created barriers for the few Deaf people who have completed teacher training to then enter teacher of the Deaf training, although in the late 1990s numerous exceptions have been made to break this cycle.

rather low expectations of Deaf teachers when I started. Anyway, I applied for the bilingual teaching position and turned out to be the only one who did, so I got it.

I was certainly happy about having this class and having it completely to myself. I worked with a Deaf woman, Pam, who was employed as a language assistant and it was up to us to work out how to run the class the way we felt it should be done from a Deaf cultural perspective. It worked! The atmosphere was more relaxed, the children were happier and more at ease with the communication we used. Their self-esteem was better too. The children in our class were communicating and signing more freely, and were more confident in initiating communication than the other Deaf children.

Teaching in a Deaf way is different. Others who teach in a hearing way often forget that Deaf children need to be visually shown what words mean. In traditional Deaf classrooms there wouldn't be enough visuals around the place, like words and pictures and so on. Hearing teachers thought more about auditory reception, which doesn't work for Deaf children. They need to see things and be taught through NZSL. The children in my class are always shown something in three ways. For example, *rabbit* is shown to a child as a sign, a word and a picture. It would be useless just signing something without showing or telling them what you are talking about. Associations need to be made between signs and the printed word. For two years Pam and I worked extremely hard, always aware that we were being observed as an 'experimental model'. We put in a lot of effort to show that the bilingual approach could and would work. We didn't want to let the Deaf community down and give the impression that sign language doesn't work. We had a lot of help with reading activities from Bea, a staff member with a background in teaching English as a second language.

Later on, David and I returned to college for the teacher-of-the-Deaf training. We were really disappointed by the course at college. It didn't cover what we needed to know about teaching Deaf children; we needed more depth on Deaf children and literacy, and models of bilingual teaching. It was so frustrating. We were at training college for one year to get a piece of paper, a diploma in teaching Deaf children, but a lot of the course was superficial and focused generically on disability, and I wanted much more focus on actual strategies for teaching Deaf children. We learned a few useful things like audiological management, and about other special needs groups.

Initially, we resisted the course orientation, saying that the issues are about Deaf, not disability. We explained that from our perspective, Deaf is normal – we feel normal, not handicapped. We are very different from those with other

special needs. To us, the greater need for Deaf people was the education itself and not all these other things. I would love to have had a Deaf professional involved in training us.

CHERYL
ANTON

My life now is certainly different from what it was when I was a housewife. Then, life was very quiet with very few involvements outside my children. I was a mother, I was there for my husband, getting dinner on the table and all that stuff. Being a teacher, I meet a lot more people, my horizons are wider, and life is more varied and challenging. At the moment I'm completing an MA in educational administration. I'm really enjoying it. Long term, I want to use my training to bring about improvements in Deaf education.* I'm doing an MA because Deaf people have to do that bit extra to prove ourselves. It's easier for hearing people to get a foot in and get promoted, but for Deaf professionals, we have to work harder, which I don't think is fair. There are only five Deaf teachers at the Deaf school I work at, and four of them have degrees. That's a far higher proportion than for the hearing teachers, most of whom do not have a degree. At the moment, I'm still trying to prove that I can do it.

---

* Since this interview, Cheryl Anton has been appointed one of four regional coordinators responsible for services to Deaf children in mainstream schools.

Discussion, National Deaf Cricket Tournament, Christchurch

Team talk, National Deaf Cricket Tournament, Christchurch

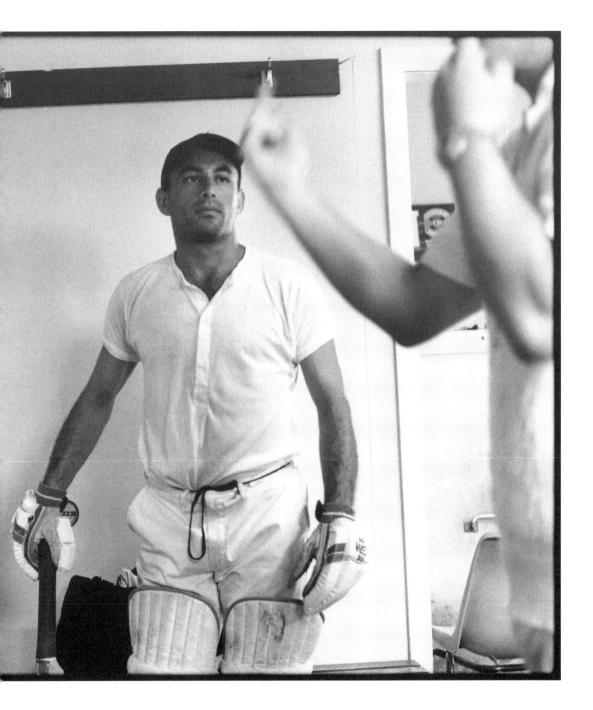

Team talk, National Deaf Cricket Tournament, Christchurch

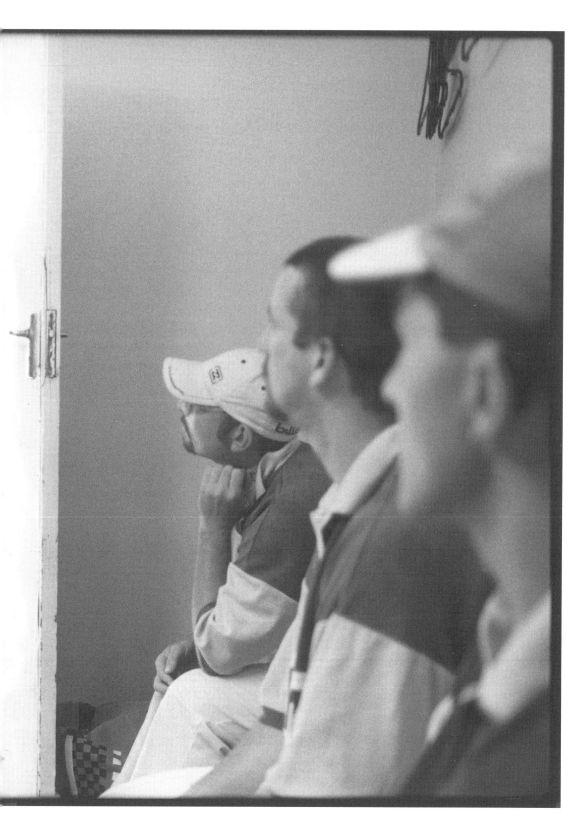

Clapping a boundary, National Deaf Cricket Tournament, Christchurch

Conversation, National Deaf Cricket Tournament, Christchurch

After-match function, National Deaf Cricket Tournament, Christchurch

Clapping, after-match function, National Deaf Cricket Tournament, Christchurch

Douglas Croskery

Born 1955

Douglas Croskery is a working family man solidly connected to the Deaf community. Like many Deaf children in the 1960s and 1970s, he was educated in Deaf schools (Titirangi and Kelston) and in Deaf units. From an early age he identified with Deaf people and sign language, prompted by friendship with a Deaf child with Deaf parents. He also tells of being thrust unprepared into the world of work and, like many of his peers, struggling with the obstacles of literacy and communication as he sought satisfying work.

I was born on 17 November 1955, healthy and hearing. Some time later I became quite ill. I was found to have a disorder with my blood, and I had to have a blood transfusion and stay in hospital for six weeks. I recovered well, and it wasn't until a bit later that my mother discovered I was Deaf as a result of the illness.

When I was about three or four, she took me to the Deaf school in Titirangi. I started as a weekly boarder at Kelston in 1960, when I was four years old. I was frightened and I kept wanting to go and be with my grandparents who lived in Auckland, but they had to leave me in the school. The first day I was pretty scared because there were a lot of Maori children and they seemed so different to me. As time went on, I got used to being there with the other Deaf children. I really enjoyed being at school for the sports, and all the different things we kids got up to together. After class had finished for the day, we'd play Tarzan on this lovely tree on the edge of the playground, or play hide-and-seek, or on the flying fox – our favourite thing. Going home with my grandparents for the weekends, by comparison, was very quiet, although my grandfather was

very good to me. My grandmother spent a lot of her time doing puzzles and talking. We communicated through lipreading and speaking.

One weekend when I was six or seven, I was helping my grandfather chop firewood. My job was to put the wood on the chopping block, and he would chop it with the axe. That day, I happened to notice that the gate to the chicken pen was open. I tapped the chopping block with my right hand to get my grandfather's attention to tell him – just as his axe was coming down to chop the log. The axe came down hard and my grandfather fainted, leaving me grasping my bleeding fingers. One finger that was cut off couldn't be re-attached, so I returned to school with half a finger missing. The children teased me with a sign that meant 'chop-finger'. For a while I got quite upset by them teasing me and pulling horrible faces about it, but I got used to it after a while. The sign for 'chop-finger' became my name sign and it's stuck with me until this day.

I was not at Deaf school the whole time. I was eight when I moved to a regular school in Waterview. My hearing wasn't too bad and I was quite good at speaking. There were seven other Deaf at the school and two of them had Deaf parents. One Deaf child's parents were New Zealanders and they were oral and didn't really sign, because during their time at school it was strict oralism. The other family, the Hunts, were from England. I really liked talking to them because they could sign fluently. One weekend Brent asked me over to his place for the weekend. His parents signed to me and it was easy for me to understand them. I learned heaps from Brent Hunt and his parents. They took me out to the Deaf Club where I met lots of Deaf people. It wasn't at all like being with the other Deaf children. The adults signed a lot different: it was so clear and easy to understand. I felt at home with them straight away. From that experience when I was about eight, I dreamed that later on I would join the Deaf Club. With the Deaf children in my early years at school, the signing wasn't like it is now – we had simple signs that we used, signs that you don't see Deaf people using these days.

All the teachers at school were oralists – strict about speaking and lip-reading. We had to keep our hands still and watch the teacher talking. The whole time we had to watch and write. It wasn't a good experience. At breaks, we'd hive off to talk secretly in sign language. Brent was teaching us stuff all the time: he was a really valuable person for us. I was hungry for more sign language and more information, keen to talk about more things. I preferred being with other Deaf children, because at a hearing school you can get along okay playing sports at lunch time but it's impossible to have a decent conversation.

I went back to Kelston Deaf school when I was in Form One. I boarded there until I was 11, when my parents separated and my mother moved to

Auckland. Then I became a day pupil, but I got really homesick for school and begged Mum to let me go back as a weekly boarder. I wanted to be with my Deaf friends at school Monday to Friday and only come home for the weekends. I have two sisters: one is a year older and the other one is three years younger, and we didn't sign at home when I was growing up.

When I was high school age, I went over to Kelston Boys' High for three subjects: woodwork, technical drawing, and engineering. I had to walk from the Deaf school across to the high school, coming and going quite a bit. I'd usually get to class late because of the distance I had to walk. One very strict teacher always ticked me off about being late, but I thought he was unreasonable because it was a fair distance. Later on I found out that he'd been a New Zealand representative athlete, and ran everywhere. I'm sure he expected me to run between the high school and his class just so that I could be on time.

When I was in fourth form, I was sent off to various places to do work experience with the other students. The work placements lasted about a week. One August holidays I was sent to a shoe factory that made heavy-duty footwear. A week went by, then two, and finally the third week. They approached me then and asked me to sign a form – which I realise now was a tax form – asking me to become an employee. I didn't know what it all meant so I just signed it. The following Monday I was up ready to go to school as usual. Mum said to me that I wasn't going to school, I was going to work. 'What!?' I'd never said that I wanted to go to work. I wasn't finished at school. I had fifth, sixth and seventh forms to go yet!

It ended up that I did work there from then on, straight into a job. I missed my school friends and being at school. Once a year, Parents of the Deaf would organise a get-together, and I would bike across Auckland from Onehunga to Kelston to meet up with all my school friends. They asked where I'd been, and I told them that I'd been sent to work, thinking it was only temporary, and then found out it was permanent. It was really distressing. I missed my mates. It felt strange that they didn't know where I was, because I just disappeared from school.

I eventually got used to working, and joined the Deaf Club when I was 17. My mother found out from the Hunt family (through their hearing daughter) that the Deaf Club met every Wednesday for a social evening of cards and supper. I was keen to go. I met some new people, and also met up with some of the older boys I'd known from Deaf school. There were very few girls there at the time; it was mostly a place where men met and talked about sports and work. I became part of that crowd and forgot all about school. This was a new stage of my life. I was now part of the Deaf community.

I got quite involved with their activities. On Monday evenings there was basketball straight after work; Tuesday, I discovered, they had badminton. I was in for that too. Then on Wednesday was the Deaf Club social evening; Thursday would be basketball games at the YMCA, and we had a good team there. On Friday nights a Deaf crowd used to frequent one particular pub in town, but because I was under age, I couldn't get in so I would meet other young Deaf and we'd go to the movies or just walk around until 10.00 p.m. when the pub closed. Then we'd get ourselves some hamburgers and sit around and talk before I caught the last bus home. This was a regular Friday event. It was the wild life!

At the shoe factory where I worked I got a lot of flak from the foreman, and we argued a lot. We'd get mad with each other. I used to make mistakes with the size of shoe tacks that I had to load into the machine, and a lot of shoes went to waste. I was slow at doing some other work too. I was there for seven months doing my apprenticeship, and this meant regular training sessions with the manager in his office. He tried his best to help me, but it wasn't really working out. The communication problem was too difficult and I was fired in the end. The foreman was about to kick me that day but I moved out of his way in the nick of time and he fell on his backside on the floor. I left immediately.

I got another job in a factory where I discovered there was another Deaf person. This was a spray-painting job, painting kitchen and bathroom benchtops. I'd always spend my breaks talking with the Deaf guy. I left there and got another job working with pool tables, through Mr Manning, a field officer for the Deaf who worked at the Deaf Club. At the new job there were two other Deaf men, believe it or not. I knew one of the Deaf guys from school; the other was English and he was a fluent signer. But he never went out with Deaf people – he didn't seem to want to for some reason.

After that I got two part-time jobs, and then decided to move to Wellington, where my first job was as a kitchen hand, washing dishes. I made friends with some hearing people but I was on the lookout for Deaf people and didn't know where the Deaf Club was. I'd met some Deaf people from Wellington before, at the Labour Weekend Deaf Games, but I didn't have their addresses, so I decided the best thing to do was to go down to the railway station and see if I could spot anyone I knew. I went and sat around munching on a hamburger, keeping my eyes peeled. Soon enough I recognised someone. I was taken out to meet other Deaf, and from there I got involved with the Wellington Deaf community.

I stayed in Wellington for two and a half years, then headed back to Auckland. I was working for a while in a steel factory, making roofs, and it was at this time that I met my wife, Pam. I met her through badminton nights and also through Deaf Club socials on Saturdays. But actually the Deaf world is small: I first knew Pam when I was about 11 and she was nine years old. I used to see her on the train going home from Deaf school to Mt Maunganui. She lived in Te Teko. Of course I didn't talk to her at that stage, because I was hanging out with boys. I talked to her more often at school when I was in fourth form, then I left school and didn't see her again until I was 21. At first we were just friends, playing badminton together, but after a while we started dating, fell in love, and got married.

I remember when I was a boy staying at my grandparents' place, I visited Patreena Bryan, a Deaf woman who lived on our street, who would take me to visit another Deaf couple. They had children, and they used to tell me that in the future I would get married to a Deaf woman and have a family of my own. I thought that was rubbish, and I told them I'd rather marry a hearing woman. Imagine, I actually said that! When I left school, I met a hearing girl at a nightclub. I saw her for a year, but there were problems understanding each other and we would end up arguing, so that ended. I decided never to go out with a hearing girl again. I mixed with both Deaf and hearing people after that, eventually met Pam ... and that was it!

She didn't like me working in a factory, getting filthy with grime every day. She suggested that I could work in an office. 'You've got to be joking!' I said. My reading and writing in English was so poor I knew I'd never be able to work in an office. I could only read things related to sports. Pam was a bit disappointed at my response. So she and my mother had a bit of a talk one day, and my mother went off and found a job possibility for me at NZ Post. They pushed me to go along and check it out. The employer asked me what job I would like to do. I said I'd like to do driving or postal deliveries. He told me that the best money was really in mail sorting, so I said I'd give it a try, and he then gave me five minutes to look over a list of New Zealand place names. I got a bit worried at this stage. I went through the list, trying to see which names I knew and which I didn't, trying as best I could. Then he took the list away and gave me a test on the place names. I tried to remember how to spell them, but if I didn't know I would just abbreviate. The man understood what I meant with my abbreviations, and he passed me. He found out in the interview that I had absolutely no school qualifications and no trade qualifications, but still offered to train me as a mail sorter. I had the job.

The day I arrived to start the training, I was really nervous. But as I was walking to the Central Post Office building who should I bump into but a Deaf person who was also going to start work there – Milton Reedy, a Maori guy I

DOUGLAS
CROSKERY

had known when he was young at school. He was now very good at wrestling and judo, and had won a medal for it. We talked on the way, and went in together to start our training. One of the training tasks was to memorise all the different place names and suburbs. Milton really whizzed through it all and was off to work before I was. I took a bit longer because I was heavily into basketball and badminton at the time and I wasn't managing all these things very well. I didn't have an interpreter there either, but I eventually passed by reading and studying for myself and went on to do the job. I ended up working with three other Deaf guys there.

Some time later, we had to go for more training related to the regulations and laws. This time it was a tutor talking to the group. He pointed to the paper he was talking about, to indicate that I just needed to refer to that. But I couldn't read! I sat there looking at it, thinking 'I can't understand this.' Then there were questions and answers as well as a practical test of our sorting speed. I was relieved to pass both sections, and so did Milton. Later I was promoted to be responsible for all New Zealand places, not just Auckland.

One Christmas time it was extremely busy and everyone was doing 12-hour shifts. One night it happened that there were eight of us Deaf people all in a row, sorting mail. We chatted away in sign language, making plans to meet at breaks. Then we'd all troop off to the cafeteria together, a whole pack of Deaf people. The boss came along one time, and told us to get on with our work. Eventually he separated us. It was quite funny. He came up to me later and had me on about it. It was all right for hearing people, he said, because they could talk and work at the same time. But when we talked, we had to stop sorting to use our hands for signing. That was a rare thing to happen, though. It only happened once or twice a year, and we had a great time.

Now I work at a courier company, in the business mail centre. I enjoy my job. Some Deaf people have suggested that if I left my job I could work in the hostels at the Deaf school. But I don't really want to work for Deaf, teaching children or anything like that. I'd love to be involved in organising sports for young Deaf, but I would not be comfortable doing a job with paperwork. I couldn't do that.

My wife and I have a little boy called Jay – he's hearing. We were interested to see what language he would use: whether he was going to speak or sign first. He's picked up signing naturally, and I can either talk to him or sign and he understands both. I take Jay along to the Deaf Club, but it doesn't worry me whether he ends up being more comfortable with Deaf or hearing people. It will depend on what he wants for himself, not on me.

Lynne Smith

Born 1954

Lynne Smith identifies strongly as Deaf, but enjoys the advantages of being bilingual and bicultural. Like many of her generation, she found her intelligence undervalued at both Deaf school and a mainstream high school. Career choices were limited, and initially made for her. Lynne's memories highlight some of the unpredictability of being a Deaf child. Balancing between the hearing and the Deaf world has always been part of her life – in a hearing family with a Deaf brother, in the workforce, and as the mother of two hearing children.

I didn't realise I was Deaf until I was about 10, when it occurred to me that there was a difference between me and other people: they were hearing. I never thought to myself, 'I am a Deaf person.' At 13 or 14 I started asking my mother, 'Why am I Deaf?' and it was upsetting for her to actually talk about it. At the time, I thought I was like everyone else, though my family communicated in a different way, using gestures. I also signed at school with other Deaf children.

My parents are both hearing and I have a twin brother who is hearing and other siblings who are hearing. My older brother is Deaf, but we're quite different in our outlook. My mother discovered my brother was Deaf when he didn't respond after she yelled at him at about 18 months old. I was diagnosed as Deaf when I was a baby.

I went to a hearing school when I was five. It seemed fine to me. I was a quiet child at home. I kept busy playing with my brothers. I don't think I had good communication with my parents. I remember my father taking me out places,

but he would only give me snippets of information and just smile at me a lot. Then one memorable day when I was six or seven, my parents and I went for a long drive. I took my doll with me. We eventually arrived at this school and I met a teacher who shook my hand, and was quite pleasant. My parents told me that they were going to show me to my room. 'Room?' I thought, 'what room?' Anyway, I followed them upstairs. They showed me to what was going to be my bed. 'Why am I being sent here?' I wondered. It was Kelston School for the Deaf. My parents hadn't explained anything to me – not where I was going, nothing at all. When I came back from seeing my room, my mother and father had gone. 'Where were they? Why had they gone?' I cried a lot then. I was pretty upset. I looked around at the other children and realised I would be staying too.

I wondered what the Deaf children were doing with their hands at first. Then I recognised that I was like them and that I signed too. I quickly picked up signing from the others and I became a lot happier. Of course, we weren't allowed to sign at all in class. We only signed at breaks, in the playground using our own signs – it was easy for us to talk, compared to how it was in the classroom where we had to mouth words and lipread, sometimes with our hands behind our backs. We would be smacked or have something thrown at us if we reverted to signing. We resented that. Even if the teacher's back were turned to us, they would always know when we were signing because of the noise of our lips smacking as we signed.

Whenever I went home I would wonder why my parents were there, while I was in Auckland. I would go home on the bus to Tokoroa, but never really be happy because nothing was explained to me. I didn't know who or what I was, really. Eventually my parents moved up to Auckland when my mother was expecting her fourth child, my sister. I was a weekly boarder at first. On Fridays my Deaf brother and I would come home for the weekend and on Mondays we were dropped off at school again. My brother actually has more of a hearing loss than I do, but for some unknown reason he was main-streamed later on, while I stayed at the Deaf school as a day pupil. I think maybe it was my behaviour that set us apart. I was told I was a difficult person who didn't listen. I didn't know what that meant. But I think it was because I was confused. I felt as if I was on a roller-coaster: I was at a hearing school one minute, then taken and left at a Deaf school, without knowing where my parents had gone and why they'd left me there.

At school once, I remember these two elderly people visited me with a bag of oranges, and stayed half a day. I wondered, 'Who are they?' I was thinking how nice it was for my parents' friends to spend some time with me. It wasn't until I was about 11 that I asked them who they were and they said they were my grandparents. I checked this out with my mother, who explained that they were my father's parents. This was one of the incidents where I was not told things. Inside, I was angry about not knowing many things, because it made life unpredictable.

In Form Three I was mainstreamed at Kelston Girls' High School, which was right next door to the Deaf school. I went back to the Deaf school for English classes for a while before they stopped that altogether. Again, I didn't know why. I was the only Deaf girl there; it was a really hard and frustrating two and half years. I didn't get a good education because I couldn't understand anything the teachers said. Some of the teachers were good to me, but they thought I was like everyone else: they treated me as if I could hear. They expected me to read out loud, but I would be so humiliated because I couldn't speak or read very well at all. I got quite frustrated when I lost the support from Deaf school. Now I think I should been much more assertive about all these things, but at the time I just went along with it and felt confused. By the Fifth Form I used to go and talk to the counsellor about what was going on and the problems I had. I wouldn't talk to my mother about anything.

Some Deaf people can be so stubborn sometimes that it can be difficult to get the message through. I think the frustration and stubbornness is because of their past experiences and the poor education they had. People say that I'm stubborn, but am I really? Perhaps I'm so determined to find out what I need to know because of my poor education and that seems like stubbornness. Through my quest to find out, I learn a lot of things that are just common knowledge to other people. It's hard work. I get really angry when I think of my past, but that's life.

I left school after fifth form and my mum enrolled me at Winters School of Hairdressing. She'd paid the fees and everything: nothing was explained to me, I was just sent there. It was like she had it all planned. Mum thought I'd enjoy hairdressing because when I was little I kept a scrapbook of different hairstyles.

We had various classes and in one of them I had a tutor who talked about colouring. I tried my best to lipread but it didn't work and I missed all the information. On the other hand, I was very quick at the practical side of hair-dressing. I could see how things were done by watching the tutor and copying. When it came time for exams, I couldn't understand the English in my test papers, so I didn't do it. I felt like I had failed. Fortunately, one older tutor knew about my difficulties and talked to the others, and the next week I had an oral exam where I was allowed to respond to questions verbally. That was how I passed. At the end of the year we had another test - this was practical and my mother was my model. I passed all aspects of that test as well as the

written section because it was multiple-choice, which was easier for me. I got three certificates at the end.

LYNNE
SMITH

Mum was the one who job-hunted and came to the interviews with me. I did get a job. The people at my new workplace realised I was Deaf, and they were very good in the way they spoke to me with clear mouth-patterns and tapping me on the shoulder to get my attention. Despite all of that I still wasn't very happy. I hadn't achieved a goal that I had chosen for myself.

I'm not a hairdresser any more. At my current job where I do data processing, I have a problem with some hearing staff. I'm quite outgoing and I always take the initiative to greet people at work. But I notice that they treat me as if I'm invisible, talking to each other and sharing information as though I'm not Deaf. They forget I'm there. Actually it's similar to when Deaf people get together and start signing away, then they realise there's a hearing person present. Whoops! The difference is that Deaf people are always quite patient. They will make the first move to ensure that hearing people feel included. Hearing people toward Deaf people are different, unless the Deaf person is quite assertive.

The hearing staff at work casually pick up what's going on, but I can't, so I need to go around and find out my own information. For instance, if I've seen people talking over a piece of paper, I'll ask what they were talking about. If they say it was nothing, I go and check it out. Often I find it's information I need, so I let my supervisor know and she will tell me the details. There are a few really good people who tell me what I need to know when I ask. I have a very good supervisor who will always talk to me individually and give me the complete details, and she encourages me by saying, 'You can do it!' I have to work on computers, which involves certain skills. If I don't know how to do something, I can't get by with just asking someone. They don't give me the detailed information I need, because their communication with me is usually limited to a brief answer. I end up reading the manual, and then I check that what I've learned is right, maybe from someone with more experience in a particular area. So it seems like more effort for me. I'm regarded as very capable at my job by my employers, but I do have to make extra effort to compensate for being Deaf.

A lot of people at work don't believe that I am actually Deaf. They accuse me of using it as an excuse. That really annoys me. I might have trouble understanding something the first time and it can take three or four goes for me to get it. When I want to check I have got it right, then people say I'm faking my deafness. They can think what they like, but it does make me mad.

I have become more assertive, but I still feel like telling them to wake up and realise that they can't expect me to be just like them: I am Deaf! I can't understand people on the phone at work, but they still tell me to 'try'. Now I just put up a front where I laugh with them and tease them back. I've learned some tips from counselling and leadership training too. The counsellor in particular gave me some good encouragement. She told me to look at myself and what I've achieved: I've raised two children on my own, I have my own house, I've travelled. This is when I realised what I'd achieved – more than these others! When I travelled to Australia on my own, my workmates were all taken aback and said that they couldn't do that, they'd have to go with a friend. I asked them, 'Why do I need someone to hold my hand? I'm capable of going alone. I'm a strong person and I'm very independent.' People at work don't really know who I am – my real character, and what my Deaf culture is all about.

I had Deaf friends while I was going to the school for the Deaf but I saw less of them after I went to high school. I missed them, though I had some very kind hearing friends. The problem with hearing friends was that there wasn't enough real communication. But I had a few close friends by the time I left school. By then I had been in the hearing world for five years. I thought that my life was always going to be that way, mixing with hearing people.

When I was 16, a Deaf couple who lived nearby and had known me as a child invited me to Deaf Club for a New Year's party. But I didn't have any contact with Deaf people for a quite while after that. Then one day I bumped into a couple of my old schoolmates from Deaf school. I was thrilled to see them again. They told me that there was a club for Deaf people, which I couldn't believe. After I left school, the thought of a Deaf Club never occurred to me. Anyway, one of these old school friends invited me to his twenty-first, and that's how I got back in touch with Deaf people. I was amazed by their sign language. By then, I was so used to speaking and lipreading that it was a big shock to be surrounded by signing again. I was hooked on going to the Deaf Club after that. I felt they were my brothers and sisters, my people, and where I belonged. They made me feel welcome. We shared the same experiences, and I knew exactly what they were talking about. We all communicated the same way. With hearing people it's always a struggle to take part in any conversation because you have to lipread different people and try hard to fit in all the time. With Deaf people you can be yourself and just relax. I got very involved with the sports events and parties and so on; there was always something on.

I was divorced from my Deaf husband when my two children were still young. These days, being a mother of two teenage boys is my first priority, and so I'm less involved in either the Deaf community or the hearing community. Sometimes I feel like I'm in-between the two worlds. I want to be involved in

the Deaf community more, but it's hard to find people who are the same type as me. I do have a few very good friends who have the same interests, like tramping, and talking about anything and everything.

When I'm in the Deaf world I feel different from when I'm with hearing people: the atmosphere among Deaf people seems happy, communication is great; things are always alive. There's always something to do there, and people to meet up with. In the Deaf community you learn from other people's different life experiences. It's easy to befriend overseas Deaf visitors because you can communicate with them - there's a natural bond with other Deaf people. Deaf have different ways from hearing people. Hugging is a favourite way of greeting between Deaf people. It's as though they're part of your family because you have known them for so many years, like brothers and sisters. Even if you've only known someone for one week, you feel as if you've known them for years. In the Deaf world you enjoy things better, you feel more relaxed. The signing, the facial expression and body language are amazing; I love it. Just watching Deaf people makes me smile. Hearing people seem dull the way they talk with a deadpan face, except for when they laugh occasionally. Deaf people are so alive! You feel part of everything so easily.

Hearing children with Deaf parents are also part of the Deaf community. CODAs are wonderful - they are like Deaf people. They have grown up in the Deaf world and know how to respect Deaf people, and how they feel. They talk like Deaf people and relate very well. They've grown up in a signing environment with their parents' friends and other CODAs. You can tell when a hearing person doesn't have Deaf parents - their signing isn't as natural and relaxed. My sons are hearing, but I would have been happy to have had Deaf children. It would be great, in fact. My brother has two Deaf children, and it's possible that my sons could have Deaf children, so future generations in our family might be Deaf. If my sons were to be involved in the Deaf world, I'd want them to be involved in the hearing world as well, because they are hearing - that is part of them. It's up to them, wherever they are comfortable fitting in.

One of my sons says I'm like a hearing person because I talk to them, though sometimes I do sign. My older son has quite good signing skills. I always let my boys have their own world, though. My sons are mature, responsible people, which I think is a result of having Deaf parents. CODA children often act more responsibly. They are like their parents' ears; they listen for them. If someone's knocking on the door, they let their parents know about it. They communicate for them on the phone, and some parents rely on them to interpret for them at the shops and other places. I will communicate for myself, but if I really don't understand then I'll ask one of my boys to help out. Some hearing children have a real struggle in the Deaf world because of their parents' reliance on them. It can get very stressful for them. I leave my boys to have their childhood. I know that if I lean on them too much, it will be hard to separate from them later.

I am strict and direct with my boys. I have seen a few children of Deaf parents who become very bossy because of the role they fall into. They gain a lot of confidence and knowledge in themselves by being the go-between for their parents in the outside world, and they actually take over and control their parents' lives. The parents don't have a problem until the children become teenagers and then the parents can't control them and the children can't control themselves. I have set limits with my boys and do things for myself as much as I can. My philosophy is that if I can do something I will do it, and if I can't I will at least try. My oldest son is quite protective of me and looks after me very well, but I prefer to be quite independent. I believe that children should have their own freedom. Parents also need some freedom from their children, although children don't always realise this. It's important to be aware of how my children are feeling. I tell them to be honest with me and tell me how things are. I tell them how I feel too.

My dream used to be to become a nurse, to look after people. I would still like that. Other than that, I would like to be involved with helping Deaf people – not as a professional, like a teacher or psychologist, but as a normal person, just as myself. I feel I have enough knowledge and experience to guide other Deaf people. If I was a professional I'd have to keep a professional distance. That's not me at all. I want to be myself, on the same level. I think Deaf people view Deaf professionals as different to themselves, because you're never the same person once you study and become a professional. You are not how you used to be because of what you've learned.

Not having good literacy skills is holding me back from working in the kind of job I'd like. I'd have to start all over again to improve my English skills and so on, and that's a lot of work. I'd also like to be a supervisor at work, but I can't: the supervisors use the phone, they can speak, they can easily take part in meetings; they can meet with the boss and then pass on the information. It's really frustrating that those barriers are there for me, because I know I could do other aspects of the job.

I really enjoy challenging those hearing people who think they know all about Deaf people and our culture. It's difficult to talk to them because they've switched off from hearing anything more on certain topics. I'm very pro-Deaf, and I get annoyed when hearing people label us so readily with what they think they know.

If I had the chance to be able to hear, the only reason would be to listen to music. I love music. And sometimes I'd like to be able to hear more of what my sons are saying – *really* saying! I've also wished I was hearing because I want to learn and know more. When you are Deaf you have barriers in your life. There's no problem in learning in the Deaf world where everyone communicates in sign. I didn't learn much at all being with all those hearing people at high school, but when I met up with my Deaf friends again I was forever asking questions: 'What's this? What does that mean?' and so on. I learned so much; it was like being fed. I'm happy the way I am. I have accepted my life and the fact that I was born Deaf.

LYNNE SMITH

Perry Meets the Law

This is the story of a memorable incident from Perry Strawson's younger life. It is included here as an example of the many anecdotes within the Deaf community about encounters with non-Deaf people which escalate into potentially hazardous situations through miscommunication. Typical is the scenario where a police officer misinterprets a Deaf person raising their hands to sign as having violent intentions, or a Deaf person gets on the wrong side of the law by apparently 'ignoring' a verbal instruction.

This story happened while I was living in Sydney. One day I went out with some friends to the pub for a drink. I went home about 11.00 p.m. and got straight into bed. I was a bit drunk and I went out like a light. Then all of a sudden the front door burst open. Of course I couldn't hear it, being Deaf. There I was in bed, with nothing on, asleep. My bedroom was the first one as you came into the house, and my Deaf flatmates had the next two rooms down the hall. Anyway, next thing I know, someone kicked me from the side of the bed, really hard. Then they jumped up and stood on my bed. I didn't know who it was so I punched him and knocked him off the bed. Oops, turned out to be a policeman – *shit!* Then more police came in and there was a big punch-up. I didn't know what they were doing there, and I was just trying to defend myself. They were laying into me and had me down. When they stopped, I asked them if I could please put my trousers on, and they let me do that. My flatmates were panicking – they didn't know what was going on either, and the police were all over them too. Then they arrested me and took

me to the police station. I didn't have the chance to say anything to them or explain anything to my Deaf flatmates.

I was put in a police van. The windows were tinted so I couldn't see out. I tried to keep calm. I was just sitting there bumping around as they drove, didn't really know what was happening. When the van stopped, I felt the engine switch off, and then there was this incredibly loud thumping on the side of the van. I could feel it echoing around the van walls. Then they opened the van and frog-marched me out, with my hands in cuffs behind my back. Geez, I thought, the Sydney police are rough!

Anyway, I got inside and they started talking at me. I just sat there and let it all go past me. Couldn't understand a thing. Then the sergeant in charge of the station tried to talk to me. He was a bit nicer and easier to understand than the others. I was still handcuffed and I gestured to him to undo the cuffs. So he ordered another cop to come and undo the handcuffs – the one who still had a bloody nose. He looked cheesed off but I didn't give a toss. Once I got my hands free I gestured that I was Deaf and the guy interviewing me said to the other cop, 'He's Deaf!' That other cop was gobsmacked – it made him look really stupid. Then the interviewing policeman asked the other one to explain what the problem was, why they'd brought me in. They had a bit of a discussion about it – I don't know what they said. Then the interviewer asked me where I lived, and asked me to write down my address. Not my name, just my address. So I wrote it down. When he saw it, he got a funny look on his face, looked real uncomfortable. He asked me to wait there and he and the other cop went off into another office. I couldn't see in – there were blinds over the windows. Anyway, I sat around till finally the big guy came back looking really uptight. He called me in and there were several cops standing there. The cop who'd arrested me said, speaking slowly for me, 'I'm very sorry.' 'Why?' I said. Then he wrote down 'I arrested the wrong person, at the wrong house.' But they said they were going to charge me with assault for punching the policeman. They asked me if I'd accept the charge and I said, 'Yeah, okay, but I want you to pay for the damage to my house.' They agreed to that. And I told them I wanted to take it further, because of how he'd kicked me in the ribs and the rest of it. The policeman in charge tried to talk me out of it, so I said, 'If you drop the charge I'll forget everything.' They had a bit of a think and a talk about that, and the big guy told the cop to apologise to me. So he came and shook my hand and said he was really sorry. I agreed to have the charge dropped and I'd forget it, even though it was really painful where he'd kicked me. I asked them to drop me home and the senior guy told the one with the bloody nose to drive me – he had to do it. When we got there he apologised again. I told him, 'Next time, don't ever kick someone like that again. Use your truncheon and give them a poke – that's what it's for! It's safer too because it keeps the person at arm's length. Don't just put the boot in next time.' He looked embarrassed – said he kicked me because he thought I was ignoring him.

Paul Buzzard

Born 1961

Paul Buzzard was born and raised in Christchurch, where
he lives now with his wife Della (see following story) and
their four Deaf children. Paul's childhood, in a hearing
family (with one Deaf sister) during the 1960s and 1970s,
was very different from the lives of his children in a Deaf
family twenty years later. Paul works today at van Asch
Deaf Education Centre and is passionate about bringing
the language and culture of the Deaf community to Deaf
children.

My brother was born first – he was hearing. Next came Ava, who was
Deaf. It was a big shock for my parents, and hard for them to cope
with a Deaf child, so they decided not to have any more children.
But then, out of the blue, there was me. My mother had German measles while
she was pregnant, and I was born Deaf. In a way it was easier for my parents
having two of us Deaf, because we were company for each other. My hearing
brother was probably a bit isolated because Mum had to give a lot of attention
to us, and Ava and I could communicate happily with each other. On the other
hand, it meant my brother matured quickly because he had a lot of adult
conversation and information that we completely missed out on. When my
parents talked on the phone, for instance, they'd often turn their backs so we
couldn't lipread them or pick up the body language. I hated that. I thought, 'If
you want to have a private conversation, then close the door.' There were lots
of little things like that at home, but overall my parents did a pretty good job
of bringing us up. They were very affectionate and loving to us.

I remember once going over to a Deaf friend's house, and all his family
were hearing. That was a big shock for me, because I was used to having my

sister and brother to sign to. In this hearing household I felt like I had to literally drop my hands and try to speak all the time, and work out what people were saying. I felt sort of paralysed. I felt lucky because at home I could communicate easily with my sister and brother, and when Mum and Dad talked to us they always used gestures and big mouth movements – they were used to communicating with Deaf. I hadn't realised until then that other hearing families were so different.

I started at the Sumner School for the Deaf when I was three and a half years old. The thing that I remember vividly from that time is meeting my teacher, who had a long scar with stitch marks across her throat. It really gave me the creeps. It made a big impression on me and made me wonder if something scary was going to happen to me too! When I was five, I moved to the Sumner Primary Deaf Unit, with eight Deaf children. We enjoyed being together. Of course at that time, signing was strictly forbidden in the classroom – we'd have our hands slapped or be sent out if we signed. The teacher was hopeless, always writing on the board and talking at the same time, so we couldn't understand what she was saying. We'd fill in the time by signing secretly to each other when she wasn't looking, and once we were out in the playground we signed freely – that's where we felt most comfortable. But because we were a Deaf group within a hearing school, we got harassed by hearing children in the playground – calling us Deaf and dumb, that kind of thing. Then in the classroom we had to switch off our signing, actually sit on our hands and put up with wearing headphones and practising speech endlessly. There was hardly any written work, and the maths we did was just copying times tables off the board, over and over again. The teacher was really useless. Then we got a new teacher, and things improved a lot. She took us on trips, gave us experiences and lots of visual activities. We really enjoyed that, but still there was very little academic work.

My speech never became very good. I think I can make the lip-patterns okay, but I haven't got good voice control. As for sign language, we picked that up easily from each other, especially through travelling on the bus to school with the other Deaf kids. That trip every day from town to Sumner was a great time for chatting. I don't remember signing much at home myself, but I watched my older sister sign to me a lot. Ava used to bring her friends home from the Deaf school, too, so sign language was going on around me. I was quite shy and reserved as a child, not very talkative at all, but I know I had a strong sign language base from being able to communicate at home with my sister.

I was at the Deaf unit for nine years, and then shifted to Sumner School for Deaf for high school. I was pleasantly surprised to find myself in a much larger

group of Deaf children, and all of them signed fluently. I could participate in everything and know what was going on. It was a bit of a shock at first to have so much communication going on, but I enjoyed the wider social life. The comparison made me realise that being in the Deaf unit with the same eight children all those years was very limiting. I didn't realise until I got to this big Deaf community at Sumner how much more stimulating it was to be able to talk about anything. I joined in everything – like sports. It was great.

I'd say nearly all of my learning at school was from other Deaf kids. I picked up a lot of information from them just through talking to them in NZSL. I learnt nothing from the teachers. I'd be given a maths worksheet, and I'd look at it and think, 'What's this all about?' I couldn't really do it because it hadn't been explained to me beforehand – there was no real teaching. When I was about 16 they took us out on worthless visits, like showing us how the lights work in a house, or to watch fencing [the sport]. It was pathetic. It was only from Deaf people that I had access to useful information – ordinary everyday information about what was happening in the news, sports or family things – or moaning about problems we'd had with hearing people.

Deaf friends often came over to my home and my parents always made them very welcome. They encouraged Ava and me to socialise with other Deaf children, and were happy to see us communicating and having a good time together. They were never disapproving about us signing or mixing with our Deaf friends. Looking back, I think that if my parents hadn't encouraged me to have friends I could have been quite isolated and lonely. I was quite shy, so I was lucky to have Ava, my sister, and the opportunity to be with other Deaf kids on the school bus every day. Those experiences were so important for my development.

When I communicated with my parents, they used clear lip-patterns, and did a lot of gesturing and pointing. I didn't see as much of my father because he had three jobs – he'd be out at work from 5.00 a.m. till 10.00 p.m. So it was mainly my mother who was responsible for us. She worried about us being Deaf, and thought the best way for us to be able to communicate was to encourage us to have friends, and for me and Ava to communicate with each other in sign. So she more or less left us to it, although she gave us plenty of love, and always made an effort to speak clearly to us. But we never had really in-depth communication.

I remember one time when we were having dinner at home, I was sitting next to my hearing brother at the table. My parents were across from us, and Ava was sitting on the end. There was a big vase of flowers in the centre of the table. My brother was listening to my parents talking, and I leaned over to try to see around the flowers to lipread what they were saying. When I leaned over, I bumped my brother and he got annoyed, saying I was hassling him. I told him I hadn't meant to hit him, but my parents started growling at me too. All I was doing was trying to see what they were saying. I felt really put down and powerless. Many years later, my parents visited my house. They knocked at the door and naturally I didn't hear them, but we had a dog that always let us know if someone was at the door. So I opened the door, hugged my parents and asked them in. And my mother said, 'I've got a sore arm from knocking so long on your door.' Seriously! 'Well,' I said, 'you should have pressed the buzzer here, it's connected to my doorbell light.' Apparently they hadn't noticed it. Anyway, they thought that was a great idea to have a doorbell light. They came in and sat down for a chat, and while we were talking I moved a vase of flowers off the table where we were sitting. My mother shifted them back again and said 'Leave them there, they're pretty.' I felt as if she was trying to take over in my home. I know they like flowers, but I moved them aside again so we could see each other clearly, and this led to a conversation with them about Deaf culture and Deaf ways. My parents were a bit shocked by the concept of Deaf culture, and I think it made them feel guilty about some of the things that had happened when we were growing up. They got quite emotional about it, but I think in the end it was a good thing. My mother told me that I'd made her cry as well as laugh, but it helped her understand my feelings much better and what it had been like for me growing up.

Later on, when I told my parents that I'd got a job at van Asch that involved meeting parents of Deaf children, they were very pleased and told me they believe it is so important to support the parents. 'We wish that when we had our first Deaf child we had met Deaf adults straight away,' they said. There were many little things that they just hadn't been aware of at the time and they wished they had met a Deaf person who could have explained lots of things, like the importance of eye contact. They didn't really know how to deal with us so they left us to our own devices a lot, but now wished they'd been able to be a bit more involved in helping us with our school work and so on. So it was good for all of us that we finally shared that information. My mother told me before she died that she was grateful we had talked those things over and learned to understand and accept each other better. She said otherwise she could have died without me ever having expressed those things to her, and her accepting me. I feel that now she's 'looking down' at me. It's important to me that before she died I talked to her about how I felt.

When I was growing up, I had a strong belief that the hearing world must be better. I was doubtful about whether the Deaf way was any good. I'd say to the others at Deaf school, 'The hearing way is much better, the hearing world's got

more to offer than you lot.' I'd get put in my place when I started saying things like that, and I'd argue with them. Now, in hindsight, I know I was completely wrong! I just wasn't aware of what I had. My whole life, I'd been given hearing role models to look up to and aspire to. Hearing people were constantly giving me the message that they were all there to *help* me. So I saw them as authorities, and believed they were very powerful people, way above my level. They had fancy language and lots of knowledge, and they always knew the right answers to everything. This was obvious at school because whatever work I did – whether it was speech or maths – was usually wrong and the hearing teacher would come along and point out the mistakes to me and tell me the correct answers. Pretty soon I saw that they knew everything and I didn't know any- thing, and I lost motivation and confidence. Naturally, I wished I were hearing. They seemed to have everything, and because they were the only role models we had, I hoped when I grew up that I would be like them, able to speak well and be clever. That's why I used to tell the other Deaf at high school, 'Oh, it's much better in the hearing world – they have more fun, and you lot are limited to the same old boring stuff.' We argued about that a lot. Much later I realised that it wasn't true at all – I was misguided!

It was when I was 18 and I met my wife's Deaf family that I learned there was much more to the Deaf world than I had known. Here were Deaf people using wonderful sign language in their home and having ordinary lives. That had a great impact on me. They were very close, very much a real family. I felt I could be fully included in that family, because things were always done in a Deaf way. They used my language, so it was a comfortable environment for me. Now my wife and I have our own four Deaf children and it's the same for us. We have a strong family bond and Deaf values.

Another important thing that happened to me was the World Games for the Deaf here in Christchurch in 1989. In 1985, I had been to the WGD in Los Angeles, and that had a big impact on me, meeting so many Deaf people with many different sign languages – it was so exciting. I gained a lot of respect for the Deaf world from that point. I was bowled over by the variety of people and the sign languages I saw: Deaf professionals, people of so many interesting backgrounds. It made me aware for the first time that Deaf people can do a whole range of things on an equal level to hearing people. I was like a vacuum cleaner, virtually sucking up new experiences, information, ideas. It was inspir- ing. Coming home to Christchurch was very unsettling. I got back, kissed my wife and told her I wanted to move to America. I told her the sign language there was so much better, and I suppose I was puffed up with all this new knowledge, a bit full of myself. In LA, I'd glimpsed a better life and I felt really uplifted. Getting home brought me down to earth with a big thump. I realised the opportunities we had here couldn't match what I'd seen in America.

But life went on, and from that experience I developed a real respect for Deaf leaders here who lobbied hard to get leadership training for the Deaf community, and to put into action some of the things I'd experienced in America. I was one of a group chosen to go to a course on teaching sign language at City Lit in London, where we were taught by a Deaf tutor. That was mind-boggling in itself – having a *Deaf* teacher! The course lasted four weeks, and it was wonderful being able to learn directly from a Deaf person. It was completely different from the frustration I felt when I was going to a hearing school and struggling against communication barriers. It hit me then that for my whole education I had been completely passive. At this course, I was told for the first time in my life that it was all right for me to challenge the teacher and to discuss things. So I got back home, started teaching NZSL night classes, and I've been teaching ever since. When I started out, I was more or less on a mission to confront hearing people with sign language and the Deaf way, as if to say, 'I'm Deaf. Look at my moving hands, this is my language! This is the Deaf way!' I was pretty staunch about it.

One big difference between my children and me is that I will not accept oppression for them. My wife and I don't want them ever to have the experience of feeling oppressed and patronised like I did. When I see a teacher from their school say, 'She's doing so well with her speech,' I'm always suspicious, because when I was at school, the teachers would praise my speech, but when I talked to people outside of school they often couldn't understand me at all. I only knew how to pronounce some words, but I couldn't actually communicate properly. So I always ask the children's teachers to explain what they mean when they say they're doing well. Sometimes my wife and I don't agree with them or we don't accept their judgement because we have a different view. While the school says they're coping well in a hearing environment and speaking very well and so on, we think, 'Hang on a minute, is the child comfortable from a Deaf perspective?' We're protective of our children's home language and culture.

When we had our first child, we took it for granted that she would go to a Deaf school with other Deaf children, because that's where she would be able to communicate most naturally. But when she was four and a half and already at the preschool at van Asch, we found out that they were using Signed English in the school. My wife and I were uncertain about that; it didn't look at all natural. But I thought it would be helpful to the children's English because it followed the word order of English. We got home and had a talk about it, and

Della was adamant that our child was not going to use it. She said to me, 'What about our own sign language?' We argued hard about it. She told me I was mixed up about my own language. Anyway, the advisor had told us we had three options: van Asch, a Deaf unit, or mainstream. We didn't really know what mainstreaming was, and when they explained that it was one Deaf child in a totally hearing school, I balked! I just said straight off, 'No thank you! Definitely not!' I wanted to opt for the Deaf unit, but my wife still thought Deaf school was better. We weren't quite sure what to do.

PAUL
BUZZARD

If we had a Deaf school with plenty of Deaf children, and Deaf teachers and the opportunity to mix with fluent signers – whether hearing or Deaf – that would definitely be the best option for our children. I feel strongly that Deaf children need the chance to be all together, to meet a whole range of different people and to have Deaf adults around. When I was growing up, I had no concept of stories or poetry. All we learned was isolated words. Where were the stories for us? Now the children have storytelling in NZSL, and they know that books are a way to get information. That's been fascinating for me to share with my children. I believe it's very important to have a thriving Deaf school, where children can learn easily and have exposure to Deaf adults.

At that point two advisors came to visit us – one was a reinforcement for the other. They stayed about three hours, discussing all the options including mainstreaming, and they offered to place our daughter at the Deaf school in a class with a child with other disabilities. I didn't want that – she isn't disabled. And at the Deaf unit, they were all oral. We didn't want that either; we wanted sign language for her. There were no decent options. We investigated home schooling by correspondence, but they wouldn't accept us because we were Deaf parents and they didn't think we'd be capable. So my wife and I talked some more and decided we should try and be open-minded about it, and at least go and have a look at our local primary school – just to see what it was like. The school had a very traditional, old-fashioned feel about it, with school uniforms and straight lines. I liked that, even though all the children were hearing. You see, at this point we felt we had no good choices. This was our last option. After a lot of agonising discussion, we decided reluctantly to start her at our local school and see how it went.

At the start, we were at the school every single day to check how things were going, even taking time off work to be there. We wanted to be absolutely sure that our daughter wasn't being teased or feeling under pressure. After a little while we felt more relaxed about it, and we noticed that the class and the teacher had learned quite a bit from us being around so much, which was great. We – mostly my wife – would spend time with the hearing children in class, and they just naturally copied what we did and learned quite quickly how to communicate with us and our daughter. We were pretty vigilant about this situation! As time has gone on, it's worked out well. It's amazing how many of the children in her class now sign fluently, including all the Deaf facial grammar and everything. When the classes have changed some years, it's taken a while to develop good communication with new children, but it seems to have worked all right.

Then it came time for our second and third daughters to start school, and again we felt we had no good options. Unfortunately there were no other Deaf children of the right age to form a group to start school together, so we went through the same process again – at the same primary school. We had a lot of struggles getting specialist support for our second daughter at school: they would continually cut the support hours because they said she could hear more with a hearing aid than they first thought. We kept trying to explain to them that this was irrelevant – we weren't interested in what she might be able to hear with a hearing aid, because in the end she is still a Deaf child learning to read and write in a hearing environment. We were concerned that she got the best support to learn and develop to her potential, while they kept telling us how well she was coping, and how well she could understand speech with her hearing aid. Meanwhile, she would often come home in tears because she missed out on what the teacher was talking about a lot of the time.

I remember one time I noticed the school had made a wall chart with a big picture of a hearing aid on it to encourage the children to remember to use their hearing aids. The school asked us to make sure the children had their hearing aids on when they came to school, but we told them, 'Sorry, but we've got three Deaf children, and we don't have time to fiddle around with six hearing aids every morning! It has to be their choice to put them on or leave them off if they choose.' We are constantly being told how important hearing aids are for Deaf children – and we *know* all that – but we draw the line at forcing them to wear their hearing aids because in the end it has the opposite effect. I had such a bad experience as a child with hearing aids that I've never worn them as an adult. How the Deaf child feels about herself is much more important than the hearing aids. I just tell these people, 'Look, you have no idea what it's like, whereas I do. I was a Deaf child and I know exactly how it feels.' So when the teacher explained that the children got a star on the chart for remembering to use their hearing aid, I said to the teacher, 'Look at it this way: your signing isn't very good. How would you feel about having a "hands" chart that we put stickers on or off every day, depending on your signing? How would that make you feel?' They had no answer for that and I asked them to remove the chart, which they did in the end.

PAUL
BUZZARD

I feel my children have good social interaction at school. They are experts at knowing how to adapt to communicate with hearing children or in the Deaf world. They do plenty of creative writing and reading; it's completely different from my own experience at school. I wish I'd had the education they're having. They're all doing very well academically. They sometimes come home a bit down when they get picked on by other kids, so my wife and I talk to them about ways they can deal with that without being too negative. Their situation is definitely not ideal, but in the end we don't have any better choices. And fortunately our children have all gone to the same school so they have each other, and the school knows them well so there is a more supportive environment for them. If they were alone, or in separate schools, it would be a much worse scenario. There is also one other Deaf child at the school, who learns a lot from our children.

My hope for my children's future is that they will be socially well adjusted and have good independent lives. I don't want them to suffer the kind of oppression that I experienced. Of course, like every parent, deep down I'd love to see them succeed and get a university education, but my wife and I agree that the most important thing is for them to have good social skills and experiences. We will encourage them to follow their own directions in life, and mainly we want them have better lives than us. We have doubts about whether mainstreaming is the best way, but we know that our children are very fortunate because no matter what, they have a Deaf family. At home they have their natural sign language, and we can support them as they go back and forth between school and home. If there are problems at school they always tell us and we deal with it. They are far better off than when I was a child and I couldn't explain anything to my parents. Everything was just held inside. Later on I learned to express all that emotion with people in the Deaf community. But that's not how it should be – feelings should be expressed and talked about within the family first. We have strong family bonds because of easy communication in sign language. My children can express their emotions comfortably at home with their family, rather than outside in the Deaf community, or with hearing people – and that's exactly as it should be.

Most Deaf children are now mainstreamed even from preschool. It's a real shame. I teach sign language to many of the parents with preschoolers the same age as my son, and I've said to them, 'Why not get the children together to form a group at the van Asch preschool, where they could be together and use sign language?' But they all say it's too far to travel, and the level is too low, and so on. They're not keen – they'd rather have their child in the mainstream until problems arise, and then they get in touch with other parents for support. So this means we're stuck without any real peer group for our youngest Deaf child. It's a worry for us. We'll have to take our chances on a mainstream situation again. But we will be watching closely, and if it's not working we'll try for home schooling. If they turn us down for that, we'll be fighting it this time. The government has an obligation to provide parents with suitable choices for their child's education, and that should include us. Where are our rights?

Obviously, hearing parents see this situation differently from us. The mainstream school speaks the same language as the parents, and so that's the environment they would choose for their child. But some parents do worry about their Deaf child becoming isolated and unhappy in a mainstream school, and that's when they realise it's valuable to make contact with other Deaf children. That's such a big debate: I could go on about it forever! I think most parents get inadequate information about different school options for their children – Deaf school, mainstream, Deaf unit – and what each one means. I'm keen to share what I know from my own experience as a parent and as a Deaf person with other parents, but it's uphill sometimes getting them together.

For many years I worked at the Toyota factory and taught night classes in NZSL, because it was something I felt strongly about. Then in 1994, my wife spotted a job at van Asch advertised in the newspaper and I decided to try for it. At the interview I was very honest and I told them straight off that my reading and writing are hopeless, and a few other things I thought were weaknesses. I felt it was better to let them know this at the start than waste their time later. But they said 'Fine, we accept that, and we'd like to offer you the job anyway.' So I started work at the school for Deaf as 'Deaf resource tutor'.

It wasn't always easy to work alongside my hearing colleagues because we had quite different perspectives. I came from a strongly Deaf orientation, and a lot of the information I was given in my training was from a hearing professional perspective. There was tension over many issues. It took quite a while for me to be willing to listen to the hearing viewpoint, and when I did, I recognised that it was a medical perspective and that's why I was so uncomfortable with it. Part of my role was to be involved with other hearing professionals – what a challenge! I struggled hard to get across a Deaf point of view. When I started my job, there was still a heavy focus on Deaf children's ears, hearing aids, speech, and TC. Teachers didn't have much knowledge about NZSL or the Deaf community, and I think many of them found it quite threatening working with a Deaf person and having to learn my language. At that time, the principal of the Deaf school was supporting a change towards bilingual education, and I saw that as very positive. But I feel on a tightrope at times, balancing my professional role at school with my personal role as a Deaf parent and advocate for

PAUL
BUZZARD

my own Deaf children, as well as being a member of the Deaf community. Sometimes it's helpful in my job having personal insight from all three points of view, but sometimes they clash!

Della and I have faced many battles over the schooling of our children. It's usually thanks to her that we find out information about what's going on in education, because she reads and picks up information. There are often issues that we need to follow up quickly to make sure our children get what they need, before bigger problems arise. Thank goodness Della can read well, because without access to written information we'd be sunk; we wouldn't be able to advocate for what we want. Through working at the school I've had to read more and I'm sure that's improved my reading, but I still struggle with it.

The most important thing in Deaf culture is sign language. Deaf culture means belonging to the Deaf community, all using the same language to communicate, keeping in touch with Deaf friends, and the way Deaf are when they get together at Deaf sports and Deaf club. It means the way we need eye contact with each other, the way we touch each other to get attention, use flashing lights in our homes, and how Deaf people have full access to information and communication when they are together. Deaf culture is our own Deaf way of doing things that's very different from the hearing way. For example, when I bought a house, I had to make sure there was an open sight-line between the kitchen and dining and living rooms so we could see each other signing. When we first bought this house, there was a wall between the kitchen and the living room, and that was impossible because we couldn't see each other, so that came down straight away. Also we have wooden floorboards right through the house so that we can stamp on the floor to call each other's attention by vibrations. We have flashing lights in the house, a TTY, so everything is accessible for us. It feels comfortable that way. At first the neighbours used to look over at our place and see all these lights flashing on and off at odd times, and I'm sure they gossiped about it – not that we cared! Then finally one of them plucked up courage and came and asked me, 'What are the flashing lights for? Do your children play around with the light switches?' I explained that they were to signal when the phone or the doorbell rang. 'Oh', they said, 'how amazing!' I said, 'Would you like to come over and see how it works? You're welcome to come in.' But they looked uncomfortable and declined. Sometimes if I'm outside gardening I'll see the flashing phone light reflect on the fence, and I'll know that a fax has come. This is how I have access to knowing what's going on, including fire alarms, everything in the house. These things make life comfortable for us. That's our Deaf way of life.

Della and Paul Buzzard give boating instructions to their children at The Groynes, Christchurch

The Buzzard family at The Groynes, Christchurch

ABOVE AND OVER: *A picnic lunch at the Buzzards, Christchurch*

*Deaf parents of Deaf children discuss
education issues, Christchurch*

Conversation, Christchurch

At the Auckland Deaf Society's Friday night Deaf Club

At the Auckland Deaf Society's Friday night Deaf Club

At the Auckland Deaf Society's Friday night Deaf Club

Della Buzzard

Born 1959

Few Deaf people share Della Buzzard's experience of a network of Deaf relatives, and she tells of the cultural advantages that a Deaf family enjoys (see previous story). Her four children are third-generation Deaf on her side. Raising Deaf children has made her very aware of both improvements and shortcomings in Deaf education over several generations, and brought her into conflict with professionals over medical and cultural interpretations of being Deaf.

I was born Deaf, like my parents and my two younger sisters. My father's parents and all his relatives are Deaf; my mother is the only Deaf one on her side. But I think she wasn't surprised about having Deaf children. Lots of Deaf people told her she was lucky, because it would be easy to communicate with us.

Because there are no hearing people in my family, I didn't have much experience of hearing people as a young child. It was a bit of a shock starting school in a Deaf unit, being in a hearing environment and with a hearing teacher for the first time. I had never thought of myself as being Deaf – everyone in my family was the same as me – so it was quite disorienting to suddenly be surrounded by hearing people who spoke and didn't sign. Before starting school I had never thought to ask at home about hearing people, but when I was older we talked a lot within the family about the 'outside' world and hearing people. We'd share our gripes about the hearing world – for example, about being taunted at school with rude gestures, or being put down by hearing people. I used to see those things as my problem, but now I realise it was actually the hearing people who had a problem with us.

DELLA
BUZZARD

My parents both went to Sumner School for the Deaf until the war, and in 1941 or 1942 my father was transferred to school in Titirangi, so they ended up at different schools. Years later, they met up at the Labour Weekend Deaf Games – the same way that lots of Deaf couples met. Soon they were married and my mother was pregnant, and they settled in Auckland. My parents separated when I was six. That was a bad time of my life and I grew up too quickly because I saw a lot of things happening at a tender age. We had a very difficult time.

I'm most comfortable and relaxed with Deaf people. Growing up, I always felt secure coming home to my Deaf family. I remember going over to friends' places and always feeling very awkward around their hearing parents. When I was young I had to keep secrets about things that were happening in my family, and I was so good at putting on a cheerful face that no one really knew what I was feeling inside. It's still hard for me to talk openly about a lot of things: I have a kind of barrier that comes from lots of hurtful experiences with hearing people putting me and my family down because we were Deaf. That made it hard for me to trust hearing people, and now I have definite limits as to how close I will get. I don't want to get too involved in their world and risk being hurt again. But with my own Deaf children being mainstreamed, most of their friends are from hearing families and I'm fine with that. It's stretched my comfort zone because I have much more to do with hearing people now, like the kids' friends coming over, and contact with other parents. So for the children's sake, I've moved on – but there is still a limit to how closely I can really connect.

My parents had lots of Deaf friends and we grew up with the Deaf community around us. Mum was involved with the Deaf Club and we went to all the Christmas parties, fundraisers, picnics and socials. My parents' friends visited each other's homes a lot. They were good times. Mum tried to encourage me to mix with hearing children, like the neighbours and so on, but I just wasn't comfortable – I always felt more at ease with Deaf friends.

I started school at Kelston School for the Deaf and soon I was moved to a Deaf unit in Glen Eden Primary, although no one told me why at the time. Later we moved to Christchurch and I was sent to the School for Deaf at Sumner, but again after a little while they transferred me to a Deaf unit class at Sumner Primary. At intermediate I was in a Deaf unit again, and then after a year back at Deaf school I was moved to the Deaf unit in a hearing high school. Most of the Deaf children mixed all right with the hearing kids, but I always found it very difficult. I was never comfortable or confident with hearing people, perhaps because of my home background.

But at Deaf school, all the pupils signed and it was easy to communicate. Everyone helped each other by surreptitiously explaining when someone didn't understand. Most of the children couldn't understand what the teacher was saying or what they were supposed to be doing, but I could usually understand quite easily, so I was always explaining to the others in sign language what the teacher had said. I even helped them in tests! You see, I had a big advantage at school. I absorbed a lot of information from talking with my family. We talked about ordinary things, like what was in the newspapers, and so we picked up general knowledge and information that the other Deaf children missed out on. That's why it was so hard for them to learn at school, because they didn't have any background knowledge to help them understand things. They came to school with nothing, compared to me. Being the only one with Deaf parents, I took on the role of passing on what I learned at home to the other kids, and they soaked up all the information I could give. When I was about 10, I was advanced for my age compared to the others and I was moved up into a class with 13- and 14-year-olds.

I remember once, in Auckland, when my parents came to my school, the other Deaf children were just blown away because they had never seen a Deaf adult before. Up till then they thought there were only Deaf children in the world. They were amazed to realise that grown-ups could be Deaf, and that it was even possible to have Deaf parents. Now, I believe it's so important for Deaf children to meet Deaf adults: otherwise, how can they imagine their future?

At school in Christchurch I had one good teacher for three years and I learned a lot from him. When I went to van Asch at the age of 11, it seemed that my education stopped – I didn't really learn much more after that. I was busy helping the other kids with their work, but there was absolutely nothing to challenge me. I was so bored that I'd get up to silly mischief, and then I got to the age where all I thought about was boys. It's incredible, but at my hearing high school I had a teacher who let us play cards in all her classes for a whole year while she read her newspaper and smoked. We thought it was great at the time, but now that I look back, it was dreadful – what a terrible waste of our education! I've run into some of my old school teachers and they've said to me, 'Oh it was a shame you played up at school because you were such a bright girl.' That really annoys me! I was only naughty because they didn't have a clue how to teach us, and didn't offer me any real education. They seemed to believe that Deaf children were just naturally troublesome, rather than looking at their own teaching. The real shame was that they were wasting our intelligence – but they can't see it from our perspective, of course.

I found being at a hearing high school quite difficult. I was with two other Deaf girls, but they were very rule-abiding and anxious about being caught signing, always trying their best to fit in and be oral. Whenever we went into

town on work experience they'd try and hush me up, saying, 'Don't sign, every-one will stare!' They were very embarrassed by my signing, so there was always friction over that. I couldn't really mix with the hearing kids either, so I was never really happy at high school, and by the time I was 15 I told my mother I was ready to leave and look for a job.

At that time my mother worked in a factory. Earlier on she had worked at the Deaf school, as a housemaid in the kitchen and dining room. She left because the hours weren't suitable for looking after children and she went to work in a packaging factory. When I left school, she asked me if I wanted to go and work there too. I did, and I really enjoyed it, although the wages were very low. I stayed there quite a while, and it was good because we moved around and worked in different areas. There were a couple of other Deaf people working there besides my mother and me – one Deaf lady had been there for about 30 years. After three years I left for a better-paid job in a sheepskin factory, because by then I was flatting and I was having trouble paying the rent and bills.

I had a hearing boyfriend from the time I was 13, and stayed with him for seven years. We started living together when I was 16, and it was good at first, but after a while we argued all the time, mainly over communication problems. I'd get really frustrated when I thought he was talking to friends behind my back. I always tried to mix with his friends, but he didn't take part in my Deaf world at all. Hearing men are different from Deaf men – most Deaf women say the same thing. Now that I'm a bit older and wiser I can see that they are good at catching Deaf women and taking advantage of them in a relationship where the man has the power. When we broke up, I went back to my roots in the Deaf community and that's where I've been ever since.

My father died in an accident, and I didn't really know where I was going in life, so I went to Australia. But I couldn't find a job and only stayed three months. When I came back I met my husband Paul, and things started to settle down. I first knew Paul as a little boy through his older Deaf sister, Ava, who was my school friend, but he was younger and wasn't interesting to me at the time. Then we met again at a party when I was 19 and he was 18, and I must admit I chased him then. Well, I had to, because he was quite shy. I was looking for the right kind of man, and when I met Paul I liked what I saw – he seemed a sensible person. We went out together for about four or five years, doing all the usual things – going to Deaf Club, movies, dinner. A lot of our time together was at the Deaf Club. We got engaged and married two years later.

I found out I was pregnant while Paul was away at the Deaf World Games in Los Angeles, and I sent him a telegram saying, 'Congratulations to the father.'

Paul read it and didn't get it at all, so he showed it to his friend who shook his hand and told him the good news that he was going to be a father. I had a doctor who I couldn't communicate with very well, so I didn't get much information about pregnancy and birth. After our first daughter was born, I had a feeling she was Deaf. Paul didn't want to accept that, and he was so apprehensive that he wouldn't come to the hospital with me for her hearing test. He stayed home working in the garden instead. I was right about her being Deaf, and when I came home and told Paul the news, he was upset. He had a hard time accepting it, partly because he remembered the problems he had to face in his own childhood, and I think his parents' reaction influenced him too. They saw it as a tragedy, and they reacted with sympathy – maybe that had an effect on him. But for me it was no problem: it seemed normal to have a Deaf baby. For me, it would be quite hard to face bringing up a hearing baby – exactly as it is hard for hearing parents who find they have a Deaf baby. It would be a shock, and take time to come to terms with. I've seen a lot of hearing couples who have a Deaf child separate because of the stress of not being able to communicate well in the family, and the mother having to give lots of extra attention to the Deaf child.

Our second and third daughters were both Deaf, and by that time Paul was quite happy about having Deaf children. When I was expecting our fourth, the family reckoned that the odds were for this one to be hearing, but I felt sure he would be Deaf, and sure enough he was. It wasn't even an issue for us by then. A lot of people were curious about our reaction to having four Deaf children, because around that time there had been a documentary on TV showing a radical young Deaf man, who had just got back from Gallaudet University in America, saying, 'If I had a Deaf child, I'd have a cigar to celebrate!' Well, that really upset a lot of hearing parents of Deaf children, and many of them asked us what we thought of that comment. For me, having Deaf children seemed perfectly ordinary and fine. I wouldn't make a big deal about it, but I was content to have Deaf children – it was what I expected. My second sister has a Deaf husband and four hearing children, because her husband wasn't born Deaf – he became Deaf at three from meningitis. My third sister has three Deaf children, and when they were little the cousins all played together a lot. My children enjoy having a Deaf grandmother – she babysits them sometimes, and she's taught them knitting and other crafts.

We've taken a lot of flak from the Deaf community because our children are mainstreamed. In fact, we felt we had no other choice, but others don't understand the whole story and they criticise us. Many Deaf people are very anti-mainstreaming and even though I do understand their point of view and their

feelings, I don't like it when they show their attitude to the children. They should be more accepting of them regardless of where they go to school, because it's not their fault. In reality it's not a simple situation. If the Deaf school improved and offered the same level of education as other schools, we'd put our children there straight away. That would be great! But there's still a long way to go with that. Some changes have been very positive - like the Deaf Studies curriculum, and the bilingual class. When people ask me why we chose mainstreaming I feel I have to be very careful about what I say - let's just say there are some major gaps in the training of teachers of the Deaf. Some things at the Deaf schools have improved, but I think it's really important that Deaf children are learning and achieving at the same level as hearing children.

I work weekends and some weeknights in one of the residential homes at a Deaf school, supervising boarders from 10 to 19 years old. My job in the family home is to look after the students, run the house just like an ordinary home, take them out and so on. Often when I take them out, I'm teaching them how to be independent. For example, some of the kids don't feel confident about going to McDonalds and knowing how to order food, so I go with them and show them how a Deaf adult does it and they can practise with my back-up. When Deaf kids go out with their hearing parents, what usually happens is that the parents take over and do everything for their children, so the kids don't learn how to manage these things for themselves. But my approach is to show them how, then to stay in the background so they get more confident and independent. I think it's so important for them to develop independence. When I was little, my mother thought nothing of sending me off to town with a shopping list to buy things for her. And I loved it - it was an adventure going to all the different shops and seeing the big world. It taught me a lot; it was part of growing up. I think the students enjoy having Deaf house-parents because it's a chance for them to talk about all sorts of things with a Deaf adult. Many of them have big gaps in their life education - things that you would expect kids of that age to have picked up, but somehow they haven't. Because we can communicate well, the gaps are quite obvious to me, and I can give them the information they've missed out on before. One area, for example, is knowing the boundaries between what they're allowed to do and not allowed to do - what's acceptable behaviour. Many of them aren't aware of basic manners - like how to talk appropriately to people in different situations, when it's not okay to swear, all those social skills. Also I teach them to cook and plan meals, and that gives them a great boost in confidence about looking after themselves - they love it. In other ways they're just typical teenagers.

So many Deaf children nowadays seem to be getting cochlear implants, it worries me. When it first started, Deaf people were speaking out strongly against it. Now Deaf people are still very uncomfortable, but they're backing off a bit, because they know it's parents' choice and they feel they can't say too much for fear of driving the parents away. My daughter was once asked if she wanted a cochlear implant and she said, 'What on earth for? I'm happy to be Deaf!' When I asked her directly if she was interested in an implant, she just said, 'Would *you* want an implant?' Of course not! Our children feel instinctively that it's not right. It's hard to explain exactly what it is that feels wrong, but the idea of implanting something in their skull – it's unnatural. It seems that the focus on the child as a person is lost, and the medical people are fascinated by the technology and the child's hearing. I worry about how an implant will affect them as a whole person. Cochlear implants are from the hearing world and a hearing perspective, and they are designed to please hearing people. What about the rights of the Deaf person, and the child's rights? The children are too young to speak for themselves at that age.

When my son was four, I took him to an ENT specialist about a lump on his neck. After the doctor had examined him, he asked me how long my boy had been Deaf, and I told him since birth. He asked me about his school and I told him that he went to van Asch preschool. The doctor's first question was, 'Can he speak?' I said, 'No, he signs,' and the doctor looked surprised and said, 'Oh, I though they taught speech at van Asch.' Next he said, 'Have you thought about a cochlear implant for him? They're amazing!' I was taken aback and annoyed by him asking me out of the blue like that, when our visit was about something completely unrelated. I told him we weren't interested, and he went on with checking my son's ear. But when he'd finished, he brought up the cochlear implant again and tried to tell me how great they were, and that we should consider it. I just told him we had four Deaf children and we were happy about that. When I got home I felt really sickened by the conversation. I felt as if there was no respect for my son as a person, because all the doctor could focus on was fixing his ears with a cochlear implant. We've been through the same old thing repeatedly with all our children: from the professionals it's been listening, speech and now cochlear implants. Frankly, I'm tired of their attitude. Doctors and medical people don't seem to realise how different our perspectives are.

Times have changed since my parents' day. Now we have teletext on TV, which is great, and we have interpreters. When my father needed to communicate with hearing people he always got out his pen and paper and wrote back and forth. He would have found interpreters really useful. It's a pity he didn't

live long enough to know about interpreters. Now Deaf people are going to university, and some have trained as teachers – that certainly wasn't possible in my parents' day. When I was young I dreamed that I would marry a nice man, have a lovely home, have my own children and a stable family. I didn't even think about a career. I've never had much time to dream about what I'd like to achieve for myself.

I hope my children will grow up with much stronger self-esteem and confidence than I ever had. I want them to be confident, independent people who can make their own decisions, and not be led by other people. I know my husband hopes that they will go to university, but I don't want to set up expectations for them that might be too high. It would be great if they want to go on with studying, but I'll support them in their own decisions. My four children all have their own personalities and they're all different in the way they learn. I feel that my own potential as a young person was completely wasted. I just don't want to see my children's potential wasted.

Patrick Wikiriwhi Thompson (Te Wikiriwhi Pokaitara)

Born 1964

Patrick Wikiriwhi Thompson is of Ngati Paoa/Ngati Whanaunga descent. Born into a traditional Maori family, he also spent part of his childhood immersed in the Deaf world, at Kelston Deaf Education Centre in the 1970s, drifting away from it as a young adult. He describes being a Deaf person among hearing Maori, a Deaf Maori in the hearing Pakeha world, and a Deaf person in the Deaf world. Patrick's journey between cultures has given him particular empathy with the challenges that young Deaf Maori face in finding their identity. He is an advocate and leader for Deaf Maori within the Deaf community, also working between hearing and Deaf Maori to improve cross-cultural understanding. *(Maori glossary, p. 175.)*

My family are traditional Maori and that was the environment I was raised in. I was born with normal hearing and became Deaf when I was two, through meningitis. I was the first Deaf person in the family, so my parents had no experience with this. When I was four, I was sent as a boarder to Kelston School for the Deaf in Auckland until I was 11 or 12, and so I was apart from the Maori world during that time. In those days at the Deaf school, it was all very hearing and they spent most of the time teaching speech and lipreading. I wasn't comfortable at all. In the third form, I shifted to Melville High School in Hamilton, where I was in a Deaf unit and partly mainstreamed with hearing students.

PATRICK
WIKIRIWHI
THOMPSON

When I left Kelston Deaf school and went home, my father took me under his wing and looked after me, tried to explain Maori things, took me to the marae, and so on. But our communication was very limited, although I did learn some things about the Maori world as I grew up. It was only after my father died several years ago that I realised how much of my father's tikanga I had absorbed. After he'd gone, I became involved in more and more situations where I had to stand and speak formally on behalf of Maori Deaf, and I found that I seemed to have naturally taken on his mana, which enabled me to take this role. I feel this is a taonga of our tupuna that has been passed on to me through my father.

When I left high school, I went to Rotorua for about eight years, then eventually moved back to Auckland and started working at Kelston School for the Deaf. My job at Kelston came about after I went back to the school for the first time in many years to attend the Deaf View Conference. Someone told me there would be a Deaf Maori group there. I was pretty curious and decided to go and see for myself. So I drove up from my family home in Kaiaua, near Thames. When I arrived there was a party going on where I met up with quite a few old friends, Deaf Maori whanau I'd grown up with, and some others I hadn't met before. The Maori group was having a haka practice and invited me to join in, so I started to pick it up. It was great to be learning with Deaf people. Then during the Deaf View Conference, I saw a presentation about Deaf identity for the first time. From that point, I started to move back into the Deaf world. I started to understand and become aware of Deaf culture. Before that I hadn't realised there was such a thing, and I hadn't really known where I fitted in. I think I was floating between Maori culture and the Deaf culture, and I was confused about where I belonged and where I was heading. I went back home from the conference and had a talk with my mother about Deaf culture, but of course she couldn't really understand or relate to what I was talking about.

So in the end I went back to Auckland and got a job at Kelston Deaf school as a residential social worker. My job was to supervise the Deaf children. Through working with them, I started to understand myself better. None of those Deaf children knew anything about their Maori identity or their whakapapa. I began to see the problem was that their families couldn't sign, and so they couldn't communicate at home. Like me, they couldn't develop their Maori identity because there was no signing or real communication with the family. They also weren't aware of the Deaf culture they had. It wasn't until I went to a course on Deaf culture that I really understood what it meant and started to feel good about that aspect of myself. It took me about eight months to work out my own Deaf identity, and now I feel proud to be Deaf.

Before this, I knew I was Deaf, but I didn't want to be because I was trying to blend in and be like hearing Maori. Because I could speak quite well, I thought I could hide my deafness. I was a bit confused. Back then, I would see Deaf people using NZSL and I didn't want anything to do with it. I hung around with hearing Maori friends, and once I pointed out some other Deaf people signing. My friends said 'Well, you're Deaf too – why don't you join them, try to sign with them?' I was pretty hesitant, but I plucked up courage and went up to one Deaf person and tried signing with him. He signed quite fast to me and I could not understand fully what he was saying. You see, the signing that I remembered was the type of language I'd known when I was a little boy at school. By now, my signs were a bit out of date and rusty. I had to keep asking him to please repeat or use different signs, as my sign language wasn't good enough to communicate properly with Deaf adults. It was so frustrating for me.

The other thing was, I didn't really have a deep understanding of Deaf culture and the Deaf world. But when Deaf people explained things to me, I started to pick up the language again and understand more. And later when they talked to me about Deaf culture – for example, the way Deaf people take ages to say goodbye – I recognised all those things in myself. I started to realise that some of the behaviours I had always felt were rude or unusual from a hearing point of view were actually Deaf ways of behaving. These were things I had always done instinctively, and now I began to feel that it was all right to be like that, it was normal; and I accepted my behaviour and attitude as a normal Deaf person. When I went to a Deaf culture workshop, I recognised a lot of things about myself.

This was the time when I really shifted my identity and my feeling about myself to being Deaf first, and Maori second. It was hard for my family to fully accept that I had this other culture I belonged to. That was a very stressful time, because I was trying to find my way and sort out who I was. I was learning more about being Deaf from the Deaf world, and also starting to learn more about Maori culture too. I had been in the hearing Pakeha world growing up, so it took me quite a while to get to my real identity. Finally I came to accept myself as a person living in two worlds – Deaf and Maori. If I chose to be with Maori first, the problem would be communication with hearing people. So Deaf will always come first, and Maori second. I'm bicultural and that's given me new strength. It's important that I accept myself and know my own cultural identity because in my job the young Deaf Maori look to me as a role model.

Deaf Maori children can be more involved in Maori culture if their family learns to sign. If there is no sign communication at home, it's pretty frustrating and difficult for them to be involved at all. Should Maori and Pakeha Deaf children be taught together, or do they have separate cultures? As Deaf people, they should definitely be together because they share a Deaf culture. And yet I think it's important to have a Deaf Maori group to learn more about their Maori background. I think Maori Deaf need to be together to learn more about themselves before they can be fully involved with Pakeha in the larger Deaf world. I'm not talking about segregation, but being apart sometimes so they can learn to understand their Maori side better and have more self-esteem. I don't think there is a separate Maori Deaf culture at this point in time.

PATRICK WIKIRIWHI THOMPSON

In a few areas of New Zealand where there are many Deaf Maori, they are developing some signs to express Maori concepts. For example, I'm thinking of a Maori sign I use myself meaning tangata whenua. If you use NZSL signs that mean literally 'people of the land', it doesn't have quite the same sense as the Maori concept tangata whenua. So we wanted to create a new sign that expressed the Maori meaning better. When I was young, I remember I was always confused by the way Deaf signed hangi – the sign meant, 'to *hang* someone'! A Pakeha hearing teacher told me that was the sign because the word looks and sounds like 'hang' in English. That really confused me. But I used that sign for many years growing up, and always felt uncomfortable about it. Years later, I was digging a hangi and thinking about it, and I realised it just wasn't right. I stopped using it and decided to make a new sign that represents food being buried in the ground. Recently, Deaf Maori had a hui and we talked about this and they understood the problem. They all went back to their own areas and they've spread the new sign around. Now there are some different signs for Maori concepts popping up in different regions; for example, there are now several signs for marae and maunga used in different areas. So it's important for Deaf Maori to have links with each other so they can develop common vocabulary, so our sign language doesn't get into a mess. It's important for Deaf Maori and hearing Maori to support each other, but they need sign language to do that, to express themselves.

The first national Deaf Maori hui we had was the most beautiful one we've seen in Deaf history! For two and a half years before the hui, I had travelled around New Zealand just off my own bat, visiting Deaf in different places. I mostly met with Deaf Maori, but at that time there were no actual groups of Deaf Maori, they were just scattered around in the Deaf community. If I met a Deaf Maori, I'd make a point of introducing myself, and finding out a bit about their background. I went to the South Island and Wellington where Maori Deaf people were around but not organised in any way. I also went to Northland, which was a bit different again – there was a strong Maori group up there, because it's a very Maori area. Maori Deaf had always got together because of easy communication, but they didn't have any real understanding about their cultures. So I went around talking and gathering information, asking Deaf Maori if they knew about Maori culture and if they were happy with the services they were getting. Quite a few said they knew about the Deaf Association but they didn't use the service because they usually went to the social welfare office and looked for a Maori face to help them. But then they couldn't communicate with the people there. Another example is that there are lots of Deaf Maori in South Auckland, but they don't go to the Auckland Deaf Club much because of transport problems, or because they feel it's not a comfortable atmosphere for them. Some Maori Deaf tend to be shy and feel a bit uncomfortable in Pakeha organisations, so they don't always participate fully in the Deaf community either. I learned a lot from the people I met.

Over those two years before the hui I wrote down some of the things I had found out and I told the Deaf Association it would be good to have more Deaf Maori involvement – that we needed Deaf Maori services like other successful Maori services that have been set up around New Zealand. But the question was how to do it. I learned a lot from my father, who was the chairman of the Ngati Paoa Trust Board. I looked at the strategic plans that he had developed for future development of Maori services for the iwi and I got some ideas from that. When I looked at the Deaf world, I could see that things were worse for Deaf Maori: all the services were provided by a Pakeha system. Maori Deaf needed more Maori involved in their services. So I wrote a proposal for the Deaf Association's AGM, listing the things that Maori Deaf wanted. The proposal was accepted, and the first action was to set up a national hui. It was a huge task organising it, and I had help from two hearing Maori volunteers at the Deaf Association.

About 80 Deaf people came from all around New Zealand. Never before had Deaf Maori from nga hau e wha come together. It was very satisfying for me. It was a chance for us to meet each other and identify important issues for ourselves, and it was really our first marae experience: we ate together, slept together, talked together in NZSL. It had a big impact on all of us, and a lot of growth happened. We learned things and we discussed what we wanted for the future. Afterwards, everyone went home feeling more empowered and stronger about their identity. Obviously you can't learn about a culture in a short time, but the participants had certainly learned a bit more about Maoritanga. We encouraged everyone to go back to their home area and set up ways

to keep learning more about Maori culture. Hui are planned again for every second year, and in the meantime Maori Deaf are trying to set up their own local groups to keep the momentum going.

PATRICK
WIKIRIWHI
THOMPSON

I always say my tribal affiliations are Ngati Turi/Ngati Paoa/Ngati Whanaunga. Ngati Turi is a name that Deaf Maori have created to mean 'tribe or iwi of the Deaf'. I have a way of expressing my standing as a Deaf Maori – 'Te Tuwhareturitoa'* – which means that being in the Deaf Maori community gives me a position of strength in the world.

Glossary of Maori Words

haka   warrior-like dance with chant

hangi   earth oven and its contents (cooked in a pit in the ground with heated stones)

hui   meeting or gathering

iwi   tribe, people

mana   social standing, power, influence

marae   enclosed compound encompassing an outdoor area in front of a meeting house – traditional venue for events in Maori community life such as funerals, welcoming visitors, meetings, celebrations

maunga   mountain: mountains are significant in identifying tribal origin.

Pakeha   non-Maori, European New Zealander

tangata whenua   literally – people of the land; local people; hosts in marae context

taonga   treasure, something cherished

tikanga   ways, customs

tupuna   ancestors

whakapapa   family tree, genealogy – vital to identifying oneself as Maori

whanau   extended family

nga hau e wha   literally, the four winds – an expression used to mean people from everywhere

---

* This appears to be a 'twist' on the name of the tribe *Ngati Tuwharetoa*, of the central North Island, named after the ancestor, Tuwharetoa. The word *Tuwhareturitoa* contains the following elements: *tu* – stand/standing; *whare* – house; *turi* – deaf; *toa* – warrior/strength; literally, 'the place where Deaf stand strong'. (Thanks to Mary Boyce for translation.)

Alistair Appleby

Born 1964

Like many mainstreamed Deaf children, Alistair Appleby grew up immersed in the hearing world but feeling 'different' – only to discover the Deaf world as a young adult. He now lives in two worlds, shifting between them. One of the few Deaf New Zealanders to graduate from university, he describes the grit required for a Deaf person to survive and 'pass' in the mainstream educational and social environment. This story was recorded in spoken English, and is supplemented in places by Alistair's own writing about his early life.

My parents emigrated from England to New Zealand for warmer weather and a better life. I was born in Devonport, Auckland, shortly afterwards, when my sister was still a toddler. Mum felt something was not quite right about me, but she couldn't quite place it. She took me to various specialists and they all diagnosed me as 'a bit slow'. And that diagnosis stuck, on and on, even though Mum tried many times to convince them there was something else. She knew that something was wrong with my language, so she had been putting little notes with the name of things all over the house – like 'door', 'wall'. That was so I could learn to associate words with things. When she talked to me, I used to put my head down close to her chest. But somehow I learned a written language. I don't know how, but Mum says I was reading before I was speaking. I became a bookworm.

I started at a normal school when I was five. I don't have much memory of school, but I remember just not caring. It was a place that I went, but I didn't give a stuff about it. As a five- or six-year-old, I was difficult to control. Apparently because of my hearing loss I did not communicate with other people easily, and quickly became bored and disruptive. I remember being in the headmaster's room and knowing that this was authority but feeling, 'Why am I here? I just don't care.'

Finally, when I was six and a half, Mum went to an ear, nose, and throat specialist and said to him, 'I know my son's Deaf, please give him a test.' 'No, I don't think so,' he said. Doctors were gods in those days; they had all the power. But he agreed to give me the hearing test to keep my mother happy, and then had to tell her, 'I'm very sorry, Mrs Appleby, but your son is Deaf.'

We were sent off to meet an itinerant teacher of the Deaf, Lynn Stancliffe, who would become an important influence throughout my childhood. I remember our first appointment clearly, going up the stairs into a building that reminded me of a hospital. While we were waiting for our appointment, I could see a big syringe sitting on a tray in an assessment room. Not long before this, when I was in hospital to get my tonsils out, two nurses had come into the ward – one with a paper bag in her hand – pinned me down, flourished the hypodermic needle from under the bag and jabbed it into my leg. So this time I thought, 'Not another hospital, I don't want injections again!' If Mum hadn't been there I would have bolted! It turned out to be a syringe for putting silicon in my ear to make the ear mould for a hearing aid. I was asked to identify words on flash cards, and the teacher of the Deaf talked to me while she covered her mouth, to check if I was lipreading or hearing. Of course I couldn't understand what she was saying when her mouth was covered, because I had already learned to rely on lipreading.

I got a hearing aid when I was nearly seven and it was just awful. It was a metal box about the size of a cigarette packet with a microphone on top of it and a cord that plugged into an oval piece with an ear mould on it. Mum made a special little harness that went around my chest, with a pouch for the hearing aid in the middle. All sorts of new sounds crowded into my life. The microphone scratched against my clothes and made a lot of noise. There was so much to learn and it all seemed a lot more complex than before. I remember flushing the toilet and running out of the bathroom in terror because of the horrible rumbling noise. It took me a long time to get used to sounds.

I knew that I was different from the other children: I had a lump in the middle of my chest where the hearing aid sat in its little harness, and two wires came out from under my clothes up to my ears. I think I damaged my hearing aid quite a few times on purpose so it would stop working. I couldn't really hear people talking anyway – hearing aid technology has improved since then. I didn't know any other Deaf people: I'd never met any. I thought I was the only

Deaf person in the world. I remember once reading about a Deaf child in the newspaper – deafness amongst children seemed to be so rare that it was only in the newspapers, it seemed. I think that if I had known other Deaf children it would have been easier.

I was a bit of an outcast at school. I had a couple of friends down the road I played with, and a boy who lived across the road. Looking back, I realise that the friendship with this boy was always conditional – he was my friend when it suited him while other times he pretended not to know me, which was quite hurtful. Because I was different, I was bullied and teased a lot, and I felt pretty alone, right through school. The year I was 14 was the hardest year of my life. I was made to feel unwelcome by my classmates from the first day, and the year degenerated into a round of bullying and social rejection that was a living nightmare. I used to come home from school covered in bruises on my arms from my classmates' punches. At that age it seems to be so important to fit in with the group, and I didn't fit in anywhere. The worst memory is standing outside a classroom and being told by all the other guys to 'go away'. At one point, I began to entertain thoughts of suicide. I would lie on my bed with a knife and wonder what it would be like to end it all. The harassment was unrelenting.

I remember discussions were held with the teachers, but it didn't start getting any better until I was in the fifth form. By that time Mum became so concerned about the bullying that she enrolled me in karate classes. I had one-to-one tuition and I think my tutor sensed what was happening at school. His response was to teach me street-fighting techniques that were extremely dirty but effective, as I found out the only time I had to use them! A student tried to push me into a running shower with my hearing aids on, which he knew would ruin them. I got desperate and kicked him in the stomach. I was scared stiff because he was a rugby player, much bigger than me. But fortunately he backed off and left me alone for the rest of the year. Outside of school, life wasn't so bad. I was lucky to have very supportive parents, and I joined the Karekare surf lifesaving club. That gave me a bit of respite because the people in the club were very friendly.

My fifth form year was much better. Somehow, over the school holidays everyone had grown up and the bullying disappeared. I became best mates with a guy who had emigrated from England, and also became friendly with Angus McDonald, another oral Deaf guy who was similar to myself in that he was a 'pseudo-hearing person'. Angus was given his own car at 15, and sometimes he would take me over to the Leo's Club in Avondale at a time when it had many Deaf members. A lot of the people used sign language and I recall thinking that this was not for me, as I only had a 'hearing impairment' and could speak.

Academically, I wasn't too badly off at school because I could read well. My reading outside of school helped me through. The teacher might talk about something and I'd miss it, but then I would read the book instead. But my maths has always been useless. In my brain, I've still got a black hole around anything to do with crunching numbers. I took statistics at university, and I took one test 10 times before I passed it!

ALISTAIR
APPLEBY

When technology improved, I got behind-the-ear hearing aids and I could hear a lot better, because sound was coming through two ears. But I always sat right at the front of the class and watched closely what the teacher was doing. It was always like a jigsaw for me: the teacher would be talking, but I'd miss something because they'd turn away and write on the blackboard, or look down or whatever, and I'd miss it. There's a blank spot, until the person looks up again and you can lipread what they're saying. In my mind, communication was like a jigsaw with many little bits missing, and I had to make bridges and then I'd get the jigsaw – actually build it up. It wasn't just a matter of putting a little piece in here or there, but more like building a little bridge and then crystallising something, and then that would branch out and fill the missing space. I was doing that *all* the time, in my mind. I still do that, I've been doing it all my life. It's very tiring because you're just thinking all the time about the different possibilities and which one fits and where it goes, and sometimes you get it wrong. Now I know that I often used to get it wrong, because I've been to lectures with an interpreter and experimented: I'll try my old lipreading system and then switch back to watching the interpreter again. The contrast makes me realise how much you miss. With the jigsaw you get the general picture, but miss the nuances such as emphasis that lets you know 'this part is important' or 'this is just an example of that', and the kinds of things that are conveyed through the voice and make up the full message. When I use a sign language interpreter I get 100 per cent.

Before I went to university as a mature student at 24, I had a whole string of different jobs, including office work in shipping companies, builder's labourer, tree pruning, factory hand, hotel porter and gardener. After an overseas trip I made the big decision to go to university. This was quite an introspective time for me and I did a lot of thinking about who I was and what I was doing. It was an ongoing process, and I was realising that there were lots of limitations. I also had some experiences at varsity in group situations where I did really badly, and I was very disappointed about that – not just disappointed with myself, but angry with the system that had set me up to fail because there wasn't any flexibility or support services at that time. I wasn't really involved in the Deaf world then, but I wrote to the Dean about the barriers I was facing; even 10 years ago

I could see the things I needed. I wanted sign language interpreters – I thought that was a logical thing to have. When I look at what I wrote now, it's still very relevant. But I never had access to those services, and I had to think about what my limitations were, from a hearing perspective. I was trying so hard to be a hearing person and it wasn't getting me anywhere. Then one day I just thought, I'm not going to expend all that energy any more. That was quite a freeing process in some ways. I thought, 'Well, even if I lose the plot and don't understand what's going on – who cares?' And it went from there. The only thing that saved me from throwing in the towel over the next three years was a deep burning desire to prove that I could succeed at university. I wanted those letters after my name to show that even though I had a hearing loss I could still achieve. This time I had chosen this education rather than having events that I had no control over foisted upon me. I worked very very hard indeed!

There's this pressure from society to be something that you're never going to be – hearing. I think there's a big mismatch between what society expects and what you can do in reality. I always thought that society expected me to be just like a hearing person and do all those things that hearing people do. And I did a lot of those things, but often only half participating. For example, when a group of people are talking and the room goes slowly dark, I'm just lost, because I can't use lipreading and I don't have enough hearing to be able to know what's going on. Or going to the movies, pretending to understand when you don't actually have a clue! But you hide a lot of that. If you deny your deafness you can hide it quite well, because no one's going to ask you straight after a movie 'Did you *really* understand what was going on?' You can just gloss over so many things, and you *think* you know what's going on, but you don't really – even though you still function all right as an individual. But are you *really*? You miss so much information around you.

I stopped the pretending stuff when I woke up one day and I realised that I was trying to be something that I wasn't. At this time, I didn't really think clearly about other people as hearing and myself as Deaf. That was further down the line. I would probably have described myself as 'hearing impaired'. I didn't really have a clear label for myself. I just thought of myself as having a hearing loss, or wearing hearing aids or something.

I decided that instead of trying to know what was going on all the time, then I would just not know. So if I was out with a group of people and I missed what somebody said, then I would just let that go and think, 'Oh well, so what – I missed it.' It meant missing more at lectures, those kinds of things. As a result of that, in my final year at university, I structured my year so it was really Deaf-friendly for me. I minimised the number of lectures right down, and I actually

ALISTAIR
APPLEBY

'assessed' the lecturers: I'd go 'He's got a beard – no thanks. He's got a foreign accent – forget it.' So I didn't choose my papers according to what I was interested in, but according to what would reduce the difficulty and the workload as much as possible. If I'd been a hearing person, I would have chosen the papers I was interested in, regardless of whether the lecturer had a beard or not. I was choosing from a completely different point of view. Doing that made the year a lot easier because I was acknowledging that I was Deaf, I suppose, and that I had to use these strategies to survive university.

I had no support. Because I was an older student, I was lobbying all the time, visiting lecturers. And some of their attitudes were shocking. I remember asking one lecturer if I could have a copy of his notes and he just said 'No'. When I asked why, he said 'Because they're my notes and I'm not going to give them to you.' He just couldn't give a stuff. But a few lecturers were really encouraging. Those are the types of people you really need to link into – the ones who are genuinely interested in the students as individuals wanting to succeed, rather than as drones, worker bees. I did a law paper with a lecturer who was very encouraging and who gave me all the extramural notes for the course, which weren't supposed to be given to the internal students. But he said, 'Just follow these and you'll see where I'm going in lectures.' I got a B+ in that paper and I liked it because I felt much more in control of the situation, even though I couldn't catch everything that was said in lectures. There was also a teacher of the Deaf in the area who gave me a lot of good support, even though technically I was too old to be in his caseload. I didn't really get support from the university. When they first got a disability support person at university, that person was only there for staff and not for students! I thought 'What's going on here?' It was stupid, and it made things difficult. That was as recently as 1989–1991.

I got a marketing degree, and I worked at Farmer's for about one year afterwards, selling clothes. That was awful, I hated that year, although dealing with people one-to-one was all right and I didn't have to use the phone or anything, so I could figure out what was going on. I've always been quite good with people one-to-one, because I can just pick up a holistic sort of thing. And then I worked for the government for two years in Wellington, and I found that job really hard, partly because I probably wasn't suited to the job and partly because – I didn't realise at the time – I was missing a lot of information in the meetings. It was a small group of 20 people in that section, and a lot of the work involved verbal communication which I just missed. I felt, 'What's wrong with me? Am I stupid or something? Why aren't I doing this properly? Is there something wrong with me, or is it the environment?' I just didn't seem to know enough. It was really frustrating trying to figure it out: all these people seemed to be doing their jobs competently, and I wondered what it was about me that meant I wasn't doing it well.

Entering the Deaf community was a very on/off process that stretched over a few years. In my mid-20s, when I was at varsity and I started thinking about these things, I tried to get involved with the local Deaf community. But it was very small and I didn't know enough sign language. That was a big barrier. So were people's attitudes: from the Deaf community's perspective, I was 'hearing impaired', which I can understand now. It wasn't much of a success at first, so I pulled back.

Then later I got involved in the What? Club in Auckland. There are a lot of people like me in the Deaf community today who are there because of the What? Club. The club was started by one guy who was hearing impaired and wanted to meet other hearing impaired people. So he made inquiries at the Hearing Association and they contacted a few other people who came together, and the What? Club was born. The people who came were mostly young people from the mid-20s through to their late 30s. It was a mixture of people – some with a mild hearing loss, some late-Deafened adults, some who were born Deaf but mainstreamed like myself, some who were very Deaf but not quite culturally Deaf. By that, I mean they didn't use NZSL, and didn't really have Deaf friends. Their parents had told them the oral way was the only way and they'd grown up with that attitude. The term 'hearing impaired' covers a whole wide range of people. From that, the group evolved. It started to get popular, and a few culturally Deaf people came across, and people in the club started learning sign language through classes, and some merging started to happen. The club was good for me because I met oral Deaf people like myself, and that was a big step forward.

When I first joined the What? Club and met others like me, I was amazed. For the first time in my life I could meet somebody, say a few words, and they understood exactly what I was talking about. It was such as relief. I realised that I wasn't the only one who'd had my experiences. It was a very strong connection. So many Deaf people out there think they're unique or alone, and they're not. It's mainstreaming which creates this Diaspora – they're spread out and don't have a chance to meet other people like themselves and talk about their experiences. The club was very strong, because there were a lot of people who had a real hunger, a real need, to have somewhere they felt safe. For a lot of people, once the need was satisfied they would go off and feel happy, and they weren't so hungry any more. Some of them didn't really get involved further in the Deaf community; and others did. It's a matter of individual choice.

When I moved down to Wellington to work for the government, I missed that interaction. So again, I tried getting involved with the Deaf community but the great barrier was my lack of sign language. It really frustrated me seeing people signing away and not understanding what was going on. By then I had realised that I wasn't a hearing person – but who was I? It was a process of identity search: if you don't fit in with one group, go and try out another group. It was an exploratory stage. What eventually pushed me to learn sign language was when I started working at the Deaf Association. In the end it was a pragmatic reason – I *had* to learn to sign for my job. Once I started signing, all these other things followed on. But before that I had made a choice that I wanted to be in contact with Deaf people. When I told my Dad I was learning sign language, he wouldn't speak to me. You see, my parents had been told by teachers for many years, 'You must not teach your son sign language.' That was the oral way. I don't talk about signing much to my parents. It's a separate, compartmentalised space and I don't let them access it. My Mum understands where I'm coming from on a philosophical level, but ... Parents are afraid of their child looking different, and my parents probably didn't want the label of Deaf on me. Throughout my childhood of being mainstreamed, I'm sure they'd been given the message that I had to be as normal as possible.

When I worked at the Deaf Association I did a lot of questioning about my identity, and that is still an ongoing journey for me. When I got to the Deaf Association, I didn't know sign language well, and I couldn't use the interpreter. But one day I had a kind of epiphany, at a big staff meeting. Prior to this, in meetings, I'd always try to listen *and* use the interpreter because I didn't feel confident about the information I would get from the interpreter. But that day I thought, 'Stuff it, I'm just going to watch the interpreter.' I switched off my hearing aids so I wouldn't be bothered with trying to process the sounds. (You really can't match speech and signing because they're different languages.) So I just sat there, and suddenly *bingo*, it happened! I could understand perfectly what was happening. It was an incredible feeling, to walk out afterwards and know that I had followed everything. I guess my sign language had reached a certain level. It had such a big impact on me. I didn't talk to anybody about it because I didn't feel that anybody really understood what I was going through. It was a very private thing. Later on, it made me wish I'd had interpreters at university in situations like tutorials or lectures where the teacher asks questions and you have to respond. It would have been so good to have an interpreter there to get the feedback of what's being said around the room, because it's impossible to lipread that.

I've been signing now about six years. It was incredibly frustrating for me learning to sign because I'd grown up in an aural environment and my brain

ALISTAIR
APPLEBY

was wired to the English way of thinking. It was hard to break out of that – it took a long time. I think it is a bit quicker for Deaf people rather than hearing people to learn to sign, that there is something innate – but I've got no proof of that. A Deaf person already has to lipread so you're used to reading facial expressions, and then you expand your perception from just the mouth area to the whole signing area – like stretching the window. And then you have to learn the signing part of it. Understanding signing and being able to sign are two different things. What improved my sign language most was having a relation-ship with a Deaf woman who was a fluent signer. I would call myself bilingual now, but I still get frustrated because there are concepts in my mind in English – my first language – and I can't translate them easily into sign language. Being bilingual is a very positive thing for me, because it opens up my options in life – the communication options. Why limit your options in life? What's the point of doing that? Why not broaden your options?

I worked for the Deaf Association until I was made redundant. Then I started work at the Hearing Association, which was a completely different sort of perspective. I found working there interesting, and because it's a small environment I felt comfortable. Some of the people I've worked with in the past have had a slightly patronising attitude, but I could live with that – I'm quite pragmatic about it. My feeling is, I don't care if I lose the battles, as long as I win the war – that's the big picture for me. So even though some people say I should be more assertive, I accept these little patronising things that go on, because that's the way it is. By patronising, I mean hearing people's view of what Deaf people can do. Way back in intermediate school – and I'm not joking – one teacher wrote on my end-of year-report: 'Alistair's hearing does not seem to have improved.' Mum and Dad were upset and angry, but they didn't feel they could do anything about it. I still get that. For example, one boss used to say, 'Alistair, can you hear me?' Another example is a reference from an employer that says something like 'Alistair is hearing impaired, but he has achieved ...' I was really disappointed. The 'in spite of his hearing impairment' thing is patronising. The next job I go to, someone's going to look at it and think, what kind of place do you come from that's got an attitude like that? It's setting up their expectations already.

At the Hearing Association I set up and ran an equipment service. The prob-lem was, my hearing was getting worse and I was having real problems on the telephone. They wanted me to develop the service in a direction that required me to spend a lot of time on the phone, and I felt I couldn't do that. I'm just not that competent on the phone. To do my job well, I'd like to have a phone relay service, and Internet access. Bill Gates had a vision that everyone should have

ALISTAIR
APPLEBY

e-mail. Without knowing it, he's probably such a Deaf-friendly guy! At least for those people who can use English as a written language, because literacy is one of the biggest issues facing the Deaf community. To access that technology, they *must* be able to use written English. If I ever go back to education, there are certain times when I need an interpreter and notetaker. And I really want access to full subtitling on television, video, Sky – it should all be subtitled. When I first got into the Internet, I got hooked and spent about six months talking to Deaf people in America and I realised what they had access to. I thought if I had access to what they have, that would make the quality of life so much better.

In the Deaf community I get social contact. Sometimes I feel I've had enough of the Deaf way, and I have a little break. And then I start feeling 'hungry'. I really miss it if I don't sign. The culture is very different from the hearing way. For example, in hearing culture, you don't touch people, and people's personal spaces tend to be a lot bigger. To be extreme, you'd be scared that if you touched somebody you'd offend them or even be accused of sexual harassment. But in the Deaf way, if you want to attract someone's attention to talk, you touch them. That's difficult for a lot of hearing people. Another thing is that Deaf people can actually be quite noisy: a hearing person who was working at the Deaf Association with me used to moan about the racket that went on! Deaf people are also very direct, and it took me a long time to get used to that abruptness and not let it offend me. I've changed, though, I'm a bit tougher now. If someone is very direct with me, I can handle it and I don't take it personally. That comes with having the sign language skills to be able to respond appropriately.

From time to time I like to get away from the Deaf world. I get bored easily, and sometimes find there's not a lot of stimulating conversation in the Deaf community. That's what I like about the hearing community – you can go and find someone who's interesting and sit down and have quite a stimulating conversation. So I go and see some hearing people who challenge me and get me thinking again, and then I feel more satisfied, and go back to the Deaf community. I switch between the two. Sometimes I'll be sitting in a bar or something, and I'm really tired and I can't understand what's going on, and I think 'It'd be really nice if people here knew sign language.' It's really about communication. That's why the Deaf world is comfortable, because of easy communication. So I swap between the two to fill my communication needs. I think this has enriched my life. You know, many people can only talk in English, but I can express my feelings in another language, so it gives me another route to express myself. That's an incredibly valuable part of me. I don't sign with hearing people because that's not their communication mode: it's spoken English, and that's my first language too, whether I like it or not.

As time goes on, I switch more and more between two identity modes. I go back and forth, although I feel really comfortable in the Deaf world. I need both. If somebody said to me, you have to choose, I'd say 'No way! I want both. It's not an acceptable choice.' Some Deaf people still say I'm hearing impaired, or I'm not culturally Deaf, and that can be really hurtful. But I just have to live with that. I'm pretty open about who I am, and I say 'This is who I am, if you don't like that, that's your problem. I accept you for who you are, and I'm talking to you in your language, what's the problem?' I'm as Deaf as they are, and if people don't like it, that's their problem.

My plan is to go to England and compare the services available there.* I'd stay there and put up with the weather and gloominess if I felt I was getting more opportunities and a better quality of life. I'd like to work in e-commerce: the Internet really interests me. Before it changes over to being voice-activated in 10 to 15 years time, there's an opportunity there for Deaf people. My vision is to make use of my marketing degree and to be a marketing manager with all the distribution channels – retail, catalogue, and website – under me. People go, 'Oh yeah, yeah', but I don't think society is ready for somebody like me to be a marketing manager; it's oppression. I would want to manage the web part of it, because it's Deaf-friendly. To start with, I'd like to work in Deaf-related products, like equipment, to get my foot in the door; but then if I could move on and work on other websites that would be great. It will take a lot of hard work, and maybe years to get there. But if I've got access to a relay service, and access to good systems, I think my goal would be achievable.

Also, I want to write a book about people like myself who live between two worlds. It's a really big group and nobody seems to have written about it. A lot of the books are about people who are confused in the hearing world, and then they go into the Deaf community and they cut off their links with the hearing community. But what about people who go into the Deaf world but still enjoy having access to the hearing community? Their story needs to be told. In both the Deaf community and the hearing community there's a lot of pressure to stay within that community and not move out. Socially, I'd like to access both Deaf and hearing people. I expect to meet different kinds of Deaf people overseas – some will be late-deafened and some, culturally Deaf. I feel that late-deafened adults are dealt a rough hand because the hearing people don't want to know about them and the Deaf people don't want to know about them, so where do they go? This happens. The Deaf world doesn't just welcome you in

* Alistair is now living in London. He is engaged and in 2001 will marry Caroline Cummings, who is English and oral Deaf. He does not intend to return to New Zealand for many years.

ALISTAIR
APPLEBY

straight away; you have to work at it, and it's not easy. I was talking to a friend similar to me, about how we learned to sign and everything, and he was also rebuffed at his initial attempts. Like me, he had to work really hard at it before he made that breakthrough. You've got to be persistent. I kept on coming back to the Deaf community wherever I was living, until finally I made the break-through. But the effort is worth it, even though it's not handed to you on a plate. Another Deaf friend like me describes himself as being in 'no-man's-land', not quite fitting completely into either world, and I know exactly what he means. When I meet Deaf overseas, I think people will assume I grew up signing and they'll accept me for who I am. They won't say 'He's an oralist who changed. He's a traitor.' Hopefully I won't meet that attitude.

A hundred years ago, if you were Deaf you were Deaf and that was it. But then hearing aids were developed which created this new group of people like me. Probably a hundred years ago I would have been culturally Deaf, because without hearing aids I wouldn't have been able to hear and I wouldn't have picked up a spoken language. But now there's this technology that creates this new group of people who never existed before. It's unprecedented in history. This group is now separate from culturally Deaf people, and yet also inextric-ably linked. Both groups have a lot of similarities because both have to struggle at school, and struggle socially. Within the hearing world you put hearing aids on and suddenly you're like a hearing person; but if you take them off, you're actually Deaf. I feel that every day. When I take my hearing aids off at night, I'm Deaf: that's my original condition.

Angela Sew Hoy

Born 1964

Angela Sew Hoy was the first Deaf person in New Zealand to gain an MBA degree (in 1998), having already distinguished herself as a skier and as the youngest president of the Deaf Association of New Zealand. She describes herself as a member of three cultures: Deaf, Chinese and Kiwi. Angela is a fifth-generation descendant of Choie Sew Hoy, the Otago goldminer and merchant who started a family tradition of successful entrepreneurs. Her family heritage and positive personality contribute to Angela's extraordinary drive to excel and to push boundaries.

I was born profoundly Deaf, which my family didn't realise until I was two. It seems that rubella was the most likely cause, as there was an epidemic around then. I was the first child. My mother had her suspicions earlier, but the family kept reassuring her and telling her not to worry. I spent the first two years of my life living in a Dunedin warehouse with my parents and extended family. When I was two, my mother took me to Wellington to visit her parents. While we were there she took me for a check-up, and sure enough the doctor found that I was Deaf. The family were very shocked when Mum told them, but they eventually came to terms with it. I'm the oldest of three daughters – the other two are hearing. I'm the only Deaf person in the entire family. Our family are very close and there are lots of us. My aunts and uncles lived in the houses on either side of us, and my grandparents next door. So I grew up in an extended family, always being the tomboy with my boy cousins next door. I'd dress like a boy and join in with them, looking at car engines or whatever they were doing.

My parents soon made contact with other parents of Deaf children. They lobbied to establish a Deaf unit class at Arthur Street School because there were 15 Deaf children of school age at that time. Many of the parents in Dunedin didn't want to send their children to Christchurch to the Deaf school. They felt it was too far away, and they wanted their children to have a family life. So that's how I came to start school at Arthur Street. There were two groups of us: the five-year-old group I was in, and then a group one year older. We shared a classroom, and had two teachers of the Deaf. I stayed with this Deaf group from kindergarten until 17, through all the stages of school. I was the last of them to leave school.

Most of my memories from primary school are good. I enjoyed being part of the group of Deaf children: whatever we did – school activities, camps, or playing after school – we hung around together and had each other's company. From about the age of five until 14 I never questioned why I was Deaf. I was just happily living my life with my cousins and family at home, and my Deaf friends at school. It wasn't until later on that I saw a Deaf adult signing, because at school we were taught orally. The Otago Education Board, as it was then, didn't approve of sign language, and naturally all the parents followed their advice. At school every day we had speech training using big headsets and microphones to teach us to speak well. My parents started me with speech therapy I think when I was about three or four. This continued every week after school for half an hour until I was about 17, when I declared I'd had enough. Some children had good speech and some, like me, did not. A teacher of the Deaf once told me she could tell I was born Deaf because the quality of my voice is very deep.

In Form One and Two, our Deaf unit moved on to Kenmure Intermediate School, with the same teacher of the Deaf. When I was 10 or 11, they had moved me out of the younger class and into the older class, whom I then went on to Intermediate with, leaving my friends behind in Standard Four. The teachers never explained why – I was just moved up. At intermediate, we spent some time in hearing classes, always coming back to the Deaf unit for the core subjects like English, maths, and social studies. I was keen on sports at school, doing a bit of everything with the hearing and Deaf kids.

At high school, things got harder. I was 13 when I started at Kaikorai Valley High School, which was right next door to the intermediate. I stayed right through to Form Seven, though most of my Deaf friends left when they were 15. Most of them stayed in the Deaf unit, but three of us – myself and two boys – were chosen to be put into the mainstream. We were placed into separate classes: my first time alone in a fully hearing class. It was a bit of a shock at first. All the kids were strangers to me, and they were all hearing. I desperately wanted to go back to the security of my Deaf friends and the Deaf unit. For a few weeks I refused to go into the hearing class, until my teacher and parents persuaded me to give it another try. I went back, very apprehensive. The teacher introduced me and tried to make me feel welcome. But remember at that time there were no interpreters or notetakers - you were really on your own. It wasn't until I was in the sixth and seventh form that I had a notetaker in class.

So I had my first experience of full-immersion mainstreaming at 13. I was very shy and uncomfortable at first. There were very few Chinese at my school, and almost no Maori or other minorities. I'd had Deaf friends all my life until then. But gradually I made friends in class, as we got used to each other. In class I communicated with students by paper and pencil and speaking some-times, as a few of them were used to my funny speech and could understand me. But we relied on writing a lot. I still missed my Deaf friends, and I'd always go and talk with them in the breaks. In the third and fourth form, I made some good friends in my class.

I did English, maths, social studies, accounting, economics, art - the Deaf class joined us for art, and I did music with the Deaf class, believe it or not. In music we learned about rhythm, high and low pitch, and we used percussion instruments like the cymbals and drums. It was the teacher of the Deaf's idea to do music, and she worked with the music teacher. We enjoyed ourselves, bashing away on the percussion and trying out different instruments. Really, we couldn't hear anything much, but it was fun to play around with all those things. We also had speech therapy regularly - 15 or 30 minutes once a week. I was a very diligent schoolgirl, spending hours on my homework to get it perfect. I truly enjoyed doing homework, without my parents prompting me at all. In fact they'd sometimes have to remind me to stop and go to bed. It's my nature to be a perfectionist in my work. I really did enjoy school. I always got the work done quickly and while I was waiting for the others to catch up the teacher would give me extra work. But English was my weak point. I'd hand in an assignment all beautifully written, thinking it was perfect, and then I'd always be disappointed to get it back full of grammar corrections. Because I was Deaf, the grammar of my English writing was not like normal English - perhaps more like sign language structure, even though I didn't really sign much at that time. My literacy skills improved when I was 10.

My parents encouraged me to do well in school and to go into commerce. It was a natural expectation for me to follow in the family business tradition - they had a big firm that was originally called Sew Hoy and Son, and it was one of the big companies in Otago. We had 500 staff and seven factories, with the

head office in Dunedin, and branch offices in Auckland, Wellington, Sydney, Los Angeles, and Hong Kong. The firm was established back in 1869 by my great-great grandfather Choie Sew Hoy, who first imported Chinese foodstuffs and was also a respected leader in the early Chinese community. In 1961 the family business changed to clothing manufacturing and exported to Australia, America and Hong Kong for many years, winning an export award in 1971. It was a very successful business for a long time, but in 1989 some changes in customs rules and deregulation meant the firm went into receivership. We lost 300 staff, including my own job as well, which I'd had since I finished my BCom in 1986. That was a sad time for us.

As a child, I used to go to the firm every day after school, not to the head office where my parents worked, but to the Chinese Foodstuffs department, where my grandmother worked and looked after me. I liked helping her, especially with packaging the various foods that were made there. When I was about 14 I was allowed to use the heat-sealing machine for packaging food – that was great fun! I was considered responsible enough by then, while my little sisters did the easy jobs. So I really started working in the family business with sisters and cousins when I was a teenager, just a few hours a week after school, and often in the school holidays, though I did have free time to go to movies and other things.

My parents started talking with me about their expectations for my future when I was about 14. I was the oldest of three girls, and there were no boys in our immediate family. My father is the youngest in his family, and his two older brothers had sons. So my parents wanted to prepare me for the possibility of one day maybe managing the firm. It was the same for my cousins. Each of the brothers has his own area of expertise in the business: my father's area is the fashion side, outerwear; one brother is in charge of lingerie; and the other one is in foodstuffs. With my future in the business in mind, I was guided into subjects like accounting and economics at school, and then commerce at university.

The seventh form was a really hard year for me. The other Deaf kids reached 15 one by one, went off on work experience and then left for jobs, leaving only me in the end. I felt a bit lost. Some younger Deaf kids came into the school but they were spread out in hearing classes. The school linked us up as 'buddies' so I could support them. I remember meeting one third form Deaf boy who, at the time, was short and round and I was tall and thin, towering over him. I introduced myself to him and said I'd be around if he needed support with anything, and he was quite pleased to find an older Deaf student at school. He had also been brought up orally, and didn't sign then. We're still good friends now, and he towers over me. I went to his wedding recently, and he's moved to Australia, but we keep in touch.

In the seventh form, we had a new common room especially for the senior students to go and have a coffee, listen to music, play cards and talk to friends. Oh, that place was so difficult for me. I just felt so out of place. I couldn't follow or join in the group conversations. Sometimes I'd ask someone to tell me what was being said, so I'd get snatches of the conversation, but more often they'd say, 'I'll tell you later' and I was left out. So the way I survived was to play cards a lot – that was the one thing I could join in with. Then one particular day, as I was sitting by the window with the sun streaming in, having a cup of coffee, I felt very depressed. I asked God 'Why did you make me Deaf? Why couldn't I have been born blind? It would have been much easier.' By then all my Deaf friends had left, and I felt very isolated amongst all these hearing people. Don't get me wrong, some of them were my friends, and there were some good people at school, but I could never be part of the larger group. I was okay one-to-one, but lost in a group. All the talk went straight past me and I couldn't be part of it. I was depressed for three months. My parents were upset later on when they realised, after I'd come out of it, but they weren't aware of it at the time. Being Deaf is a rather invisible problem. Outwardly, I was busily involved in sports and other activities, and I went out with friends. But the school social scene with the common room was very tough. So that's when I really faced that aspect of being Deaf. I don't remember exactly how I recovered from that low period, but somehow the thought came to me – I don't know where from, perhaps God put it into my mind – that the purpose of my being Deaf was to be an example to others. From that point, I accepted this as my reason for being Deaf, and decided to get on with my life positively as a Deaf person. After that I did go on to achieve as much possible.

I realised then too, I would have to learn to sign if I was going to be involved in the Deaf community. My Deaf friends who had left school before me were already involved with the Deaf community, and they were a link for me – we'd get together at the Deaf Club, which used to be in an old villa before it moved to a bigger Deaf Centre later. We had social nights there, Deaf Club meetings and organised sports; sports is really how I first joined up. I started playing basketball for Otago Deaf Society when I was 18, when Dunedin hosted the NZ Deaf Games. It was a real eye-opener to meet lots of different Deaf people from around New Zealand, because my experience of a Deaf community had been limited to Dunedin, which is very small. It was exciting to meet and talk to all these others. I was still oral then, but knew a few signs, just like my other Deaf friends from school. I picked up signing quickly, and I was really keen to learn.

ANGELA
SEW HOY

Once I'd left school, I asked my parents if I could learn sign language and they said, 'Okay, go ahead.' They accepted that I was Deaf and it was important for me to be with Deaf friends I could communicate with. But they also said, 'Make sure you don't lose touch with the hearing world,' so I agreed to keep my connections in both.

I hated that seventh form, bursary year. I was depressed and I found the subjects really hard. There was a lot of new vocabulary to learn. I had to do lots of extra study using my dictionary and thesaurus to try and work out the meaning of all the new language. It felt as if I had to virtually translate everything into language I could understand before I started. I would ask the teacher a lot, or just look it up for myself. But when it came to the exams I did not do well: I failed everything. I think it was a combination of difficulty with English, trying to access the class teaching, and the subjects themselves.

At the time, I never imagined myself going to university. I envisaged becoming an air stewardess, or an artist, or something fanciful like that. I told my parents I wanted to go to art school, but they talked me out of it, explaining that not many people could make a living out of art. I had never thought about the practicalities of having to pay bills and feed myself, and so that was good advice. They wanted to see me go to university. I said 'Me – go to university?!' That wasn't my ambition. But in Chinese culture, education is important and you also respect your parents' wishes. I couldn't say 'no'. So I did go to Otago University, to do commerce.

Starting at university in 1983 was a huge shock compared to being at high school. I felt overwhelmed at first by the size – there were 6,000 students in my time. The classes were held in huge lecture theatres with hundreds of students – far too many for me! I tried to sit right at the front, because there were no interpreters or notetakers; it was awful, I didn't understand a thing. It was totally impossible to lipread the lecturer pacing up and down the front. The lecturers wrote on the board sometimes but I missed everything that was explained. I endured it for almost three months, then I told my parents I was dropping out, as I wasn't getting anything out of it. They went and found someone at the university to sit down and talk to me, who explained that lots of new students go through a phase of wanting to drop out, and encouraged me to stick it out a bit longer. So I stayed, and in the end they were right – I did get more used to university life. University opened up a new world for me.

The way I tried to overcome the difficulties was to always arrive 15 minutes before the lectures, grab a seat at the front, and sit with a few friends who were willing to write notes for me to read as the lecture went along. Whenever the overheads went up, I'd frantically scribble them down before they disappeared.

After a while I started asking the lecturers for copies of the overheads and other lecture notes, and they were willing to do that for free. Years later, I heard that they charged Deaf students for copies of notes, but I was lucky enough to have them given to me – probably because I was the first Deaf student at Otago. At the beginning of each course, I'd have to go along and introduce myself to the lecturers and explain I'm Deaf and what I needed. Most of the lecturers were very good, and willing to support me. Only a couple of younger assistant lecturers were very uncomfortable: one actually shut the door on me because she didn't know how to cope. There was no such thing as a disability co-ordinator then. I just had to front up and ask for what I needed. It was pretty frustrating.

At home, I communicate with my family with a mixture of speech, some home signs that we've made up, and mime. I lipread them and if they don't understand my speech we use pen and paper or write words in the air. As a child, my parents spoke Cantonese to each other. When I was watching them, I would know they were speaking Cantonese by the way they moved their mouths, but I couldn't understand any of it. I was taught and spoken to in English only. If I had to talk to an old person in the family, I'd have to get someone else to come and translate for me into English and then back into Cantonese. At family events like meals or parties, my relatives mainly spoke Cantonese as their first language. The older generation usually spoke Canton-ese, while the ones of my generation would usually speak in English. When the younger ones spoke to the older ones it would be in Cantonese, and if the younger one didn't understand, the older person would throw in English words for them. That's how my sisters learned Cantonese, although our parents felt it was very important for us to speak English well so they prob-ably used more English at home. My sisters understand Cantonese well, but can't write it. We also started going to a Cantonese Sunday school when I was about seven. I liked it because we learned to write some Cantonese characters, and we had Bible stories. Now I can write only very basic Cantonese numbers, and recognise some written words, but I can't write them. I forgot most of what I learned.

When I'm with family, I consider myself part of Chinese culture; but in the Deaf world I am first and foremost Deaf, and I use sign language there. When I'm in the hearing world at work, I try to speak and use English, or communi-cate by writing. But I still take part of my Deaf culture with me to work, because hearing people have to do things like tap me to get my attention, or flick the lights, or bang on the floor or wave to get me to look. They're used to me and they know how to do those Deaf communication things. So I'm Deaf first,

Chinese second, and then Kiwi. Really I was born to three cultures. It depends on which situation I'm in as to which one I identify with. But mainly I'm Deaf and Chinese. When I've been overseas in China and Malaysia, I've noticed that the older people there are very traditional in their Chinese culture and I'm quite Westernised. So I'm aware that I'm a New Zealand-born Chinese, and I share a Kiwi culture which makes me more comfortable here than in an Asian country. In China I was seen as a foreigner – yes, I look Chinese, but my style and behaviour are obviously Western to them.

In New Zealand, I think Chinese people see me essentially as Chinese, but my family and people who know me well do see me as Deaf. Those who don't know me think I'm just Chinese, because I look the same, eat the same and have the same ways as them – except for language, obviously. In the Deaf community, I think Deaf people see me first as a Deaf person and also as Chinese which is something unique about me. There are very few Chinese Deaf in New Zealand: I only know of about six. When I was younger, adults in the Deaf community gave me a name sign that means 'Chinese', because that's how they saw me. I didn't like it. Later, some other Deaf people up north gave me a new name sign meaning 'Angel', which was much better. When I told Dunedin people that I didn't want the old name sign used any more they agreed that it was more appropriate to use the new sign. I don't think they realised before that the slanted-eyes sign was insulting to Chinese.

When I was born, I was named the traditional Chinese way. My parents asked my grandfather on my father's side to choose a name for me. I was given Way Lin Choie: 'Way Lin' means Beautiful Lotus flower; 'Choie' is my last Chinese name. My sisters have related names that translate as Jade Lotus and Phoenix Lotus, so we share the Lotus flower part of our names. Perhaps my parents thought I was a beautiful baby, or maybe it's because I was the first born. I don't know!

When we were younger, I felt the same as my sisters. As we got older, we started developing our own interests. For example, my sisters were interested in music, playing the piano and singing. That wasn't for me, being Deaf, though I had art and skiing. But we shared our interest in sports – we all played netball, basketball and volleyball. When I was 14, I took part in the New Zealand Chinese Sports Tournament for Chinese youth, which is held every Easter in different cities. I was an Otago rep for netball, basketball and volleyball. I was also on the organising committee with 10 hearing people in 1987.

At 14 I got really keen on skiing, and dragged my family into it too. I became a New Zealand rep in Disabled Skiing, starting off through the local branch in Otago. Through Disabled Skiing I met other Deaf and disabled people and saw how positive they were. They didn't consider themselves disabled, and they were having a pretty good life. That had an impact on me. I got better and better, and won a medal in the New Zealand championships. In 1988 I was selected for the New Zealand team to go to the 1991 Winter World Games for the Deaf in Banff, Canada. We trained first in New Zealand and then at Winter Park in Colorado with the International Disabled Ski Training Programme. There were Deaf skiers from all over the world – it was fantastic making friends with them. We clicked straight away, especially with the American Deaf, although it was pretty hard-going with their American Sign Language. I'd have to ask them to slow down, and I tried to teach myself some from a library book at the same time.

I was the only New Zealand Deaf skier at the 1991 Winter Games. I had to be quite assertive – finding myself a coach, and looking after myself. But everything worked out smoothly, and it was a marvellous experience to represent New Zealand. The competition at the Deaf games was much stiffer than the Disabled Skiers. What was really a big learning curve was attending the team captains' meetings, where I had to take on the role of the team manager for myself! These were big meetings, with debate and decisions at an international level – it was a challenge for me to be involved at that level.

After the Games I travelled in Canada and the USA. I met up with a Deaf teacher who had been a gold medallist in swimming at the Summer Deaf Games. What struck me about Deaf people in America and Canada was that they seemed to be able to do anything. There were lots more well-qualified Deaf people there; when I was a student there were only four other Deaf people at university in the whole country: one in science, I think; one in home economics; and two in commerce. That was it. In America there seemed to be loads of Deaf people with university degrees and sporting achievements. I was inspired. It made me think, 'Why can't we have that in New Zealand too?' My Deaf role models have been people like the Australian swimmer Cindy-Lu Fitzpatrick: I was penfriends with her. Another one was the famous American actress Marlee Matlin, who was in *Children of a Lesser God*. There were some Deaf adults from the Otago Deaf Society in Dunedin who were also role models – Roy Williams, the chairperson; Mary Johnson, an older Deaf woman; and Ron Dick, also a committee member. I learned a lot from them.

In 1991 after I'd been overseas, I wanted to do something for the New Zealand Deaf community, but didn't know exactly how. Three weeks after I got back from Canada, I went to a National Foundation for the Deaf conference in Wellington and started finding out about Deaf politics. I went back to Otago and got involved in organising the New Zealand Deaf Games, which were being

held in Dunedin again. A few months after that, they chose me as the Otago delegate to attend a Deaf Association AGM in 1992, and shortly afterwards I became the Otago councillor. I was nervous about going to the first council meeting. I was surprised to find that most of the members were much older, and were oral – although some were signers. They seemed like an older generation to me. Even though I was nervous, I decided to go for it and take part in the meeting. By the time the AGM came around a couple of days later, I was asked to be on the executive committee. I didn't really know much about it, but I thought, 'Why not?' I'd give it a go. In 1993 the president Jennifer Brain stepped down, and they elected me as president after only one year's experience.

I felt rather out of my depth at first, but I decided I'd just do my best, and went on from there. It was a huge challenge to be thrown in the deep end. I had to learn fast. But I must admit I enjoy that kind of challenge. The most difficult time I went through was when the Deaf Association had to respond to major government reforms in health, welfare and education systems. We had to move our services away from welfare into needs assessment and service co-ordination.

After I was elected, the executive made a national tour of the regions, and I had to give presentations and talk to Deaf community groups. At a meeting in Christchurch, a Deaf person who knew I had grown up oral came up to me and said: 'I've known you since you were a child, and it's great to see you now in the Deaf Association and showing Deaf pride. Your NZSL has improved a lot!' I was grateful for that comment. It shows how much I had changed since I'd joined the Deaf community. When I took on the presidency, I'd had a few worries in the back of my mind as to how I would be accepted, especially as I wasn't a fluent signer. But I didn't really have time to dwell on them – I was too busy just getting stuck into the job. It was a period of rapid change for the Deaf Association. Faxing was how the executive committee communicated information and discussed urgent issues. I'm sure the committee lived in dread of my endless faxes pouring out of their machines at home while I was the president.

In 1995 I decided to enrol for an MBA at Auckland University. For a long time I had wanted to do something for myself. I was looking for a post-graduate degree, and I wanted something challenging. I graduated in 1998. Looking back, I would say to any Deaf person considering doing such a thing: think carefully about your ability to be assertive and confident in participating in discussion, debates and working in a hearing team. It's a very demanding environment for a Deaf person. I was also the youngest woman in my class, and the third youngest in the entire class, so I felt very much the new kid on the block. My MBA class of 47 students got a bit of a shock when they first met me, but they did accept me quickly. My doing the course certainly raised the university's awareness about Deaf people, because the university had to find a lot of resources to provide interpreters and notetakers for my classes. The disability co-ordinators at university did a great job for me – it was very different from my earlier experience studying at Otago, without proper support. One of the big problems for Deaf students is that there are very few sign language interpreters who have university qualifications themselves, which can make it difficult for them to deal with the high-level language and subject matter they have to interpret.

It was exhausting trying to balance work and study, doing a double shift. I had to work at least 16 hours a day through the MBA, which left hardly any time for a social life. I'm grateful that my family gave me a good grounding in the business world, so at least I went in with some practical background, otherwise it would have been like starting a new job from scratch. I believe a Deaf person can succeed in business; it just takes a bit of assertiveness to ask a workplace to make small adaptations, such as having someone to make phone calls for you, or to use an interpreter for that. E-mail and fax are other ways of getting around the telephone. That's really all you need to be able to get on with the job. That's what my skills and qualifications are for – to do the same job as anyone else. At the moment I'm working as a company accountant in the family business, Glacier Investments Ltd, doing business analysis in a range of areas, such as preparing tax and financial reports. I enjoy the variety. I'm also keeping an eye out for a new job, a challenge that will utilise my MBA training and give me new opportunities to move up in the world. Ideally, I would like to use my management skills in serving the Deaf community, perhaps in a position like CEO of the Deaf Association some day – who knows? Or otherwise to get to senior management level in a hearing organisation.

One day, of course, I'd like to marry and have a family. I don't mind whether I have a hearing or Deaf partner: what's most important to me is to have good communication, honesty and trust. My partner would need to fully accept me first of all as a Deaf person. A few years ago some of the elders in my family were starting to get concerned that I was still not married. My parents sat me down for a little talk. I reassured them that I did want to get married at some stage, but I didn't want an arranged marriage! They told me, 'We understand that it won't be easy for you to find a partner, and we don't mind if you marry a European or Chinese or Deaf or hearing.' Even though it was a bit embarrassing for me, I was relieved they acknowledged that I'm Deaf and the situation is different for me. They were really giving me permission to make my own choice. My family has such a strong cultural tradition that normally we would

all be expected to marry Chinese. But Chinese Deaf men are rather scarce in New Zealand, so that would be a bit limiting for me! I don't have a fixed idea of whether my future partner will be hearing, Deaf, Chinese or European – I'm flexible on that. Someone who brings laughter would be good.

ANGELA
SEW HOY

Kelston Deaf Education Centre, Auckland

Kelston Deaf Education Centre, Auckland

ABOVE AND OVER: *Kelston Deaf Education Centre, Auckland*

Kelston Deaf Education Centre, Auckland

Kelston Deaf Education Centre, Auckland

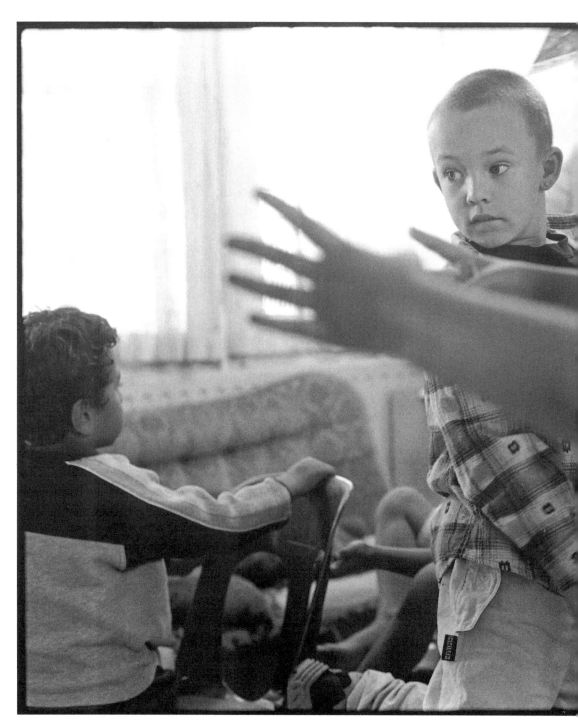

Kelston Deaf Education Centre, Auckland

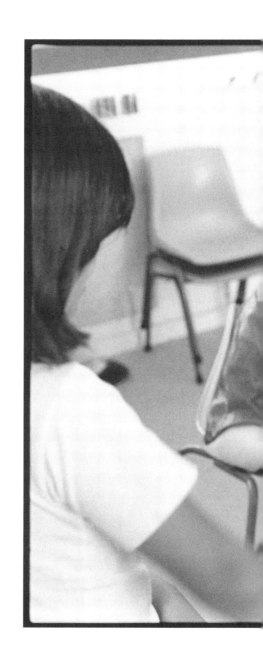

Kelston Deaf Education Centre, Auckland

John
Born 1965

Deaf people are okay. They have their faults, but I feel equal with other Deaf people. We understand each other because we've been through the same things ... We're the same kind.

'John' was born into a hearing family with its own difficulties. Poor teaching in the mainstream and poor communication at home left him well behind his age group (and ability level) by the time he went to van Asch Deaf Education Centre at 14. After a rocky young adulthood, finding his place in Deaf culture as an adult has helped John to enjoy a more settled life. This story is told anonymously, to preserve the privacy of his family.

When my mother was about six months pregnant with me she had a visit from her neighbour. The neighbour was also pregnant and she had German measles at the time. My mother didn't realise this, and when she got sick a while later she didn't go to the doctor for a check-up. I was born four days after the woman next door gave birth to a boy. They moved soon after that but kept in touch with my mother. One day she rang very upset because she'd just discovered that her boy was Deaf: she'd fired a toy gun and he didn't react. This made Mum think that I could be Deaf too. She'd already noticed that I didn't seem to respond, even to a loud noise, and was a bit worried about it.

My parents took me at nine months old to see a specialist who confirmed that I was Deaf. My mother was quite upset. She was having problems with my father, and me being Deaf added one more burden. Hearing tests, hearing aids, speech therapy and all these other things had to be done for me. It was a lot of effort for my mother. When I was a baby, Mum had problems with me waking and being noisy at night. At three I started at a kindergarten with four other Deaf children; one of them was my ex-neighbour's son. I've known him my whole life.

After about a year there I was moved to a primary school to be in a new Deaf unit with six others. I was a frustrated and stubborn child at that school. I had no confidence. I had no sign language. The teachers all spoke at us while we sat there clueless and bored. At home I would try to understand my mother by lipreading but it was pretty hard work. A year before this my mother had taken me to the hospital for a hearing test where she asked about how to communicate with me. She was told that she must speak to me and that signing was very bad. My mother blindly followed their advice and still couldn't communicate with me. My sister signed a bit when she was talking, but it was still a big effort for me to try and understand her.

My parents couldn't concentrate on me because of their own problems. My dad was an alcoholic and so there was a lot of stress and violence in the family. Between the ages of four and six I was placed in a children's home twice. I hated it. Some of the staff abused the children. We were locked in and I felt as if I was in prison. It was really frightening and lonely for me. My parents split up for a while and I was such a frustrated child that my mother couldn't cope. We couldn't communicate; she just didn't know what to do. If I was naughty, she sometimes threatened to send me to the children's home again.

At seven I was taken to a Deaf unit in another primary school. I loved that because there were many Deaf children there – about 30 of us from ages four to 13. The teachers only spoke to us, but the Deaf children signed to each other anyway. When I was about eight, my teacher slapped me for signing and told me to use my voice. My family did the same thing through my childhood. I was always being put down for my poor speech. If a Deaf friend came over who had better speech than me, my mother would say, 'Why can't you speak like him?' I'd feel really miserable. I don't know why they did that. Maybe it was because they'd never met Deaf people who signed, so all they could imagine was being oral.

I never actually saw children with Deaf parents, but somehow older Deaf people had passed signs on to the younger ones and these younger ones were passing them on to other children. I would watch the signs the children used and picked them up quickly. One day, some kids told me to come and look at a dead bird they'd found on the ground. One of them signed *bird dead*, drawing his finger across his throat for the sign *dead*. That's the first sign I remember learning. My confidence grew too. Going home was a really unhappy experience because there were all these problems at home between my father and mother and I hated it. I had a favourite teacher who was lovely to me when things were bad at home, and when I came to school with no lunch she'd give me some.

The year I was 10, I expected to be returning to the Deaf unit. Mum had got me ready for school and I was waiting for the school bus that usually came with my friend in it too. A taxi came, but it wasn't the usual one. The driver showed my mother a piece of paper that said he was to take me to the old primary school that I used to go to. Mum was quite shocked that we hadn't been told about any of this. Anyway I got in the taxi, pretty unhappy. We arrived and the teacher greeted me. I saw two Deaf kids I knew, but when I went into the class I was disappointed to see only six children there. I was the oldest of them all, too. I felt really sad and upset that day.

I would always fake that I needed to leave class for some reason or another. The first day, I pretended I had to go to the toilet, but actually I was covering up that I was crying. The teacher noticed I had red eyes and she sent me off to the sick bay for an eye-wash, thinking I had sore eyes. I wanted to go back to the Deaf unit. I liked it there! I really didn't want to be in that school. One teacher was nice enough, but the other was very tough on me. We had fun playing, but the work was fit for babies. I was given the same work as the younger ones, as though that was all I was capable of. That's why I got into trouble all the time – I was just so frustrated with everything. From 10 years old on, I was an angry kid, stroppy, so they knew I wasn't happy. Having a rough time at home was bad enough without being picked on at school too.

When I was 11 there were so few of us that it didn't seem worth having a unit, and I think they wanted to send us elsewhere. One day the teacher showed me a map of Auckland, saying that Kelston School for the Deaf was there; and then she showed me Christchurch and told me about a Deaf school there also. She knew about the problems at home and she was keen to get me away from it all. She pointed at Auckland on the map and asked me if I would like to go. I remember this well. I was looking at it, wondering what this was about – I didn't have any information to help me understand – and I nodded vaguely at where the teacher was pointing. Next thing, everything was arranged for me to go to the Deaf school. I was still unclear about it as the teacher told me to pack up, but I did want to go. I went home and got Mum's attention, to let her know something had happened, but I didn't know what to say. It was like my mind was empty.

A few days later another girl and I were sent into the mainstream. The move to a Deaf school had apparently been cancelled. I found out much later that when I was five my mother had decided to send me to Sumner School for the Deaf, then changed her mind. Later, when I was seven our whole family went on a trip to visit St Dominic's School for the Deaf. My parents decided it wasn't good enough, too old-fashioned for their liking. They decided to keep me at home and I'd be mainstreamed.

That was the start of a really bad time in my life. From the age of 11, my life got screwed up, sadly. In the mainstream I did no work. The first teacher would give me work and I learned at least something – he couldn't sign or anything, but he did try with us. With a new teacher we were completely ignored. I would go back and forth between the Deaf unit and the mainstream classes. The Deaf unit teacher would get really angry with me because I never brought any school work with me. I would start to explain why, but she would tell me off. What could I say?

When I was 12 I was still the only Deaf kid in the mainstream class. A Deaf boy I knew came back to the class next door, and then two other Deaf kids came along, but the crazy thing was that we were all put into separate classes on purpose, although we hung around together at breaks. Hearing school was a total waste of time for me. I was basically just killing time until playtime and lunchtime. Sometimes in class I would lean over to ask someone what was being said, and they would accuse me of cheating by looking at their work.

When the teacher of the Deaf visited I did some work, but that was very little. It was a disaster. I had trouble in my maths class. Maths was hard. I would always be in the corner to do my work while everybody else was facing the normal direction. Once I had finished my work, the teacher would come over and tell me it was all wrong. Of course, because I wasn't taught anything! I became violent from all the frustration. The year before starting intermediate we were given tests to find out our levels. I was given a paper with all these words I didn't understand on it. A teacher tried to give me instructions by telling me to circle the answers. I just circled any old words, not knowing what I was supposed to do, and then handed back my test.

The next year I went to intermediate school and Mum and Dad were happy for me, thinking I was excited about it. I was actually quite frightened. There were all these new kids to face. I pulled up my socks and just sat there, scared as anything. There were hearing children next to me, all around me, when the teacher started talking to me. I was so embarrassed with all these children just staring because I knew I wouldn't be able to understand the teacher – he had a big beard and moustache so I couldn't possibly lipread him. I was given things to read and I didn't understand them. I had a teacher's aide to help with communication, but they didn't sign – they just spoke. After a year I was trans-ferred to another class where I had another teacher. She would give me a little brown pad and give me the most basic tasks to do. Then she'd come over and tick it off: right, right, wrong, and off she went. That was it! No wonder I got so annoyed and unhappy at intermediate.

I was 14 in Form Two. I had a really intimidating male teacher, a big guy who would stand over us and do some pretty cruel things. I was always scared of him. I was hardly given any work either. All we did was draw Maori designs and other time-wasting stuff. Once when we were doing handwriting he checked my 'quick brown fox jumps over the lazy dog' sentence and got really furious. I don't know why, because it looked all right to me. He made me put my hands flat on the desk and he whacked them hard. I just sat there crying, none the wiser. This was just one of many times like that. I desperately wanted to take off. It wasn't just me he was cruel to, but everyone. I got into quite a lot of trouble being rude, swearing, bringing bad things to school. I was frustrated and I didn't know better. I was a bad influence on other children.

At home, I didn't fit in either. I would sit there quietly and watch my parents and sister all talking – I could see their mouths moving and I tried to copy. But I didn't understand what was going on most of the time. I had a hard time because my sisters could always have their say with my parents and I couldn't. They would believe my sisters and I always ended up getting the blame. It was maddening. One time when I was about 12 or 13, my parents were out and my sister called me into their room. She had spilled something on my mother's beautiful dressing table and couldn't get it off. My sister asked me to help her clean it off. I scrubbed away at it, but it just wouldn't come off. As soon as Mum and Dad got home, my sister blurted out about the mess and blamed me, and of course they believed her because I couldn't communicate enough to defend myself. Mum and Dad were mean to me. There were lots of times like that.

One time my Deaf friend (the one who lived next door when we were little) came to see me at school, telling me how great school was down in Sumner School for the Deaf. He was signing to me and I was soaking it up. I remember feeling uncertain about going to Sumner because I didn't know what was down there, but in May of 1979 I decided that I wanted to go to a Deaf school. The choice I had was either Kelston School for the Deaf in Auckland or van Asch in Christchurch. I chose to go to van Asch.

Mum made the arrangements and in July the principal came up to interview me in preparation for going to the school. As soon as I found out I was going to van Asch, I stopped going to Intermediate and took a break for six weeks, since I didn't like the school anyway. On 10 September 1979, with my bags all nicely packed, I flew down to Christchurch with my Deaf friend and another Deaf guy, and my parents and grandmother. It was a long way to the school, which was surrounded by big hills.

The first day I arrived I was given tests to see which class I would be in. I didn't understand them very well, and pushed them away. The teacher looked quite puzzled. But I didn't know how to do them; I hadn't been taught enough at school before. I could hardly read! It was then that I realised I'd been kept back for too long. I mean, I was 14 in Form Two! I'd never done most of the subjects they had at van Asch. I had no idea of multiplication.

When I was 15, I had a good teacher and started to really learn a lot. The teacher realised I was bright, because I would always have the answers to the questions. Before that I'd just been pretty lazy and not really tried - just opted out. But in that class I realised I had some brains, I was a quick learner, and my reading and writing started to improve a lot. At van Asch they used signing - TC - in class, which was better than having no signing at all before. I hadn't had a chance to learn before, with no communication. When I was 16 and 17 though, the work got very boring. They gave us work suitable for primary children - it was insulting and frustrating. I was bored so I got into trouble again. I was getting the strap and being sent to the headmaster regularly. And I was fed up with their TC signing. It's so confusing and mechanical looking, and it just felt unnatural. You get bored before the end of the sentence. I put up with it for a couple of years, but by the time I was 18 I refused to do it any more, so I used my voice instead and a few signs, and said I was going to sign my own way. Our own signing was actually NZSL, I realise now. The hearing teachers tried to make us sign their way, but I wouldn't. When I went home, Mum was trying to learn sign language from a book. It was too late for her to do that - I was already grown up. I should have had signing from when I was little so we could have communicated at home.

When I went back to school after the holidays I was 18, and I was horrified to find that they'd decided to put me in the special needs class with kids who were Deaf-blind, or slow learners, or had other problems. I knew I wasn't one of them. I couldn't understand why they had put me in that class. I refused to take part in class. On the first day I just sat by myself off to the side and ignored them. The teacher asked me why, and I said, 'I don't like being with them.' They were retarded, crippled, blind! I wasn't. So after half a day the teacher called the principal in, and they agreed to put me back into the bright class with the others. That was when I got a really great teacher and I learned heaps. I was motivated and doing well. This teacher was university-educated. He told us about Helen Keller, and taught us about current events at that time. I learned so much with that teacher because he would tell us stories and describe things to us. It was like the teacher I had when I was nine who used to explain about the news.

I'd really had enough of school by the time I was 18. I went to an Outward Bound course for a week, and then to a rehab course for four months to learn some work skills. I was meant to be going back to school, but before I did, a teacher came to see me to ask if I wanted to return the next year. I replied a sullen, 'No!' I didn't want to go back to school thank you very much. The teacher was adamant I should go back, and I was determined not to. Then I had problems at the hostel. Most of the teachers weren't that great, but the hostel staff were terrible. In the dorms I would swear at the hostel staff because they were so tough and intimidating to the children, just using their power unnecessarily. They were violent when children did naughty things. They would grab you around the throat, twist your arm behind your back, punch you in the face. I was throttled and hit in the face when I was a boarder. Some of the staff were very nasty. We were made to do strenuous tasks like cleaning walls of entire rooms over and over. If I said I'd finished, they would tell me to shut up, and if I spoke again they would make me do the whole thing again. It was cruel! I got into so much trouble at that school, I was nearly expelled many times. I was just so angry and miserable with the way staff treated us, as if we were all bad. When I was 16 a staff member tried to mess around with me. I loathed their cruelty and their power over us. I hate those memories I have, even though I loved being with my Deaf friends. The best aspect of Deaf school was having Deaf mates I could communicate with easily in sign language.

One time, after swearing at one of the hostel staff in an argument, I walked off to my room. I was lying on the bed when a teacher came in, not angry or anything, and calmly told me I had to leave the school in two weeks' time. That was fine with me. The teachers knew I wasn't happy there. They were very good about it and didn't tell my parents that I had been expelled. My father said that if I were ever expelled I'd get a hiding. That's why the staff suggested that I 'leave'. They knew what would happen. It was holiday time so everyone thought I was going home as usual. I got home and my parents didn't look like they knew anything about me leaving. My mother said I couldn't, we argued about it, and I left the house. I went and visited a Deaf friend who'd left school too. He took me to the Department of Labour, where I signed up for the dole. I went home, showed my Mum and she gave in. I was so happy when the battle was over with my parents to go back to school. I couldn't handle any more. My father suggested that I could go and work with him, in his own business.

My grandmother is half-Deaf, my uncle is half-Deaf and my cousin's partly Deaf. I remember when I was about five, seeing my grandmother use a few signs and being able to pick up what she was saying to me because she made some gestures that I could understand. That had a big impact on me, that she was Deaf too. For a long time I didn't want to be Deaf, I didn't accept it. From what I could see, hearing people had all the good things going for them. Hearing people were more clever than me, they could understand everything that I couldn't, and they seemed to have everything. I really wished I was hearing. My hearing sisters passed School Certificate and I didn't. I couldn't hear and I couldn't understand or learn anything. When I was growing up, my sisters used to taunt me, saying 'you're Deaf and dumb'. Even my mother said that too. Before I went to Christchurch I was uneducated and had limited language. In Christchurch I soaked up everything so fast, I was learning and I kept on learning after I left school. It was hard work, though. As I got older I accepted that I'm Deaf, and now I'm comfortable that signing is my language.

After leaving school I moved back home with my parents, who were still having their own problems, and I had communication problems with them too. I went on the dole to give myself some space. I joined a softball club and spent my time with hearing people. My parents eventually separated and I moved out to get away from all the hassles going on. I moved into a flat with three Deaf people. I had no idea how to cook, so I got really thin and scrawny. I should have learned but no one had taught me how. I was also doing drugs, drinking, and dressing like a punk.

In January the next year I got a job doing upholstery. We were getting into trouble in our flat at this stage, so we all moved out. I went back home to the same old problems. I stayed at my parents' for a year before finding another flat of my own. I'd go back and forth to my grandparents who cooked for me since I didn't know how. I was still mixing with both Deaf and hearing – I don't mind being with hearing people I can trust. I played softball and spent my time between that and going to the Deaf Club. The hearing people I mixed with would teach me things, and with Deaf people I could hang out and have a good time. I was split between both worlds. I met a friend through softball and she taught me lots of English, like what words like 'trust' meant. School never taught us anything like that. I was a member of the softball club for five years and had some good times there, but that's where the alcohol problem started really. I was drinking quite heavily.

I think the reason I had a drinking problem and why other Deaf do too is because of the bad experiences we've had. We try to suppress our feelings about it, like I did, and the alcohol holds the feelings down. Deaf people get in a crowd and think they're drinking to have a good time, but they don't know what they're drinking. I've wasted so much money on alcohol, not thinking about my future at all. As I got older I realised all this.

I got very low pay working at the upholstery firm. I remember the interview with this woman in the Labour Department. The Deaf social worker came along with me. I wanted the job, and it was arranged that I would work for three weeks on a trial basis. I got incredibly low wages but my parents said it was because I was doing an apprenticeship and after four years I would get more money. I was doubtful about that. My friends said that if I was doing an apprenticeship I should be going off to polytech as well. I was confused about it all. I was 22. After a while I met a new social worker for the Deaf who saw from my face what an angry person I was. All the alcohol hadn't helped. She also said that an apprenticeship meant going to polytech, and came with me to talk to my employer and clear it up. So I asked my boss if I was doing an apprenticeship and the reply was 'no'. I was devastated! For two years I'd been earning a pittance for nothing. I worked really hard to get $117 a week. When I left after two years it had gone up to $195, which was still pathetic. I endured that for two years. My parents had a row with the employers and blamed the first social worker and the employer for not offering me an apprenticeship so that after four years I could have gained something at least. I worked so hard! I was gutted by that experience.

I left that job and got another one. I was there for a year but I was having problems: I couldn't sleep, I was on drugs, drinking; I was a mess. I decided after a year to move to Auckland and start a new life. I stayed there for almost two years before coming back home. It was much more interesting there, but again I got into too much heavy drinking. In Auckland it was great to be with older Deaf people who would talk to you and tell you about things you wanted to know. Here, I think there's a generation gap, so the tough younger ones can't relate to the older people. In Auckland they don't have that problem. It's disappointing – I want lots of people to go to the Deaf Club so it will be more interesting for everyone. When left Auckland I was still drinking, so I started going to AA and things got much better.

Now I work in a factory. I like the work but I have a problem with staff getting smart behind my back. It makes me wild. They don't understand anything about Deaf culture. They are so cheeky to me. One person said she loved me, teasing me so everyone thinks I like her now. I'm not even interested. I don't want a hearing girlfriend. I had one before and there were just too many problems, partly to do with communication, although she could actually sign. She used me for things she wanted. Through that relationship I slipped back into drinking and dope again. I felt like I had to start all over again before I recovered. That's why I steer clear of hearing women now.

I really want to get my own house with a Deaf partner and have children.

It's not just a dream for me but a real desire.* I've had enough of this place and I'd like to move and start a new life somewhere else. It will take time to get to that stage though. I've got no savings, and I need to sort out a few things here first. As far as work goes, I would like to be a storeman responsible for taking care of stock. Where I'm working now is okay; I just bear with it and think of the money I need to survive.

Most weekends I stay home. I go to the Deaf Club sometimes. I like using sign language: it's my language that I can express with my body and hands. When I'm signing with a Deaf person, we're equal. Communication is completely on the same level. I draw, have people over to visit, and I fax and write to people. I play rugby league at a hearing club, and I also play for Deaf, but they don't have any training whatsoever. They just turn up on the day and play the game. The competition is completely different. All the photos of Deaf sports teams in my living room are part of my Deaf culture. I also keep lots of photos from school days. My hobbies are photos and photography, modelling, jigsaw puzzles – I like doing them, just taking my time. I cook and clean now. I'm 33 now and I'm a lot more settled than I was before – what a mess that was! I take just one day at a time.

I identify myself strongly as Deaf, but there's still more for me to become as a Deaf person. I'm not sure about the hearing world really. Deaf culture means lots of things to me: I think it includes the frustrations that Deaf people all share, and Deaf people trying to get what they want by being more assertive. Deaf culture is about the right to Deaf sign language: it's ours, like Maori and Chinese languages belong to them. Another thing we know is that Deaf people can do anything. We are not stupid. *Seeing* is what Deaf people do; everything is visual for us. That's how we access and understand everything best – through our eyes. For example, I'm a great reader of body language. I can sense by the way a person looks if there's a problem.

What I wish is that my family were Deaf and understood about Deaf culture. The communication gap with my parents is vast. I could never talk to them their way. It's sad. The doors of communication and information opened for me when I could sign.

I see Deaf children now and many of them sign well, but some are more fluent than others. The luckiest ones have Deaf parents. They have fluent NZSL and they're bright at school. The ones with hearing parents are much more of a mixture. If I had Deaf children it would be hard to know what to do. I'm not sure if the education for Deaf is any better now at Deaf schools, but there's no

* Since this interview, John has become a parent with his Deaf partner.

way I would mainstream a Deaf child after my experience. Mainstreaming was so bad for me. If it ever happened, I might send my child to a Deaf unit - if there was a good teacher. I'd be involved in teaching them as well. I wouldn't mind if my child were Deaf or hearing. If they were hearing, they could help me by making phone calls and letting me know if someone was at the door and other things. But I wouldn't use them too much - I'd still have flashing lights to help me.

Deaf Club's good because everyone's Deaf. We have sports, do things to help the Deaf community, and other things. I like going there because it's easy and comfortable to communicate. If I'm with hearing people, it's boring and I'm left out. When I'm with Deaf friends, we talk and joke, tell stories and have a really good time. People in the Deaf community are all different: they have different levels of intelligence; different backgrounds, depending where they went to school; and different age groups. The oldest Deaf people teach the middle-aged ones, and they pass things on to the younger generation, and so it goes on. They support the next generations of Deaf, and we learn from each other.

The hearing way and the Deaf way are very different - our cultures are different. My family never go to Deaf Club, but I don't want them to. Before, my mother wanted to go, but I didn't like the idea and I stopped her because the Deaf Club is my space, where I'm comfortable in the Deaf way. It's not their place. It's the same in my own home: all my visitors are Deaf - hearing people hardly ever come there. It's my Deaf place. I feel best with other Deaf people - we're the same kind.

Sara Pivac

Born 1979

Sara Pivac is a young second-generation Deaf woman who

is already stepping into leadership roles in her community.

Her parents, Lynette and Kevin Pivac, have been advocates

in Deaf education since their arrival from Lynette's home

country, Australia, in 1987. Their two Deaf daughters grew

up confident in the Deaf world. Educated in the 1980s and

1990s in Deaf unit and mainstream classes, Sara spent her

final high school year in Chicago before going on to

Auckland University. The opportunities open to young Deaf

people at the end of the twentieth century contrast with

some of those recorded earlier in this book, but Sara's story

vividly describes some of the challenges still facing Deaf

New Zealanders in achieving their aspirations.

I was born in Sydney, Australia, and I lived there till I was eight. My parents suspected I was Deaf when I was about three months old because I didn't turn my head to noises. They were Deaf themselves, so they accepted it when it was confirmed at five months. My younger sister was born Deaf too and we were good playmates for each other. My father has no other Deaf in his family, but Mum has two Deaf brothers, so we're second-generation Deaf. My parents were happy to have Deaf children – it seemed natural.

I started preschool at the Farrar Public School for the Deaf, just down the road from home, when I was two and a half. I went there for five and a half years, with 45 Deaf children. This was the 1980s, so they were using Signed

English at school. I was too young to know the difference between Australian Sign Language and Signed English, but I realised quite young that there were different ways to sign with my parents, with the other Deaf kids, and with the teacher. The way we signed at home (in Australian Sign Language) was more relaxed – the school way felt stiff. Now that I look back, I realise code-switching was a natural thing we learned from watching our parents. For example, when we went to visit Mum's parents we copied the way she and my Deaf uncles talked to them in a mixture of gestures and speech or really slow signing. My parents never actually told us, 'Your grandparents are hearing.' We just knew they were different by the way our parents and uncles communicated with them. My sister and I used to go to daycare after school with hearing children, and we noticed that they all spoke to each other. I knew instinctively that some people were Deaf like us and others were different. I would see my parents telling stories and mentioning other people as 'Deaf.' I knew that the taxi driver who took us to school was hearing because he couldn't sign properly. 'Hearing' to us meant people who couldn't really sign, and 'Deaf' meant the people you could sign fluently with. We always knew which was which by whether they could sign or not.

At school we spent a lot of time on speech lessons, right from preschool. The teacher asked my parents to make sure I used my hearing aids and FM aid at home too. My parents weren't too comfortable about that at first, but they went along with what the school had told them to do. So I'd go round at home wearing my FM aid, which was weird in a Deaf family! I'd plug it into the TV and turn the TV right up to maximum volume. Mum and Dad let me do it, but they must have thought it was pretty silly. I'd always say, 'I can hear it', to show off. But I was actually very Deaf – profoundly Deaf in one ear and severely in the other – so I can't hear anything much. With my aids on, all I could hear when the TV was turned up full was a noise of people talking; I had no idea what they were saying. I was just fooling around. Later, when I was at inter-mediate school, I used to go over to my hearing friends' places and see them listening to music on the radio. I thought it was cool to feel the vibrations when I put my hands on it, so when Christmas came, I persuaded my parents to buy me a radio of my own. But after a couple of days, the novelty wore off and I lost interest completely. I really just wanted the radio to be cool like my hearing friends. Later on when I got to high school I sold it to a friend for $15, but the aerial was broken off because I'd yanked it out further and further trying to make the radio go louder!

The year I was seven, I was moved up a year at school because they thought I was advanced for my age. The new class were all nine- and 10-year olds. I was

distressed to be leaving my old friends, but it was a more challenging level for me, because I had advanced writing and reading skills through having Deaf parents and good communication at home. My parents also bought a lot of books for us, and encouraged us to read books every day when we were little. Some of my Deaf friends have told me they didn't really have books at home, just toys. My sister and I played with toys too, but we could talk to each other about what we were doing, and do imaginary things like play teachers, while my Deaf friends mostly played with toys on their own.

When I was eight we moved to New Zealand. I started off for a few months in the Deaf unit at Kelston Primary School with a group of Deaf kids. Then I was moved to Glen Eden Primary School, where I was in the Deaf unit but in mainstream classes for some of the time. I was nervous about it because I'd always been with other Deaf children at school in Australia. I remember the first day I was introduced to a hearing girl who was picked to be my buddy. Off we went to a hearing class, along with a person who was meant to inter-pret for me, but within a few minutes I ran out upset and crying. The inter-preter came after me to find out what was wrong. It was hard for me to explain it to her, but I just felt so out of place, because I couldn't follow what was going on in the classroom. Before that, I'd been used to being with Deaf people who were signing, and I could easily talk with everyone and feel part of what was happening. But this class was a shock for me; I felt completely stranded. I'd always been in a small class, and now I was in a room of 30 kids, with a hearing teacher and an extra teacher of the Deaf to interpret for me. It was a bit traumatic and I went home crying and told my mother, 'I don't like being in that hearing class.' Mum encouraged me to give it a try. I was unhappy for a while, but I gradually got used to it, learned how to cope in a hearing group and I made some hearing friends by teaching them to sign.

In my last year at primary school they decided to reverse mainstream and bring six hearing children into the Deaf unit every afternoon. At first we felt that it was *our* class and that they were outsiders, and it created a bit of friction sometimes. The idea was for the hearing students to learn to mix with the Deaf kids; and they did learn to sign quite a bit, because the teacher always signed while she was talking. The teacher had us seated in mixed groups with one Deaf student in each group. The hearing children were chosen to include all the ones who had been picked as 'buddies', so my former buddy and my sister's buddy were there. I think we communicated with each other pretty well - we did a lot of activities together that were easy to communicate about, like cook-ing. When the hearing students came into our class, rather than vice-versa, the Deaf students felt more confident and more in control, because they were in our territory. When it was the other way around, if I was in a hearing class in a group of six hearing students, they would all talk to each other flat out and I couldn't join in because I'd have to concentrate on the teacher who was signing for me to know what was going on. At high school I was often assigned to do the artwork for group projects while they talked about their drama or something that I couldn't join in.

I was relieved that my buddy from intermediate was put in the same class as me in the third form, because she already knew sign language. She helped introduce me to the other students, and I explained to them that I was just the same as them but that I used sign language instead of talking, and told them not to be nervous about asking me about signs. Pretty soon they were coming up to me, keen to learn sign language. Third form was an important year because that's when I established friendships that lasted through high school; I'm still friends with some of them.

There was one other Deaf girl as well, but I made an effort to make friends with the hearing kids and taught them a lot of sign language. Some of them asked me why I didn't use my voice to talk to them, because at primary school and intermediate I had used my voice with hearing friends. At high school I decided to switch it off, because if they had to use their eyes and not rely on my voice they learned to sign better. Also, it was a real strain for me to use my voice all the time. From the time I started high school, I hardly used speech and my speech skills probably went downhill, but it wasn't important to me because in the weekends I socialised with Deaf friends, at home my family were all Deaf, and at school my hearing friends learned to understand my signing.

I coped all right at high school because by then I was used to being mainstreamed. In class I had a teacher of the Deaf who came in and signed for me. The good thing about it was that I was working at the same level as the other students. The Deaf unit can't match that because there is only one teacher to teach all the subjects, and usually they teach at a much slower pace and lower level. But I wish there had been a group of five or six Deaf in my class – if the class had been a quarter Deaf and three-quarters hearing, that would have been cool. I was just lucky that the kids in my Form Three class were accepting and they stuck with me as friends. By the time I was in Form Six and Seven most of my hearing friends were quite good signers, and often the teacher of the Deaf (who was meant to interpret for me) would ask one of my friends to sign while she had to go off to another class. They were quite keen to do it because they enjoyed signing, but really, it was supposed to be the teacher's job not the students'. In fact sometimes when the teacher was there I'd still ask

my friends to interpret, because they signed better than the teacher. Mostly they didn't mind, but occasionally they'd moan, 'Oh, do I *have* to sign for you?' Really, my friends did a better job, because the teacher only knew Signed English whereas they'd learned to sign my way, from me. I remember there was one teacher aide who would watch me sign with the other kids and try to correct them, saying it should be signed this or that way. I'd argue with her constantly about it. The hearing kids knew there was a difference too, but because she was an adult, most of them listened to her more. When we got to Form Five, Six, and Seven, my friends realised they should have followed my advice in the first place and not the teacher aide's.

It wasn't until I was at high school that I started to consciously understand the difference between NZSL and Signed English and to object to Signed English. I became more aware mostly through watching my parents talk with friends, and through a TV documentary. I was completely used to code-switching between signing with my Deaf friends, my parents, hearing students and the teachers. But lots of Deaf children don't really come into contact with NZSL until they're much older at high school or they start to mix in the Deaf community. Now, all my Deaf friends use NZSL because they've had input from older Deaf people in the community.

My sister and I always had each other for company. I know that hearing kids often go over to their neighbours to play, but it's different for Deaf people – we didn't. Our Deaf friends have always lived all over the place and we go out to visit them or they come here.

Hearing friends and Deaf friends are two separate groups. If I'm with a hearing friend, it has to be one-to-one, not in a group. I'm lost with a hearing friend in a group once they start talking to each other. But with my Deaf friends, I'm really comfortable in a group. If a hearing friend joins our group, I'm always aware that they can feel left out, so I feel responsible to make sure they are included and to be the go-between if they don't understand something. It's really a lot easier for me to mix with Deaf and hearing people separately.

One problem with hearing friends sometimes is actually knowing what to make conversation about. With Deaf friends it's easy to talk about absolutely anything, or nothing. We have so much in common, that you can just assume that everyone is up on the same information or involved in the same things. But with hearing friends, it's quite different because we don't share so much of our everyday life experience and we mix in different worlds. With Deaf friends, we might talk about what's happening with a Deaf person that we know overseas, or the next Deaf Olympics in 2001, or stuff like that. Hearing people don't know about any of that and if I mention something like this to a hearing friend, they'll go, 'Oh really, that's interesting', and that's the end of the conversation –there's nothing much to say. But with Deaf friends we share a lot more.

All my Deaf friends are signers. I met oral people from time to time growing up in the Deaf community, but when oral kids came to our school they'd pretty soon learn sign language from the other kids and become part of the group. If they stayed oral, the Deaf kids were busy with their own socialising and didn't have much time for them. They didn't fit in. I don't mean to be rude, but I don't have much to do with oral Deaf people because I don't need to, and it's hard work communicating with them. I have plenty of good friends in the Deaf community and a Deaf family and so there's not much motivation for me to mix with oral Deaf. Maybe if I came from a hearing family I might feel differently and make more effort to relate.

On the other hand, it's interesting to learn about the hearing world from hearing friends and their families - things that I'd never learn from the Deaf community. Being brought up in a Deaf household, we weren't aware of being noisy. For example, once I was over at my friend's place and everyone sat down for a roast lamb dinner. In my family it's perfectly okay to pick up the bone and suck the marrow out of it when you're finished. Well, I did this at my hearing friend's place and I must have made heaps of noise. My friend didn't say a word, but I think the family were a bit disgusted. Anyway, when I got home I told my family about the lovely roast dinner and I was skiting that I got the bone, because my sister and I used to fight over who got it. That was when Mum told me that you mustn't suck the bone when you're out because it's really noisy. I was so embarrassed when I realised; I felt like an idiot. Her family must have thought I had no manners at all, but I just didn't know about the noise because no one had ever told me. Another thing that worried me about going to hearing homes was getting up quietly in the night to go to the toilet. Deaf children who have hearing parents learn to walk quietly on tiptoes when they walk around at night; and I'm never sure whether I can flush the toilet at night when I visit a hearing family. In our house, we flush 24 hours, seven days a week, but when I visit a friend with hearing parents I have to ask them, 'Should I flush or should I leave it until the morning? What are the rules?' And shutting doors quietly, things like that, I'm not very comfortable with. I always feel uncertain about what's the right thing to do - it's quite unnerving. I've asked Deaf friends with hearing parents to show me how to handle these things because they've had a lot more experience with keeping quiet than me.

Not many of my friends growing up had Deaf parents like me, so whenever

I went to their houses there was very little conversation with their parents. Just a superficial 'Hello, how are you?' and that was about it. I couldn't chat with them the way I did at home. When Deaf kids came to my place, they loved to talk with my mother and father. They saw my Mum and Dad as parents to them as well, and my parents treated them as if they were their own children. Friends were always envious of the communication we had at home. One Deaf friend recently said to me: 'Your Mum's so cool, she's really open-minded and I can talk to her like a mother.' It wasn't until I was older and my friends started saying these things that I really appreciated how lucky we were to have Deaf parents. We always just took it for granted.

My home life was very different from theirs. In my house, we have flashing lights to signal the phone and the doorbell, and when we were babies we had a baby-cry light. I remember my parents using the light until my sister was a toddler. We used to trick them by making noises into the microphone to make the light go and get them to come running, until they got fed up and turned the monitor off. Another thing we had in our home was an old flashing light alarm clock that woke us all up in the mornings. Whenever my hearing friends came over, they were fascinated by our phone and doorbell lights because all the lights in the house would flash on and off at once. Then they'd want to know how we knew the difference between the door and the phone signals, so I'd give them a demo of how everything worked. And when my Deaf friends came over they were envious that we had this equipment that made life much easier. They didn't have those things in their homes, and they had to rely on their parents to let them know if someone was at the door or the phone was ringing.

When I was a child, I was drawn to other kids from Deaf families because they were fluent signers like us, and we were better matched. But now, as the Deaf children have grown up, it's harder to tell who is from a Deaf family and who isn't, because they're all more fluent in NZSL. When I went to America as a high school exchange student, I could easily tell who was from a Deaf family by the way they signed, even though I was an outsider and it was a foreign language to me. Maybe because I was standing back and observing, I could pick it straight away. I found myself magnetised to the kids with Deaf parents. I can't explain exactly why, but I had a rapport with them and I usually found them more interesting – they could talk about anything and in more depth than the others. In New Zealand, I don't really make a distinction between who has Deaf parents and who doesn't, maybe because there aren't many people with Deaf parents here. But in America, it's a definitely a status thing to have Deaf parents or family because it means you're very fluent in sign language. When people found out I had Deaf parents and a Deaf sister, they seemed impressed.

With friends who have Deaf parents, we talk more about family things. For instance, the down-side of having Deaf parents is that you mix in the same community and your parents know too much about you and your friends, because all the gossip gets around to them. Having no privacy is a bit of a pain. If I go to any Deaf social events, my parents are there too, noting how much I drink or which boys I'm talking to. Kids with hearing parents don't have that because their parents aren't in the same social scene. We feel like our parents' eyes are always somewhere in the background. That's one thing that every Deaf person who has Deaf parents moans about – their parents knowing too much stuff about their social life!

I guess the only other real disadvantage about growing up in a Deaf family was trying to make arrangements with friends to go out. Most of my friends had hearing parents, so they could ask their parents to ring a friend's parents. But mine were Deaf so they could never ring up for me to make plans in the weekends or holidays. We were a bit stuck because there was no telephone relay service and most people didn't use fax machines then. So I'd have to get my parents to drive all the way over to a friend's house, or sometimes I'd walk or run, knock on the door and hope they were home. I could contact my Deaf friends no problem because they had TTYs or fax machines, like us, but it was a problem trying to get in touch with hearing people.

I had a system with one hearing friend: if she asked me to go out and I needed to ask my parents for permission, I would ring her at a time we agreed on. She would make sure to answer the phone and I would say into the phone either 'No!' once or 'Yes, yes!' She could understand me enough to tell the difference between a no and a yes answer. I was never sure exactly when she had picked up the phone, so I would just dial the number and start repeating 'yes, yes, yes', or 'no' into the receiver, then hang up. Once I rang early in the morning and she was still in bed and her mother answered; I had no idea who was on the phone so I just said, 'yes yes yes' into the phone. Her Mum was pretty startled by this voice and she had to go and wake her daughter and say 'I think it's your Deaf friend.' My friend listened and got the message fine – but she told me later I was pretty loud on the phone!

It's much easier now because two of my hearing friends use e-mail, and since we left school my other hearing friends have fax machines at work. A relay service would make life much easier: that's when you phone an operator who has a TTY and a phone and they relay phone calls between a TTY and a voice phone so Deaf people can talk to hearing people and vice-versa. When I

was in America, I used the relay service if I had to do a school research project and I needed to call somewhere to get information, or if I wanted to make travel bookings, or call a Deaf friend's parents to check if they were home, and things like that. It was great to be able to call anywhere I wanted to, any time.*

I've had Deaf adults around me since I was a baby. My parents took us to parties, and there were often Deaf friends visiting the house. Lots of them had hearing children, and I used to play with them because when you're little it's easy to play together. By the time we were teenagers we'd grown out of playing games and we drifted off into our own groups of friends, hearing and Deaf. But as we lost touch with the hearing children of our own age, we started to take more interest in their Deaf parents. There were three stages in this transition: the first stage was my sister and me going with our parents and playing with their friends' hearing children; the second stage was when we stopped playing with the hearing children and hung around watching what the Deaf grown-ups were talking about; the third stage was when we developed a social life with our own Deaf friends, and by that time we knew everyone in the Deaf community – the older ones right down to our own generation, and we had taken in the history and the stories of the older Deaf people. When we started going to the Deaf Club with our friends as teenagers, we already knew all the adults there, and they all knew us because they'd watched us grow up. But our Deaf friends who had hearing parents didn't know anyone at the Deaf Club because they hadn't grown up in the community, and so people would come and ask them who they were and all about their backgrounds. It was a very different kind of relationship. To us, our parents' friends in the Deaf community are more like aunts and uncles than our blood relatives are (except for my Deaf uncles on my mother's side.) The Deaf adults are like our extended family, because we grew up around them – we'd been to the same parties, we shared the same stories, and we knew each other's history. When my Deaf friends came over, sometimes I'd dig out Mum and Dad's old photos and tell them stories about the people in my parents' generation. Mum would say, 'Put those old things away!' but it was fascinating to our friends because they had no idea about Deaf life before their time.

I got interested in the idea of going overseas as an exchange student through

---

* The New Zealand Human Rights Commission recently found in favour of a claim that the major telephone service providers are in breach of a legal obligation to provide a relay service, under the terms of the Human Rights Act, which requires that services be made available with 'reasonable accommodation' to enable access for people with disabilities. Deaf people (and hearing people who want to phone them) in Australia, the UK, and USA already enjoy free access to such a service.

meeting different Deaf people from overseas. The first was David McKee, who was working with my mother and told me about Deaf life in America. Then I met several Deaf exchange students from America at intermediate and high school who made a big impression on me. The reason I was so motivated to go was because I had spent my life in the Deaf community here and I already knew everyone – I wanted to experience different people and opportunities. I think it's different for Deaf with hearing parents because they haven't already had a lifetime in the Deaf community and so there's something new to look forward to. But I was ready to meet new people. Also, around that time I met the president of the Swedish Deaf Association who was visiting New Zealand, and he told me all about all the educational options they had in Sweden. I'd been studying German at school, and the idea of going somewhere with a different written language and culture seemed exciting. I thought about America and Sweden for almost a year, and in the end I picked Sweden as my first choice.

But then my fate changed: two months before I was due to leave, they informed me that I couldn't go to Sweden and that I'd be going to Chicago instead. Worse still, they told me I'd be going to a mainstream school. It was a bit of a shock. I'd had my heart set on going to a Deaf school, because I'd been mainstreamed since I was eight, and I wanted to go to a Deaf school before I was too old.

I had visions of Chicago as a gangster town, and it was worse when everyone kept telling what a dangerous place it was and warning me to be careful. I was almost expecting it to be like something out of a scary TV programme! I had requested to stay with a Deaf family, and they notified me that my host family would be a Deaf couple with hearing children. I was relieved, because Deaf parents would know how to guide me and introduce me to people and so on. I've seen a lot of my Deaf friends clash with their hearing parents because their parents don't understand the things they want to do, and won't let them go out with friends, and I knew that Deaf parents would have a better understanding of Deaf life and what was appropriate. When I arrived, I found the parents were nice, but of course they signed in American Sign Language (ASL), so I communicated with them in gestures at the beginning. My host mother was the only Deaf teacher at my school.

I felt really left out on the first day of school because all the Deaf kids were using ASL, which was a foreign language to me. Also, being the first day back after the summer holidays all the students were busy catching up on what everyone had been doing. It was the first time in my life I'd felt such an outsider and I didn't know where to put myself. At home I knew everyone in the community, but now I felt like I didn't belong. It made me realise how an oral Deaf

person probably feels. And that's when homesickness really hit. The others thought I was either really quiet or a bit thick because I couldn't say much. I wanted to say plenty, but I didn't have the language to get it out. After a little while, when I started to get involved in things, it got better. And once they'd forgotten about the summer holidays, I was a novelty and suddenly everyone wanted to be my friend! There was one Deaf guy in my class who had Deaf parents, the same as me, and I stuck with him. He was like my guide, and he introduced me to the others, because the students with hearing parents didn't take much notice of me at first. I felt comfortable with him because of our similar backgrounds. I wasn't shy in trying to learn ASL – I'd constantly be asking, 'What? What?' when I didn't understand or needed to know how to sign something.

There were about 40 Deaf students in a school of around 1,500, and they were either fully mainstreamed with a qualified interpreter or had a mixture of mainstream classes and Deaf unit classes. There was also a small group with extra disabilities who needed to learn basic living skills. I was put in the mainstream with some other Deaf students and an interpreter, but it was really tough at the start because I'd only been in the States three weeks and I didn't have a good grasp of ASL. I'd sit there pretending to understand, with no idea what the interpreter was signing. Sometimes I got caught out because in American schools the teachers expect the students to participate much more than they did in my New Zealand school. In New Zealand, we didn't seem to have much discussion, it was mostly book work, whereas in America the book work was done at home. I often felt like an idiot because I didn't understand enough ASL at the beginning and when I knew the answer it was frustrating not to have the language to express it properly. The Spanish class was interesting: in that class we fingerspelled all the time. The interpreter was Mexican and she was fluent in Spanish. It was a complicated process for me, because I was learning Spanish through American fingerspelling and signs, but in my head translating that into NZSL or English – so I had about four languages going on in my head at once. It took a *lot* of figuring out! In the end I loved that class – it was one of my favourites. After my experience learning ASL, I realised that if I had gone to Sweden it would have been twice as difficult because I would have faced a new written language as well as the sign language. It took me two or three months to cope with ASL reasonably well, and that was hard enough.

In America I suddenly had a lot of Deaf friends my own age at school. In New Zealand, I was used to spending lunchtime with a few Deaf friends and the rest of my class time with hearing kids. But now there was a much bigger Deaf social scene at school. I didn't bother to mix with hearing students, because I didn't need to. After school there were clubs and activities for Deaf students, like the Deaf volleyball team and junior NAD [National Association of the Deaf]. I really enjoyed all those activities. The only contact I really had with hearing people was with my teachers through interpreters. I wasn't interested in making hearing friends there, because I knew those friendships wouldn't last, whereas Deaf friends last forever. That's the way Deaf people are. Also, I had a much bigger choice of friends in my age group to hang around with. In New Zealand I was used to mixing with people from 15 to 25, because there were so few of us; but in America, there were enough people that I could spend most of my time with people in my own age group and a bit older. I noticed though that the Deaf students in Chicago had less experience of an adult Deaf community than me – they socialised mainly in their own peer group and they didn't go to a Deaf Club.

Another difference was the American students' expectations about education. They'd complain about their interpreters over the most trivial things. I couldn't believe it, because I had never had a real interpreter in my whole school life. I had only had a teacher who used poor Signed English and sat right beside me in class. I didn't have independence like they had. I told them they should be grateful because they were better off than Deaf people in almost any other country in the world. I think I made them aware of how many things they took for granted. They were shocked when I told them we didn't have all our videos and TV programmes subtitled in New Zealand the way they did. They had no idea. At the end of the year some of my friends said, 'Thanks for making us realise what life is like for Deaf people in other countries – now we know how lucky we are.' They'd grown up with all these things, like interpreters, relay services, subtitling, and they just assumed that was normal life until I told them they should be grateful and proud of what Deaf people have in America.

At the end of the school year, all my friends were discussing which university they wanted to go to. They didn't know how lucky they were to have so many options. I didn't have any real choices when I returned to New Zealand, because I would more or less have to go wherever I could get an interpreter, or I could just go to university and hope for the best, not knowing whether I'd have an interpreter or not. I was envious of the choice they had. The only things they had to consider were whether they liked the size of the university, the fees, where their friends were going, and the social life. They never had to stop and think, Will it provide support services for Deaf students? Will I be able to get an interpreter? They could take that for granted wherever they went.

It was definitely worth going to America for a year. I had a marvellous time and I learned lots more than I could have done in a year in New Zealand. I

learned a new sign language. I studied Spanish and a lot of other new subjects; and I was involved in all kinds of activities that weren't available at home. It was fantastic, the best experience of my life, but when I got back home I felt less restless and more satisfied with my life here somehow. It gave me an appreciation of the positive things we have here – like having a close community and a Deaf Club, and how easy it is to see friends here because the distances are smaller. And now I appreciate how beautiful our green environment is. In Chicago everything was concrete and man-made, but here we can easily go tramping or go to the mountains or the ocean, there's so much to choose from.

SARA
PIVAC

Coming home also made me appreciate my family, and especially how lucky I am to have a Deaf sister, because I missed her in America. I was lucky to have only a Deaf sister, because if there had been hearing siblings there might have been more competition between us, or jealousy about parents giving one more attention than the other. But with just the two of us, we were always treated equally by our parents. We've mostly shared the same group of friends through school and done almost everything together. People thought it was funny that when we went out we never really talked to each other, but of course we didn't need to because we saw each other all the time at home – it was more interesting to talk to different people when we were out. Plus, that way we got better coverage of everything going on and we could swap gossip when we got home. Ever since we were young, we were always invited out as a pair. People thought we were a cute pair – two Deaf sisters – and I think they liked inviting us because we were usually the 'life of the party', always had plenty to talk about and livened things up. Now that we're older, we still share the same group of friends and go out together, but we're not so much the leaders of the group. Others have grown up and got more confidence, and new ones have moved in from other places, so we're more a part of the crowd now.

One of the main ways of getting together with Deaf people is through sports. Deaf sport is really important for social reasons – that's where I meet up with my friends and talk. I've loved sports since I was young. It's much easier for me to be part of a Deaf team than a hearing team. In a hearing team I'm on the fringes, waiting for the others to tell me what to do and being a follower. In a Deaf team, I'm right in there making decisions and joining in everything that's going on. The great thing about Deaf sport is that because the Deaf community here is so small and there are never enough good players it's relatively easy to get selected for a team and have chances to travel to matches. I've been involved in a quite a few Deaf sports: at the moment I play netball, and I was in the New Zealand Deaf basketball squad. I did athletics all through my childhood and I was keen on badminton and orienteering at one stage. I wanted to play badminton in the World Games for the Deaf, but then I got this other dream of being an exchange student and I realised I probably couldn't achieve both.

Since I was little I've also enjoyed art, but when I got to high school I had to focus more on academic subjects and think about future jobs, so I didn't really develop my art skills. I don't mean to be negative, but job opportunities for Deaf people in New Zealand are quite limited, so I had to make realistic choices about which subjects at school would lead to something in the future. My first ambition when I was young was to be a teacher – I used to practice on my little sister. My parents never had to teach her maths because I'd already taught her to count and add. After the teacher phase I had all sorts of ideas about what I wanted to do when I grew up. Now, I'm not certain, because these days most people tend not to stay in one job for life. My mother, for example, really wanted to work in science, but she started out working in accounts at a bank, and then she worked at a Deaf school, and now she teaches sign language, so it's hard to predict where you'll end up. I know that I'll probably do several types of work in my life, and that's good because I like new challenges. I hope to work somehow with Deaf people, maybe in education or in the social services area. There are more chances now for Deaf people to work anywhere, but I want to do something that makes a difference to people's lives.

At the moment I'm studying for a BA, and I've taken papers in education, history, sociology, and linguistics. I also tried a Maori paper, because I enjoy languages, and I'd like to take a paper in Croatian, because I'm half Yugoslav Croatian on my father's side.

University is very different from school: everyone is more independent and it's harder to make friends – not just me, but the hearing students too. People say, 'hi', but that's about it. Sometimes I'll have a conversation with someone by writing. There's another Deaf student at varsity who I see quite often. If there were more Deaf students we could set up a club, but you can't have a club with only two people. Most of my life is still in the Deaf world. I've got my sports, and the social scene in weekends. I have some hearing friends that I might meet for lunch or a chat, but I don't go to parties with them or hang out in their groups. I don't feel a great need to make more friends at university because I already have a good social life in the Deaf world. That's where my culture is.

Deaf culture to me includes the sort of things that other cultures have, like our technology (flashing lights and TTYs), jokes, sign language. Deaf culture doesn't have anything to do with skin colour; people from all backgrounds come together with the common feeling of being Deaf; they share communication

in sign language, and lots of them have been to school together. Deaf culture means keeping the same friends forever. The most important thing in Deaf culture is obviously sign language; signing is how we communicate, how we express our humour, how we do drama, how we teach. Sign language is part of almost everything in Deaf culture.

Like most people, I've got plenty of dreams! I hope to finish my BA by the time I'm 21 or 22 - that's the most important thing at the moment. It'd be nice to go to Gallaudet University, but financially it's probably out of the question for a while. More realistically, I want to go to Europe and travel the world, learn more about other countries - maybe get to Sweden this time. Mainly, I hope I'll have a happy life and be successful.

I love New Zealand of course. Going away to America prompted me to get around to finally becoming a citizen. New Zealand will always be my home, although I feel a link with three countries: I'd call New Zealand my first home, America my second, and Australia my third home. I guess where I end up will depend on what kind of work I do, and who I marry.

As for marriage, I expect to marry a Deaf man. If I married a hearing person, it wouldn't be completely equal - I wouldn't know who he was talking to on the phone, and when hearing people visited they'd talk and it would be hard for me to join in, or my husband would have to interpret and I'd be uncomfortable about that. I'd feel much more equal with a Deaf partner. As long as he's Deaf, his family background doesn't matter so much - hearing family or Deaf family. Of course it'd be nice if my partner came from a Deaf family, but the person himself is the most important thing. I'm 19 at the moment and I plan to take my time! It'd be good to have Deaf children, because that's my own background and it's quite possible because of my family's genes, but that depends on who I marry. If I had hearing children, that would be a really new experience for me. Naturally I'd use NZSL with my children, whether they were Deaf or hearing, because they'd need it to communicate with my parents and my sister, as well as me.

Some of my Deaf friends say they wish they were hearing, but I've never felt like that. For me being Deaf is natural; I can't imagine being any different. It's different for Deaf people in a hearing family because they're constantly being reminded of the fact that they are Deaf. I know in the working world it might be different, being with hearing people, but it doesn't worry me. So far I've always been happy to be Deaf and I wouldn't want to change, because I've had such an interesting life - probably more interesting than a lot of my hearing friends' lives.

I know that I'm very lucky in many ways. My parents tell us how much better off we are than they were: we had sign as our first language all our lives at home and school, whereas they had to put up with oralism. They say we've had a much better education than them and that we're lucky to be able to go to university. In their day there wasn't much support in education, so there are things we can do that weren't possible for them. They are what they are now because of their experiences, and we're lucky that we live in different times. We've had access to a lot of information that they didn't have when they were growing up. My parents both had hearing parents (although my mother was lucky to have two Deaf brothers), so it meant they missed out on a lot of ordinary talk at home. But we were part of everything that was going on, and picked up information much younger than they did. Another difference is that they went to boarding schools, while we could live at home with our family, so they aren't really as close to their parents as we are. We know our parents much better, and of course they know us better too, so we're lucky to have a much closer family relationship. We don't have to work quite as hard for everything as our parents did.

Kelston Deaf Education Centre, Auckland

ABOVE AND OVER: *Kelston Deaf Education Centre, Auckland*

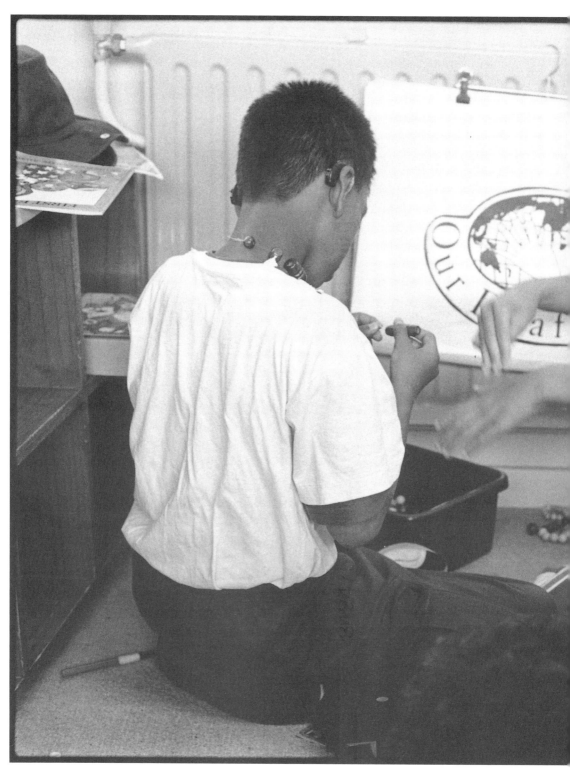

Kelston Deaf Education Centre, Auckland

OVER: *Singing, Kelston Deaf Education Centre, Auckland*

Basketball, Kelston Deaf Education Centre, Auckland

The Buzzard family at The Groynes, Christchurch

List of Terms

CODA is an American-coined term that stands for 'Children Of Deaf Adults', i.e., the hearing offspring of Deaf parents. CODAs often see themselves as in-between Deaf and hearing cultures – being automatic members of the hearing world by being able to hear and speak, yet having a strong cultural and language affiliation with Deaf people from having been raised in the Deaf world.

Deaf Association of New Zealand (formerly New Zealand Association of the Deaf) is an organisation of and for people who identify as Deaf, mostly people born Deaf. Its goals and services reflect the interests and culture of the Deaf community.

Deaf unit is a class established within a regular school for the purpose of providing specialised teaching (by a teacher of the Deaf) to a group of Deaf children – usually of mixed ages. Deaf units proliferated in the 1960s with the aim of keeping Deaf children closer to home and promoting social integration with hearing peers. The establishment of Deaf units led to a major decline in residential school enrolments from this period. Relatively few units (or 'resource classes' as they are now called) remain today; the majority of Deaf children are individually placed in mainstream classrooms.

Fingerspelling is a way of representing letters of the alphabet on the hands, also sometimes referred to as a 'manual alphabet'. Fingerspelling varies from one sign language to another – for example, the British-related languages (including New Zealand Sign Language) use a two-handed alphabet, while most European and American sign languages use one-handed systems. Not all sign languages include the use of fingerspelling, and they vary in the extent to which fingerspelling is used within the language. Fingerspelling only became a commonly used part of NZSL after the introduction of signing to schools in 1979. Prior to this, many New Zealand Deaf adults had never experienced the use of fingerspelling.

FM radio aid is a device that can enhance the quality of sound received through a hearing aid. A selected sound source is picked up by a small microphone worn by a person speaking (or plugged into a TV, for example), while the hearing aid user wears a small receiver device with a direct connection to their hearing aid. Sound is transmitted via FM radio frequency, reducing background noise and producing a clearer sound signal at a greater distance. FM aids are often used by Deaf children in school classrooms.

Hearing Association of New Zealand advocates for the needs and goals of those who identify themselves as 'hearing impaired' or 'hard of hearing', usually having acquired a hearing loss later in life.

IHC: Intellectually Handicapped Children's Society, an organisation that provides advocacy, educational and vocational support services for persons with intellectual disabilities.

Kelston Deaf Education Centre (KDEC): see Titirangi School.

Mainstreaming, in the New Zealand context, refers to the enrolment of individual Deaf students (or other students with special needs) in regular school classrooms where they are expected to learn and integrate with non-disabled students. Various kinds and levels of specialist or para-professional support (such as visiting teachers, teacher aides) may be provided to assist the student. Mainstreaming is currently the most prevalent type of placement of children with special needs in New Zealand, including Deaf children.

Name signs: Most people in the Deaf community are known to others by a 'name sign', which is given by other Deaf people rather than chosen by the person themselves. Name signs in NZSL often describe a physical feature (such as *finger-chopped-off* in Douglas Croskery's case) or a behavioural characteristic. Alternatively the meaning of a name sign may be related to the spelling or sound of the person's spoken name (such as *Angel* in Angela Sew Hoy's case, or *Battery* for for Patrick – based on the lip pattern). It is common for name signs to be acquired from Deaf peers at achool, and to be changed later in life by a different group of friends. Name-sign systems arise in Deaf communities around the world, but vary in the form that name signs take and the type of information they encode (see R. McKee and D.McKee, 'Name Signs and Identity in New Zealand Sign Language', in M. Metzger (ed), *Sociolinguistics in Deaf Communities*, Vol.6, Gallaudet University Press, Washington D.C., 2000).

New Zealand Sign Language (NZSL) is the indigenous language of the New Zealand Deaf community, which has developed amongst Deaf people over approximately the past 100 years. It is closely related in vocabulary and structure to British Sign Language and Auslan (of Australia), which can be seen as related dialects.

Notetakers provide service to Deaf people in educational settings (or meetings) where it is impossible to watch a sign language interpreter or lipread a speaker and take notes at the same time. Trained or volunteer notetakers are usually provided for Deaf students in large tertiary institutions, ideally in addition to a sign language interpreter.

Oral is used in the Deaf community as an adjective to describe a Deaf person who mainly communicates through speech, rather than signing. This may be because they have not grown up in contact with sign language, or they choose to communicate in speech only, or because they belong to the oldest generation of Deaf people who typically use less signing than younger generations. The meaning of *oral* in relation to these older Deaf people differs from its implication when applied to Deaf people who have grown up amongst hearing people and never been exposed to sign language (e.g., as a result of being mainstreamed). In reality this older 'oral' generation use a mixture of signs combined with English lip patterns and voice as their normal communication mode within the Deaf community. This accords with Cheryl Anton's description of how her grandparents communicated – 'oral, but also used gestures and signs a lot', though they didn't perceive themselves as signers. *Oral* is also used by Deaf people to describe communication or school instruction through speech and lipreading, to the exclusion of signing, and sometimes as a verb meaning 'to speak (without signing)'. When used to describe schooling, the sign *oral* usually carries a negative connotation because it is associated with unpleasant experiences of intensive speech training, of not understanding teachers speaking, and of not being able to sign and communicate freely.

Sign Language Interpreters facilitate communication between Deaf and hearing people by translating from speech into sign language, and sign language into speech. Interpreters serve Deaf and hearing people in a wide range of situations, ranging from everyday personal appointments to educational situations, public meetings, legal or medical situations, and conferences. Interpreters require specialised training and a high degree of fluency in both languages and cultures, as do interpreters of spoken languages. (See Chapter 1 for background on interpreters in New Zealand.)

Signed English is a system for coding spoken English on the hands by signing each word in an English sentence, usually simultaneously with speaking. Specially invented signs are used to represent tense endings, plurals, and other grammatical particles of English. This form of signing bears little resemblance to the way Deaf people communicate in New Zealand Sign Language (or other natural sign languages). Australasian Signed English was widely introduced in New Zealand in 1979, with a change to the **Total Communication** approach for teaching Deaf children, Much of the vocabulary for **Australasian Signed English** was adopted from Australian Sign Language (the language of Deaf people in Australia), while some signs were created by a committee or borrowed from articifial sign systems in America. The philosophy of Total Communication originated in the USA in the 1960s, and espoused the use of spoken, signed and written modes to encourage better language and cognitive development in Deaf children. As Signed English was the most conspicuously new part of this approach, the sign system itself has become widely referred to in New Zealand as 'TC'.

St Dominic's School for the Deaf, a private Catholic school, first opened in Wellington in 1944, and moved to its permanent site in Feilding in 1952. Unlike its earlier-established counterparts in Australia, the school used oral-only teaching methods, in accordance with the New Zealand government policy in Deaf education. St Dominic's closed in 1989, after several years of operating a non-residential Deaf unit only.

Sumner School for the Deaf opened in 1880 as the first government school for the Deaf. It was re-named van Asch College in its centennial year, 1980, after the founding principal Gerrit van Asch, a Dutchman who established a strictly oralist teaching regime. The school, now renamed van Asch Deaf Education Centre, is referred to in the Deaf community as both Sumner and van Asch, depending on the age of the signer or the period being discussed.

Telephone relay is a service whereby a person using a TTY (see definition below) can make a phone call to a person without a TTY (and vice versa) via an operator who receives and relays messages back and forth between two parties on line. The operator reads aloud the text message from a TTY call to a voice caller on the phone, and types the voice caller's words back to the TTY user. This service enables Deaf and hearing people to call each other directly, without relying on an interpreter or another person to make calls on their behalf. Free relay services are well established in several countries, but not yet in New Zealand.

Titirangi School opened in 1942 in the Titirangi hotel building (now Lopdell House), as a temporary extension of the Sumner school. As the population of Deaf children steadily expanded in the North Island, the Auckland school became a permanent, separate institution, and eventually moved to a purpose-built residential school at Kelston in 1958 – now known as Kelston Deaf Education Centre.

van Asch Deaf Education Centre (VADEC): see Summer School.

TTY stands for Teletypewriter: a machine with a keyboard, a small LCD screen display, and cups on which the phone receiver is placed. Two TTY users can type messages to each other, transmitted via the phone line through an acoustic coupler device.

World Games for the Deaf (WGD) is a large-scale international sporting competition organised by and for Deaf people, including a wide range of Olympic sporting events. WGD have been held regularly in various countries since the 1930s. Summer and Winter Games are held on an alternating four-yearly cycle, so that an international event is held every two years. In 1989, the New Zealand Deaf Sports Association hosted the Summer WGD in Christchurch – the largest Deaf event ever to have taken place here. The majority of participants and spectators at the WGD share the common experience of being members of a Deaf community and communicating in sign language.

Select Bibliography

Annual Reports of the Ministers of Education to Parliament, 1879-1906, cited in M. Collins-Ahlgren, 'Aspects of New Zealand Sign Language', PhD thesis, Victoria University of Wellington, 1989, p. 17

Baker, C. and R. Battison (eds), *Sign Language and the Deaf Community: Essays in Honor of William C. Stokoe*, National Association of the Deaf, USA, 1980

Baynton, D. C., *Forbidden Signs: American Culture and the Campaign Against Sign Language*, University of Chicago Press, Illinois, 1996

Collins-Ahlgren, M., 'Aspects of New Zealand Sign Language', PhD thesis, Victoria University of Wellington, 1989

Dugdale, P., 'Being Deaf in New Zealand: A Case Study of the Wellington Deaf Community', PhD thesis, Victoria University of Wellington, 2000

Forman, W., 'Towards a Critique of the Exclusive Use of the Oral Method in the Education of the Deaf in New Zealand 1880-1923', *New Zealand Journal of Disability Studies*, 7, pp. 40-56

Gannon, J., *Deaf Heritage: A Narrative History of Deaf America*, National Association of the Deaf, Silver Spring, Maryland, 1981

Geering, L. in N. Glasgow (ed.), *Directions: New Zealanders Explore the Meaning of Life*, Shoal Bay Press, Christchurch, 1995 (Foreword, p. 10)

Gregory, S. and G. M. Hartley (eds), *Constructing Deafness*, Pinter, London, 1991

Higgins, P. C., *Outsiders in a Hearing World: A Sociology of Deafness*, Sage Publications, Beverly Hills, 1980

Jacobs, Leo, *A Deaf Adult Speaks Out*, Gallaudet College Press, Washington DC, 1974

Kennedy, G., R. Arnold, P. Dugdale, S. Fahey, and D. Moskovitz (eds), *A Dictionary of New Zealand Sign Language*, Auckland University Press with Bridget Williams Books, Auckland, 1997

Lane, H. *When the Mind Hears: A History of the Deaf*, Random House, New York, 1984

Lane, H., *The Mask of Benevolence*, Alfred A. Knopf, New York, 1992

Lane, H., R. Hoffmeister and B. Bahan, *A Journey into the Deaf World*, Dawn Sign Press, San Diego, 1996

Levitt, D. *Introduction to New Zealand Sign Language*, National Foundation for the Deaf, Auckland, 1985

McKee, D. and G. Kennedy 'A Lexical Comparison of Signs from American, Australian, and New Zealand Sign Languages', in K. Emmorey and H. Lane (eds), *The Signs of Language Revisited*, Lawrence Erlbaum, London, 2000

McKee, R. and D. McKee, 'Name Signs and Identity in New Zealand Sign Language', in M. Metzger (ed), *Sociolinguistics in Deaf Communities*, Vol.6, Gallaudet University Press, Washington D.C., 2000).

Monaghan, L., C. Schmaling and G. Turner (eds), 'The Development of the New Zealand Deaf Community' in *Many Ways to be Deaf: International Linguistic and Sociocultural Variation* (forthcoming)

Padden, C. and T. Humphries, *Deaf in America: Voices from a Culture*, Harvard University Press, Cambridge, Mass., 1988

Penman, P., 'Deaf Way, Deaf View: A Study of Deaf Culture from a Deaf Perspective', Masters thesis, Victoria University of Wellington, 1999

Pritchett, P., 'A Survey of the Reading Comprehension of a Sample of New Zealand Children with Prelingual Severe/Profound Hearing Loss', MA thesis, University of Melbourne, 1998

Sacks, O., *Seeing Voices: A Journey into the World of the Deaf*, University of California Press, 1995

Sameshima, S., 'Deaf Students in Mainstream Universities and Polytechnics: Deaf Student Perspectives', MA thesis, Victoria University of Wellington, 1999

Stewart, D., *Deaf Sport: The Impact of Sports within the Deaf Community*, Gallaudet University Press, Washington DC, 1991

Taylor, G. and J. Bishop, (eds), *Being Deaf: The Experience of Deafness*, Pinter, London, 1991

Townshend, S., 'The Hands Just Have to Move: Deaf Education in New Zealand - A Perspective from the Deaf Community', MA thesis, Massey University, Palmerston North, 1993

Woodward, J., 'Implications for Sociolinguistics Research among the Deaf', *Sign Language Studies*, 1, pp. 1-7